Go-Live
Smart Strategies from Davies Award-Winning EHR Implementations

Edited by

Margaret Schulte, DBA, FACHE, CPHIMS

About the Editor

Margaret Schulte, DBA, FACHE, CPHIMS, serves as adjunct faculty in the Northwestern University Masters of Science in Medical Informatics program and is Editor of *Frontiers in Health Services Management*, a publication of the American College of Healthcare Executives. Previously, she served as Associate Professor in the Graduate Program in Health Administration at Grand Valley State University in Grand Rapids, MI, as Vice President of Education for HIMSS, as Vice President of Research and Development for the publishing subsidiary of the American Hospital Association, and as Director of Education for the Healthcare Financial Management Association. Prior to moving to Chicago, Dr. Schulte served on the faculty of the Mercer University Graduate Program in Health Administration, as adjunct faculty to the Mercer School of Medicine, and as a planning consultant to hospitals and physician practices. She has also served as Director of Certificate of Need for West Virginia, in various management positions in hospitals and as Director of Planning and Development for a multi-hospital organization. Dr. Schulte holds a doctorate in Business Administration from Nova Southeastern University, Ft. Lauderdale, FL, and a master's degree in Business Administration from Xavier University, Cincinnati. She wrote *Healthcare Delivery in the U.S.A: An Introduction* in 2009, published by Taylor and Francis, collaborated with HIMSS in the preparation of the CPHIMS Review Course, and is a certified instructor in that course.

About the Contributors

Nancy R. Babbitt, FACMPE, started her career in the healthcare field in 1982. She has been in her current position as the Administrator of the Roswell Pediatric Center, in North Atlanta, for 22 years. She is a Fellow of the American College of Medical Practice Executives. She started two local Medical Group Management Association (MGMA) chapters, the Georgia Pediatric Practice Managers Association, and the North Fulton Hospital Office Managers Association. She served for several years on the Georgia MGMA Board, through the position of President and was then elected to the Southern Section Executive Committee. She is currently serving on the MGMA National Board of Directors. She has served on the HIMSS Davies Awards of Excellence selection committee for Ambulatory Care Practices. She serves on the American Academy of Pediatrics Pediatric Practice Managers Leadership Team. Ms. Babbitt is a public speaker on electronic health records.

David Collins, MHA, CPHQ, CPHIMS, FHIMSS, is Director of Healthcare Information Systems with HIMSS, where he holds responsibility for the Davies Awards Program and serves as staff liaison to the HIMSS Patient Safety & Quality Outcomes Committee. Prior to joining HIMSS, Mr. Collins served the Virginia chapter of HIMSS for five years (President in 2003). Mr. Collins previously served as Project Manager for the Doctor's Office Quality-Information Technology project at Virginia's Quality Improvement Organization. Other employment has included Trigon Blue Cross Blue Shield, Accenture Consulting, and service as an EMS provider for seven years, three years of which he served as an advanced life support provider. Mr. Collins attended Virginia Commonwealth University and completed his Master's degree in Health Administration in 2000. He holds the designations of Certified Professional in Healthcare Quality and Certified Professional Health Information Management Systems. In 2004, he served as US Senate Productivity Quality Award Examiner in Virginia.

Louis H. Diamond, MB ChB, FACP, FCP (SA), FHIMSS, is Vice President and Medical Director at Thomson Reuters Healthcare (part-time) and is self-employed as President, Performance Excellence Associates. He currently serves as Co-Chair, Strategic Directions Committee, Executive Committee, Physician Consortium for Performance Improvement; Chair, Quality, Measurement, Research and Improvement Council, National Quality Forum; Chair, Patient Safety, Quality and Outcomes Steering Committee, HIMSS; Chair, Policy Steering Committee, eHealth Initiative; President, the End-Stage Renal Disease Network 5; and Delegate for the Renal Physicians Association to the American Medical Association House of Delegates. He previously held leadership positions at a variety of healthcare organizations, including the National Patient Safety Foundation, Medical Society of D.C., and the American Society of Internal Medicine, and the American College Medical Quality. He was previously chairman of the Georgetown Department of Medical Affairs at Georgetown School of Medicine and Professor of Medicine, Georgetown School of Medicine. Mr. Diamond is a graduate of the medical school of the University of Cape Town, South Africa, Fellow, American College of Physicians, Fellow, College of Physicians (SA).

Barbara M. Drury, FHIMSS, is President of Pricare Inc, a national independent consulting firm founded in 1982 and based in Colorado. Pricare's mission is to provide clear and independent options for physicians making decisions about the use of computers in their offices. This has included researching and advising practices about the acquisition and growth of practice management systems and electronic medical record systems. Ms. Drury is a frequent lecturer on electronic medical records at national and regional events. She has achieved Fellow status with HIMSS and serves on the HIMSS Davies Ambulatory Award Committee, as well as on multiple HIMSS task forces. She currently serves as Education Chair for the Colorado Chapter of HIMSS. She is a frequent speaker at the HIMSS Annual Conference and is the recipient of the December 2004 and the April 2009 Spirit of HIMSS Award. Ms. Drury is a member of the Colorado Consumers Advancing Patient Safety Steering Committee and the Health Level 7 Records Management and Evidentiary Support Work Group.

Joan R. Duke, BS, MA, FHIMSS, has been involved for more than 30 years in all aspects of healthcare information systems. In 1990, she founded Health Care Information Consultants (HCIC) to assist organizations in health IT management. HCIC focuses on solving problems relating to systems management, organizational readiness and technology integration. She has assisted a variety of organizations, including health systems, hospitals, home care, long-term care, hospice, behavioral health, clinics, physician groups, healthcare information exchange, healthcare technology vendors and non-profits to unify their organizational and information, technology resources. In 2003, she was appointed to the HIMSS Davies Award of Excellence Task Force to evaluate organizations for recognition of exemplary implementation of electronic health records systems. She is a Fellow of HIMSS, past President of Maryland Society of Healthcare Information Systems Management; and participates in the American Medical Informatics Association Healthcare, Technology Network of Greater Washington, Health Information Standards Panel (HITSP) and Health Level 7 Working Group (HL7). Ms. Duke obtained her Bachelor's degree in Mathematics from the University of Maryland in 1965, and her Master's degree from Johns Hopkins University in 1973. Ms. Duke has delivered papers and published in national forums on such topics as systems planning, systems evaluation, terminology standards, HIPAA, electronic health records (EHR) and health information exchanges (HIE). She is author of two chapters for *Aspects of Electronic Health Record Systems, Second Edition,* published in 2006.

Daniel Griffin, MD, was the founder of Alpenglow Medical in Fort Collins, CO, and the winner of the 2006 Davies Award in Ambulatory Care. He trained as an Internist and is currently at the North Shore Long Island Jewish Health System on Long Island, NY. Dr. Griffin is an Elmezzi Scholar at the Elmezzi Graduate School of Molecular Medicine and is doing Immunology Research in the Department of Oncology and Cell Biology at the Feinstein Institute. Dr. Griffin is also a teaching attending for the Internal Medicine Residency Program at the indigent clinic that served as the beta site for the roll out of the largest ambulatory EHR implementation to date. Dr. Griffin is a recognized national expert on electronic health records, being the speaker for CMS's first Transformational Grand Rounds and speaking at regional conferences and in Washington, DC. Dr. Griffin is the current Chair of the Davies Ambulatory Care Award Selection Committee.

Susan Heichert, BSN, MA, FHIMSS, is currently Senior Vice President and CIO at Allina Hospitals & Clinics in Minneapolis, which was selected for the 2007 Davies Organizational Award. Ms. Heichert has been involved in health IT for more than 25 years, working with both providers and vendors. She is active in her state HIMSS chapter and currently serves on the Davies Organizational Award Committee. Ms. Heichert received her Bachelor's degree in Nursing from the University of Maryland at Baltimore, and her Master's from the University of Minnesota.

Brian R. Jacobs, MD, is Vice President and Chief Medical Information Officer and Executive Director of the Center for Pediatric Informatics at Children's National Medical Center in Washington, DC. He is also a Professor of Pediatrics at George Washington University. In this capacity, he directs the Children's IQ Network®, a pediatric health information exchange in the DC metropolitan region. Prior to joining Children's National Medical Center, Dr. Jacobs was a Professor of Pediatrics at the University of Cincinnati, as well as the Director of Technology and Patient Safety at Cincinnati Children's Hospital Medical Center. While at Cincinnati Children's, he oversaw the implementation of their electronic medical record and was the principal author and winner of the HIMSS Davies Award. Dr. Jacobs specializes in pediatric critical care medicine and has authored numerous journal articles, book chapters, abstracts, and scientific presentations. He frequently shares his knowledge in the pediatric space as a guest lecturer at conferences, leadership forums, and hospitals. He is a fellow of the American Academy of Pediatrics and the American College of Critical Care Medicine. He also is a member of the Society for Pediatric Research, the Association of Medical Directors of Information Services and is the current chairman of the HIMSS – AMDIS Physician Community. Dr. Jacobs received his Bachelor's degree in biology from the University of California, Los Angeles; his Master's degree in biochemistry from the University of Oregon; and his medical degree from Oregon Health and Sciences University. He completed his residency and chief residency in pediatrics at Naval Regional Medical Center, San Diego. Prior to completing his fellowship training in critical care medicine at Children's National Medical Center, Dr. Jacobs served as a physician in the United States Navy, for which he was distinguished as a decorated Persian Gulf War veteran.

Alice Loveys, MD, FAAP, FHIMSS, is Chief Medical Information Officer of the Monroe County Medical Society Health Information Technology Service Bureau, overseeing the implementation of EHRs for 240 physicians in the greater Rochester, NY, area. She also is a practicing pediatrician with Pediatrics @ the Basin. This practice won the HIMSS Ambulatory Care Davies Award for implementation of electronic health records in 2004. Dr. Loveys has chaired and remains actively involved with the HIMSS Ambulatory Davies Committee. She won the Spirit of HIMSS Award for her work as part of the HIMSS Katrina Phoenix Project, helping medical practices destroyed by hurricane Katrina with disaster recovery and conversion to EHRs. She is active in the American Academy of Pediatrics Council on Clinical Information, on the MSSNY HIT task force and is the former vice-chair of the Greater Rochester RHIO board of directors. Dr. Loveys is an innovator in the field of health IT. Her focus is on the practical applications of technology in the small-office space that will improve the quality of both the delivery and impact of healthcare processes. She uses Google Sites as an effective tool to assist in bringing health IT into these small offices. In 2008, with grant support from the New York State Department of Health, she built a health IT support center that targets the privately held, small physician office within the framework of a local physician-trusted entity, the Monroe County Medical Society (MCMS). She is currently CMIO of the MCMS Health Information Technology Service Bureau (SB). The SB first project was to provide support for medical practices adopting EHR technology. Given a relatively small budget and support staff (3.1 FTEs), she was able to lead the implementation of EHRs for 240 physicians in the greater Rochester area. The practices used nine different vendors and all connect to the RHIO and do clinical quality reporting all while keeping in step with the NYS directives on health IT and complying with federal government regulations. A solid implementation takes a coordinated approach between IT support vendors, EHR vendors, RHIOs and the practices. Getting practices to EHR from paper lays the foundation for further advancements using technology.

Denni McColm, MBA, is Chief Information Officer for Citizens Memorial Healthcare. Ms. McColm has been at Citizens Memorial since 1988, serving as Director of Human Resources and Director of Finance before moving into the CIO role in June 2003. Ms. McColm served on the Certification Commission for Health Information Technology as a Commissioner from 2006–2008. She also served on the Davies Awards of Excellence Organizational Selection Committee from 2006-2008 and again in 2010. Ms. McColm is a member of the Editorial Board for *Healthcare IT News*, published in partnership with HIMSS. Ms. McColm holds a Master's of Business Administration degree from the University of Missouri-Columbia.

Justin Ott is currently working on his Master's in Health Administration at Grand Valley State University. During the writing of this book, he served as a graduate assistant to Dr. Margaret Schulte. As a graduate assistant, Mr. Ott conducts research on a wide array of topics concerning health information and management.

Patricia B. Wise, MA, MS, RN, FHIMSS, is Vice President, Healthcare Information Systems for HIMSS and has oversight of the HIMSS Nicholas E. Davies Awards of Excellence in electronic health records in hospital organizations, ambulatory practices, and public health agencies. Additionally, she leads the Society's work in ambulatory care and acute care, studying the challenges of EHR implementation and the return on investment. Prior to joining HIMSS, Ms. Wise was on active duty for 28 years with the United States Army, serving in a variety of worldwide positions. She is a retired Colonel and former Chief Nurse Executive and Deputy Commander of Eisenhower Army Medical Center in Augusta, GA. While on active duty, Ms. Wise was selected for a legislative internship in the office of Senator Daniel Inouye. Following retirement from the Army, Ms. Wise joined Computer Based Patient Record Institute-Healthcare Open System and Trials (CPRI-HOST) as Executive Director, a position she remained in until the CPRI-HOST merger with HIMSS in 2002. Ms. Wise received her Bachelor's of Science in Nursing degree from Villanova University and her Masters in Nursing degree from the University of Maryland. She is a graduate of the US Army War College in Carlisle, PA.

Dedication

In honor of Nicholas E. Davies, MD, and each of the Davies Award winners.

Contents

Preface

Margaret Schulte, DBA, FACHE, CPHIMS

This is the day of widespread implementation of electronic health records (EHR), and of investments in health IT. While these investments reach deep into our pockets and financial reserves, this technology offers tremendous opportunity to improve the way in which we do business and, importantly, the way in which we deliver care. Yet, the journey into the EHR is complicated, time-consuming and disruptive.

HIMSS is fortunate to have "the nation's largest collection of first-hand accounts"[1] of EHR implementations in hospitals, health systems and physician practices in the United States. Each year, providers who have implemented an EHR and have been able to report clinical process and outcome improvements and complete an exhaustive application for the Nicholas E. Davies Award. This collection of applications is the source from which the authors in this book have drawn to describe a plethora of best practices and lessons learned (i.e., what not to do and "fix-it" pointers) for each step that you will carry out as you undertake your EHR implementation. The book is designed, chapter by chapter, to provide "how to" insights for each of those steps. These insights are not theoretical, but come directly from the experience of hospitals and physicians who have implemented an EHR.

Several themes will emerge as you read this work. The first reflects the universal emphasis on leadership as the one critical element that will define the success, mediocrity or failure of your EHR implementation. Without wholehearted leadership commitment of time, resources, enthusiasm and determination, your investment does not have a chance of success. This means leadership that begins at the top of your organization. "No Davies Award winner has achieved a successful EHR installation without the vision and support of their organization's top leaders, as well as its supervisors and managers."[1]

A second theme that will emerge is one of change. Everyone in your organization (even patients) will be touched by the EHR implementation. Each needs to be encouraged, sometimes prodded, other times pushed, in the change and adoption/adaptation they will need to make. The workflow to which they have become familiar will need to be assessed from the outset of your EHR journey and throughout the implementation. Each person needs to be prepared to change his or her approach to work and to effectively use the technology. This will take time—don't take shortcuts, but don't dally either. There will be a point at which it's all or none—meaning, as so many of the Davies Award-winning organizations have found—at some point, all will either have to adapt or will no longer fit the environment. Patience and determination will go a long way in this process, so will lots and lots of training and support.

A third major theme that will emerge as you read is that the EHR offers the essential platform for clinical and business performance improvement. It will provide the data, measures and results reporting that will ultimately influence quality improvement. These metrics can't be efficiently accessed through a paper record. In the current environment—in which financial incentives are being provided to those who implement an EHR and demonstrate the meaningful use of that EHR—those metrics are key to financial success, to making the investment in the technology more palatable, and to clinical quality improvement.

ABOUT THE NICHOLAS E. DAVIES AWARD

The HIMSS Nicholas E. Davies Award of Excellence is one of the most coveted awards for excellence in EHR adoption in the United States. Since 1994, the Davies Award has recognized excellence in the implementation of and value derived from health information technology, specifically EHRs. There are currently four award categories: Public Health, Organizational, Ambulatory, and Community Health Organizations. This book draws upon the Organizational (hospitals and health systems) and Ambulatory Care (physician practice) Awards. The applications that are submitted to HIMSS for these awards are case studies that provide rich detail of how to successfully implement an EHR.

Originally created by CPRI-HOST in 1994, the first three recipients of the Davies Organizational Award were recognized in 1995. Today, management of the Davies Award program continues under HIMSS, with which CPRI-HOST merged in 2002.

The Award honors Dr. Nicholas E. Davies, an Atlanta-based practicing physician, President-elect of the American College of Physicians, and a member of the Institute of Medicine Committee on Improving the Patient Record, who tragically died in an airplane crash in 1991, with Senator John Tower. Dr. Davies was an accomplished physician who believed that the computer-based patient record was needed to improve patient care.

The Davies Award is based on an evaluation framework that involves a two-step process. It is modeled after the Baldrige Award for which applicants are asked for assessment and documentation of their progress based on four key areas, including management, functionality, technology and overall value. The application process serves as an introspective self-assessment that is valuable for planning an EHR implementation. A committee of the applicant's peers, many former Davies recipients, independently score the applications and then convene to determine site visit candidates. On those site visits, they are able to assess first-hand the applicant's integration, use and commitment to the paperless environment. They are able to see how the hospital, health system or physician practice is using the EHR to improve care delivery.

The Davies Award program objectives are to:
• Promote the vision of EHR systems through concrete examples.
• Understand and share documented value of EHR systems.
• Provide visibility and recognition for high-impact EHR systems.
• Share successful EHR implementation strategies.

WHAT THIS BOOK IS *NOT* ABOUT

This book has not attempted to suggest particular technologies that are available or should be used. It addresses the importance of standardization and the importance that you will place on identifying applications that are in compliance with standards and that support interoperability in your organization. However, a discussion of the many technologies that are on the market today is not a focus of this work. To the contrary, its focus is on the organizational elements, the really hard part, of an implementation. Should you want to read about the technologies that any of the Davies Award winners installed, you can find this information on the Davies Web site at www.himss.org/davies. All the winning applications are there for your use.

SUMMARY

Many hospitals and physician practices have successfully made the EHR journey and find that post-implementation, the process continues with upgrades, change and process improvement. They discover they are able to extract ever more knowledge from the system. On a very positive note, they are seeing results in their business returns, efficiencies in their processes, improvements in their clinical outcomes and better balance in their lives and lifestyles.

We at HIMSS hope this book will shed some light on, and answer some questions about, the decision making and implementation questions that arise for those who are approaching this process for the first time and for those who are ready to move onto upgrades and expansion of IT functionalities.

As Editor, I would like to thank each of the authors who contributed to this book. Many of them are Davies Award winners who have guided their organizations, not just through the process of applying, but also through the EHR implementation journey in their own organizations. Thank you. I have been honored to work with you on this project.

- Nancy R. Babbitt, FACMPE
- David Collins, MHA, CPHQ, CPHIMS, FHIMSS
- Louis H. Diamond, MB ChB, FACP, FCP (SA), FHIMSS
- Barbara M. Drury, FHIMSS
- Joan R. Duke, BS, MA, FHIMSS
- Daniel Griffin, MD
- Susan Heichert, BSN, MA, FHIMSS
- Brian R. Jacobs, MD
- Alice Loveys, MD, FAAP, FHIMSS
- Denni McColm, MBA
- Justin Ott
- Patricia B. Wise, MA, MS, RN, FHIMSS

Thanks also to Fran Perveiler, Vice President, Communications, HIMSS (and publisher of this book) as well as Matt Schlossberg, Manager, Publications. Your patience and ongoing support have been amazing!

Reference

1. *Improving Quality and Reducing Cost with Electronic Health Records: Case Studies from the Nicholas E. Davies Awards.* 2007. HIMSS: Chicago IL.

Profiles of the Nicholas E. Davies Organizational and Ambulatory Care Award Winners

Justin Ott

Having the latest technology and tools is essential, particularly if an objective of your organization is to become recognized as a distinguished institution. In an attempt to achieve this level of greatness, electronic health records (EHR) are being released in healthcare systems throughout the United States. Implementation of the EHR has proved to be one of the most effective and efficient methods to yield higher return on investments, more efficient organization skills and improved patient care.

This section provides a list and brief profile of the HIMSS Nicholas E. Davies Award of Excellence winners, whose real-world experience, strategies and challenges are presented in this book. There are two subsections of winners—Organizational (hospital and health systems) and Ambulatory Care (physician practices)—who are briefly described next. Descriptions can include name, location, patient volumes, staff totals, bed size and a brief explanation of what the EHR is doing for their organization or practice.

NICHOLAS E. DAVIES ORGANIZATIONAL AWARD WINNERS

MultiCare
Tacoma, WA
2009 Davies Organizational Award Winner
A not-for-profit organization based in Tacoma, WA, since 1882. Evolution and integration of technology has occurred at MultiCare in order to fulfill their quality oriented mission statement which reads: "Quality is achieving optimal outcomes for our patients through exceptional customer service and effective use of human, technological and financial resources." MultiCare has 8,908 employees with 327 employed physicians utilizing their EHR to help accomplish their mission. In 2008, MultiCare had 37,626 inpatient admissions, 416,190 outpatient visits and 154,354 emergency department visits throughout their entire system.
http://www.multicare.org/

Eastern Maine Medical Center
Bangor
2008 Davies Organizational Award Winner
Beginning with only five beds, Eastern Maine Medical Center (EMMC) has since grown into a 411-bed comprehensive medical care center, with more than 3,000 employees and a

medical staff of more than 400. Their mission statement guides EMMC to "strive to provide exceptional primary and specialty healthcare with a passionate pursuit of excellence in patient safety, clinical quality and service. Our mission is to care for patients, families, communities, and one another." In 2007, EMMC had 19,656 total inpatient admissions, 456,575 outpatient visits and 67,937 emergency department visits.
http://www.emmc.org

Allina Hospitals & Clinics
Minneapolis
2007 Davies Organizational Award Winner
Allina Hospitals & Clinics (AHC) is a not-for-profit network of hospitals, clinics and other healthcare services, providing care throughout Minnesota and western Wisconsin. With nearly 24,000 employees, more than 5,000 healthcare providers and 2,500 volunteers, AHC is able to fulfill the mission: "We serve our communities by providing exceptional care, as we prevent illness, restore health, and provide comfort to all who entrust us with their care."

After taking into consideration 85 clinics and 11 hospitals, there are a total of 1,821 inpatient beds in the Allina system. These clinics and hospitals are linked together through their EHR. AHC's facilities are located throughout much of the Minneapolis area, as well as some outlying communities. In total, AHC had 103,171 inpatient hospital admissions, 799,925 hospital outpatient visits, 220,483 emergency care visits and 52,702 hospice visits in 2006.
www.allina.com/ahs/home.nsf

Center for Behavioral Health (aligned with Centerstone)
Bloomington, IN
2006 Davies Organizational Award Winner
The Center for Behavioral Health (CBH) is a group of outpatient clinics located in eight states in the southeastern United States. CBH has built a large continuum of residential services, mainly for clients having some form of serious mental illness, such as schizophrenia. Because clients' levels of impairment vary, CBH offers a wide range of residential facilities, ranging from an acute stabilization unit (Transitional Care Facility) through group homes with 24-hour oversight, to apartment complexes for those who need little assistance. As of 2006, CBH had a staff of more than 280 employees, nine of whom are physicians. The EHR they use keeps their staff updated and linked and supports the organization's research orientation and commitment to evidence-based treatments. In 2005, CBH provided 313,136 clinical transactions and served 7,861 clients.
http://centerstone.org

Generations+/Northern Manhattan Health Network
New York City
2006 Davies Organizational Award Winner
A health group located in New York City, Generations+/Northern Manhattan Health Network (GNMHN) aims to serve underprivileged communities in the Manhattan area. GNMHN provides services through three acute-care hospitals, as well as three

neighborhood family health centers that provide community-health services. Additionally, there are 38 facilities (family health centers, child health centers, school-based clinics) located in the area that work in collaboration with GNMHN to provide maximum care.

Throughout the entirety of GNMHN, there are 7,261 employees and 2,383 healthcare providers. Annually, these employees and providers service 253,398 emergency department visits and 1,582,216 ambulatory care visits. GNMHN has a total of 947 beds.
http://building.nychhc.org/Default.aspx?page_id=30&item_id=74

Citizens Memorial Healthcare
Bolivar, MO
2005 Davies Organizational Award Winner
Citizens Memorial Healthcare (CMH) is an integrated rural healthcare delivery system, with 1,538 employees and 98 physicians. The system includes one 74-bed hospital, five long-term care facilities, and 16 physician clinics and home care services in nine counties. CMH describes itself as a fully integrated and nationally recognized healthcare system.

With the mission of "caring for every generation through exceptional services by leading physicians and a compassionate healthcare team," CMH had 130,031 visits to the physician clinics in 2004, 19,888 visits to the emergency department and 14,455 home care visits.
www.citizensmemorial.com

NorthShore University HealthSystem (formerly Evanston Northwestern Healthcare)
Evanston, IL
2004 Davies Organizational Award Winner
Founded in 1891, and headquartered in Evanston, IL, NorthShore University HealthSystem (NUH) is a comprehensive, fully-integrated healthcare delivery system comprising multiple facilities to provide care. With more than 900 beds in all facilities combined, this integrated health system has significant capabilities in a wide spectrum of clinical programs, including cancer, heart, orthopaedics, high-risk maternity and pediatrics. NUH employs more than 600 physicians who practice in 75 offices throughout the area. Its medical staff includes more than 2,000 physicians across the four acute-care hospitals. In 2001, NUH's chief executive officer began to prioritize the system to acquire an EHR, so they could handle their increased patient volumes. NUH operates in a completely paperless environment. With 1,005,282 outpatient visits and 116,063 emergency department visits in 2009, NUH has increasingly valued the EHR since its implementation in 2001.
www.northshore.org

Cincinnati Children's Hospital Medical Center
Cincinnati
2003 Davies Organizational Award Winner
Established in 1883, Cincinnati Children's Hospital Medical Center (CCHMC) is a full-service, not-for-profit pediatric academic medical center with 511 registered inpatient beds. With a vision to become the leader in improving child health, CCHMC is directed

by three cornerstones to achieve this vision: to dramatically improve the delivery of care; to greatly increase the impact of its research; and to implement new models of education for pediatric professionals, patients, families and the public.

Nationally, among comparable pediatric institutions, CCHMC ranks second in number of surgical procedures, second in number of outpatient clinic visits, fourth in number of emergency visits, and fourth in number of inpatient admissions. In 2008, CCHMC had 1,292 active medical staff physicians and 10,680 total employees. The hospital served 925,944 patient encounters including:

- 29,168 surgical procedures.
- 93,456 emergency department visits (including level 1 trauma patients).
- 27,392 inpatient admissions.
- 14,147 home care visits.

www.cincinnatichildrens.org

Maimonides Medical Center
Brooklyn, NY
2002 Davies Organizational Award Winner

Located in southwest Brooklyn, NY, Maimonides Medical Center is a not-for-profit, voluntary hospital and the third largest independent teaching hospital in the country. Maimonides is the Brooklyn Clinical Center of the Mt. Sinai School of Medicine and academic affiliate to neighboring Coney Island Medical Center and Lutheran Medical Center. Founded in 1911 as the New Utrecht Infirmary, Maimonides is the product of a 1947 merger of Beth Moses and Israel Zion Hospitals. Today, Maimonides is a 705-bed hospital and provides care for 36,861 discharges, 77,118 emergency department visits and 253,316 ambulatory visits. With a staff of 4,612 employees, the hospital's 277 staff physicians coordinate care with a network of 978 community physicians throughout the borough.

www.maimonidesmed.org

NICHOLAS E. DAVIES AMBULATORY CARE AWARD WINNERS

Virginia Women's Center
Richmond
2009 Davies Ambulatory Care Award Winner

Virginia Women's Center (VWC) is able to serve as the largest women's health center in central Virginia mainly due to having a provider staff comprised of 25 physicians, one clinical psychologist, 12 nurse practitioners/midwives and two registered dietitians, and a clinical and support staff of 158 employees. The healthcare providers offer services within and beyond traditional obstetrics and gynecology to include female urology, pelvic reconstructive surgery, clinical research, psychological counseling, nutritional counseling and genetic counseling. For 2009, each healthcare provider saw on average 2,672 patients. With their mission statement being to provide a lifetime of skilled and compassionate obstetrical and gynecologic care, to advance the practice of that care wherever possible, and to offer convenient access to other services that complement that care, VWC believed an EHR would be the best way to honor that statement.

www.vwcenter.com

Cardiology Consultants of Philadelphia
Philadelphia
2008 Davies Ambulatory Care Award Winner

Cardiology Consultants of Philadelphia (CCP) has 21 office locations around the Philadelphia area, making it the second largest cardiology practice in the nation. With 121 providers and 297 employees, CCP is able to manage all of the offices located in four counties, utilize their 13 imaging centers, and see 2,710 patients per provider annually. In an interesting side note, CCP has the only catheterization laboratory in the state, and their imaging centers are able to perform nuclear imaging and stress testing. Given that their mission is "to improve the health status of our patients through the provision of the highest quality cardiovascular care, research, and education," CCP found it necessary to acquire an EHR that could be effectively utilized by each team member to perform at a high level of excellence and still be able to create an effective and caring environment for the patient.
www.ccpdocs.com

Oklahoma Arthritis Center, PC
Edmond
2008 Davies Ambulatory Care Award Winner

Founded in 2000, the Oklahoma Arthritis Center (OAC) is a rheumatology practice located in the Oklahoma City area with a focus on arthritis and, in particular, diseases such as lupus, fibromyalgia and osteoporosis. With only 26 employees, three physicians and two physician assistants, OAC is a small clinic that sees a high volume of patients (3,900 per provider annually). OAC implemented their EHR to ensure continuity of care within the practice.

Palm Beach Obstetrics & Gynecology, PA
Lake Worth, FL
2008 Davies Ambulatory Care Award Winner

Palm Beach Obstetrics & Gynecology, PA, was founded in the mid-1990s and offers women's routine health services. The practice has grown to incorporate six healthcare providers, including four physicians, one nurse practitioner and one nurse midwife, and 19 employees working in four hospitals and two offices. With 41,115 patient visits in 2007, the practice sees an average of 3,558 patients per provider in multiple locations. Its EHR serves to link their facilities and practitioners.

Valdez Family Clinic
San Antonio, TX
2007 Davies Ambulatory Care Award Winner

The Valdez Family Clinic (VFC) has one location in southern San Antonio, TX, and is managed by one provider with near-future hopes of recruiting a second provider. There are six other staff members employed by VFC, which saw approximately 9,600 patients for the year 2007. VFC implemented an EHR to provide organization and efficiency in practice operations.

Village Health Partners (formerly Family Medical Specialists of Texas)
Plano, TX
2007 Davies Ambulatory Care Award Winner

Founded in 2001, Village Health Partners (VHP) is a three-physician traditional family practice in a suburban community. When VHP decided to implement an EHR, the practice had three healthcare providers seeing an average of 10,000 patients annually. Today, there are seven providers, and they see many more patients as a result of their EHR implementation. The EHR selected is suited for VHP's mission, which is to provide unsurpassed customer service and clinical quality.
https://secure.villagehealthpartners.com/portal

Alpenglow Medical, PLLC
Fort Collins, CO
2006 Davies Ambulatory Care Award Winner

Located in Fort Collins, CO, Alpenglow Medical is a freestanding, privately owned clinic offering basic outpatient services. Opened in 1999 with one provider, Alpenglow has two providers and six other employees to serve their annual average of approximately 10,000 patients. IT serves a patient base of 70 percent Medicare beneficiaries; 28 percent privately insured; 2 percent private pay or uninsured; and less than 1 percent Medicaid. The patient population is 85 percent Caucasian, 10 percent Hispanic and 5 percent African-American, as is the community. Alpenglow's goal is to deliver efficient, quality healthcare with no patient waiting time and 100-percent patient satisfaction. The EHR was implemented to aid the clinic with achieving their goal.
www.alpenglowmedical.com

Cardiology of Tulsa
Tulsa, OK
2006 Davies Ambulatory Care Award Winner

Cardiology of Tulsa (COT) is a full-service practice that offers comprehensive noninvasive diagnostic and therapeutic care, ranging from disease prevention and testing to interventional cardiology and electrophysiology. Having been in existence since 1969, COT now employs 101 staff with 26 healthcare providers that encounter 57,548 patients annually. Due primarily to the expansion of the practice by helping construct the St. Francis Heart Hospital, COT deployed an EHR. COT values the EHR and how it has streamlined work processes, eliminated paper charts and made access to information easier to receive.
www.cardiologytulsa.com/index.html

Piedmont Physicians Group (PPG 775)
Atlanta
2006 Davies Ambulatory Care Award Winner

Piedmont Physicians Group comprises eight board-certified internal medicine physicians, two of whom are also board-certified rheumatologists, who provide both primary care and rheumatology consultative services, as well as two physician's assistants. The clinical

functions of the office are supported by 20 clinical staff full-time employees, including RNs, LPNS and MAs, and by four full-time lab and radiology staff. The administrative and business functions of the office are supported by 10 full-time staff. PPG 775 has a patient base of more than 40,000 patients.
www.piedmontphysicians.org

Southeast Texas Medical Associates
Beaumont
2005 Davies Ambulatory Care Award Winner
Founded in 1995, Southeast Texas Medical Associates (SETMA), a primary care practice located in Beaumont, TX, has approximately 263,000 annual patient encounters. An EHR keeps all locations and staff members connected, as well as achieving excellence in clinical care. SETMA has three clinical locations and 36 clinical personnel, including 23 full-time-equivalent physicians. In addition, SETMA has separate locations for each of the following: billing office, physical therapy department, hospice, home health and mobile x-ray. SETMA operates a level two, moderately complex reference laboratory, which is completely integrated electronically. SETMA's 24 physicians are primarily primary care, family practice, internal medicine, pediatrics and nurse practitioners. They are supported by rheumatology, general surgery, pulmonology, ophthalmology, radiology and sports medicine, as well as a colorectal surgeon, ENT surgeon, nephrologist, podiatrist, neurologist and endocrinologist. SETMA employs 260 personnel and has a patient base of more than 80,000, with approximately 263,000 annual patient encounters. In addition, through electronic means, SETMA provides management services to the critical care areas of two local hospitals.
www.setma.com

Sports Medicine & Orthopedic Specialists
Birmingham, AL
2005 Davies Ambulatory Care Award Winner
Sports Medicine & Orthopedic Specialists (SMOS) was founded in 2000 as a solo practice on the campus of Baptist Medical Center-Montclair in Birmingham, AL. With a concentration on sports medicine, the practice was established to provide a new type of service, with an emphasis on athletes and care of injuries in an active population. Today, SMOS has four healthcare providers with 15 other staff members. SMOS has a volume of approximately 20,000 annual patient visits.
www.orthodoc.aaos.org/bsmos

Wayne Obstetrics and Gynecology
Jesup, GA
2005 Davies Ambulatory Care Award Winner
Wayne Obstetrics and Gynecology (WOBGYN) was founded in 2003 as a single-physician practice. While WOBGYN is still a one healthcare provider practice, there is now a supporting staff of nine to service an annual patient volume of 6,000 direct encounters and more than 3,600 indirect encounters (e.g., phone contacts). WOBGYN installed an EHR at their office, which has increased the efficiency of patient care within the clinic.

Old Harding Pediatric Associates
Nashville, TN
2004 Davies Ambulatory Care Award Winner

Old Harding Pediatric Associates (OHPA) has two locations in Nashville, TN, with a total of 14 healthcare providers and 76 staff members. There are annual patient encounters of approximately 72,500 between the two clinics. An EHR was implemented primarily to improve the quality of patient care; however, OHPA also achieved increased staff efficiency, greater patient satisfaction and an increase in office profitability.
www.ohpa.com

Pediatrics @ the Basin
Pittsford, NY
2004 Davies Ambulatory Care Award Winner

Pediatrics @ the Basin (PB) has one location in Pittsford, NY. Founded in 2002, PB was formed and is managed by two healthcare providers, with eight other employees working with the providers. PB has approximately 44,200 annual patient encounters. PB implemented an EHR and PMS (practice management system) because they work in league with another clinic, and these help the two entities stay linked into each system to improve efficiency at each of the offices.
www.pedsbasin.com

North Fulton Family Medicine
Alpharetta, GA, and Cummings, GA
2004 Davies Ambulatory Care Award Winner

Comprising two facilities located in Alpharetta and Cummings, GA, North Fulton Family Medicine (NFFM) is a primary care practice. With 16 healthcare providers and 38 staff members between the two locations, NFFM is able to serve 51,000 patients annually. NFFM implemented an EHR, with the goal of saving time and money but also had improvement in quality and efficiency. The EHR has proved useful in the variety of services offered at NFFM such as physical examinations, onsite x-rays, cardiac exercise stress testing, flexible sigmoidoscopy exams, pulmonary function testing, school and sports physicals, immunization updates and worker's compensation examinations.
www.nffm.md

Riverpoint Pediatrics
Chicago
2004 Davies Ambulatory Care Award Winner

Riverpoint Pediatrics (RP) was founded in 1978, and is managed by one healthcare provider and six other staff members. Now located in Chicago, RP has moved locations four times since it opened. In total, RP has an annual patient encounter volume of 7,375, both in the facility as well as over the phone. The EHR has made it possible for RP to go almost entirely paperless, run a more managed care practice and shrink reimbursements.
www.riverpointpediatrics.yourmd.com

Roswell Pediatric Center
Alpharetta, GA and Cummings, GA
2003 Davies Ambulatory Care Award Winner

Founded in 1978, Roswell Pediatric Center (RPC) has three locations in Alpharetta and Cummings, GA. With 16 healthcare providers and 66 other employees, RPC is able to serve an annual patient volume of 82,000. An EHR was chosen primarily to achieve the following: universal access to the chart, quality of documentation, intra-office communication, workflow, and forms and referrals processing. Linking the three offices together has been the greatest asset and accomplished with implementation of the EHR. *www.roswellpediatrics.com*

Cooper Pediatrics
Duluth, GA
2003 Davies Ambulatory Care Award Winner

Cooper Pediatrics is a one-site solo-practice located in Duluth, near Atlanta area. Founded in 1992 at another location, Cooper Pediatrics is staffed by a single physician, as well as a part-time physician's assistant and two nurse practitioners. The office manager is supported by a staff of five—a receptionist, exit clerk, and three billing specialists. One part-time student assistant scans documents into the EHR. The practice currently serves 12,431 active patients from all social classes–from the indigent to the wealthy–from all over northern Georgia. Medicaid patients make up about 10 percent of the practice. Cooper Pediatrics deployed an electronic health record on December 4, 1995. Eighteen months after going on-line, the office stored its paper charts off-site. Except for scanning and storing documents, it is a paperless office. The office performs the following services: well child care, immunizations, hearing screenings, vision screenings, minor injury management, sick visits and daycare/school forms. *www.cooperpediatrics.com*

Evans Medical Group
Evans, GA
2003 Davies Ambulatory Care Award Winner

Georgia-based Evans Medical Group specializes in newborn care, child care, adult medicine, geriatric medicine and adolescents. The practice went live with its EHR system in 1996. As the practice grew, they continued to increase their investment in both hardware and software. Upon realizing that EHR was more than just a medical record but also a database, the practice made attempts at measuring and improving quality. Notable accomplishments since going live include: being a "paperless" practice since 1998; increased provider and office staff buy-in; improving quality of care; increasing the practice's patient base; and increased profitability. *www.evansmedicalgroup.com*

CHAPTER 1

The Case for Electronic Health Records

Brian R. Jacobs, MD

"Information is really the lifeblood of medicine ... Health information technology is its circulatory system."

—David Blumenthal, MD, MPP, National Coordinator for Health IT

INTRODUCTION

It has been more than a decade since the Institute of Medicine reported that up to 98,000 deaths per year are a result of medical errors[1], but little progress has been made in addressing this critical situation in healthcare. Even more alarming, we now know that this number significantly underestimates the true impact of medical errors in the United States.

Though much progress has been made in reducing hospital-acquired infection rates and length of stay for common conditions, positive sustainable culture change in quality and safety has been painfully slow.

In 2007, the Agency for Healthcare Research and Quality (AHRQ) published their *National Healthcare Quality Report*, which noted an average improvement of less than 2 percent per year from 2000–2005 in patient safety indicators, despite the release of several important evidence-based safety publications.[2] The Congressional Budget Office estimated that 5 percent of the nation's gross domestic product (GDP)—or $700 billion per year—is spent on unnecessary medical tests and procedures that do not actually improve health outcomes.[3] These figures *exceed* the estimated resources required to cover the entire healthcare costs for the uninsured population of the United States.

Now more than ever, we need to ensure that the highest quality care is delivered to every patient in every healthcare environment, every time. Congruent with this notion, the National Quality Forum in 2010 established these six national priorities:

1. Enhance patient safety primarily through the prevention of medical errors.
2. Improve care coordination across the community and within healthcare organizations, encompassing medication reconciliation, avoiding unnecessary emergency department visits and preventing hospital re-admissions.
3. Improve patient and family engagement, including informed decision-making, patient self-management and an improved patient care experience.

1

4. Improve palliative care, focusing on the relief of physical symptoms, help with psychosocial and spiritual needs, effective communication regarding treatment options and access to high-quality palliative and hospice care.
5. Avoid overuse of inappropriate healthcare, which includes medications, laboratory and diagnostic testing, warranted maternity care, procedures and consultative services.
6. Improve population health such that all Americans receive effective preventive services and adopt healthy lifestyle behaviors, and having national health indices established.

Congressional health reform proposals are re-emphasizing the necessity of moving forward with integrated healthcare. This rationale capitalizes on studies from academic centers and experience from integrated healthcare organizations suggesting that when patients receive healthcare in organized settings, costs are greatly reduced and adherence to evidence-based guidelines is far greater.[4]

Physicians and other healthcare providers are often ill-informed regarding the quality of the care they provide. Recent data suggest that only one in four physicians receives personal performance data and fewer than one in five physicians receives information on outcomes for their patient population.[5] It is unreasonable to expect the healthcare system to improve when providers are not aware of their actual performance, expectations of their performance and opportunities to improve.

Health IT is often referenced as a centerpiece of the health reform movement, and will likely play a significant role in addressing many quality issues. As more healthcare organizations purchase, implement and meaningfully use health IT, opportunities for improvement will be discovered, analyzed and refined. And this information will be widely disseminated, resulting in significant improvements in the quality of care delivery.

Discontinuity of Healthcare Delivery

Healthcare in the United States is most often delivered in silos. Individuals who develop an illness or injury typically begin their transit through the healthcare system in an urgent care center before being transferred to an emergency department. Then, they are admitted as an inpatient to a medical/surgical care unit or intensive care unit. Upon discharge, patients follow-up with their primary care physician.

Clinicians at each care venue in this transit need to make evaluation and treatment decisions, but are often hampered by insufficient information from the previous healthcare environment. It can be challenging—and is inappropriate—for a patient to accurately recall diagnoses, laboratory and radiology testing results, and prescribed medications. Written records, if they are transferred with the patient, can be incomplete or hard to decipher. And the process of obtaining medical records from a previous provider can be so challenging and delayed as to not be effective as a resource in optimizing diagnostic and treatment decision-making.

The impact of discontinuity on healthcare delivery is extensive.[6] Laboratory tests, radiology studies and procedures are often repeated, incurring additional care delays, unnecessary costs and patient dis-satisfaction.[7-9] Diagnostic decisions are made with incomplete and/or inaccurate information. Treatments may be started or continued that are not in the patient's best interest.

Inefficiency

In most areas of the country, access to care remains a significant problem. Patients must often wait weeks for primary care or specialty appointments.[10] Emergency department throughput inefficiencies can result in excessive triage-to-doctor and doctor-to-inpatient-bed wait times.

In the ambulatory setting, patients are generally dependent on getting through to an office during regular working hours to initiate the process of appointment negotiation, rather than having direct electronic access to appointment slots. Appointment schedules are burdened by last-minute patient or provider cancellations, late patient arrivals and manual appointment reminder systems, if they exist at all. Furthermore, in preserving their autonomy, providers are not always amenable to efforts aimed at improving their efficiency.

Finally, the dynamics of patient and provider workflow within the office or hospital setting are complex and often filled with waste. Some of the simpler processes, such as refilling medications or obtaining a laboratory requisition, typically require that a patient endure a process that involves placing a telephone call, leaving a message and waiting for the call to be returned—or even traveling to the clinician's office for service. Hand-written prescriptions brought to pharmacies are delayed by manual insurance verification prior to medication preparation labeling and dispensing, which also involve delays.

Ineffective Care Delivery

It has been estimated that only 54 percent of the care delivered to patients is evidence-based care.[11] Treatment inconsistencies between providers for the same conditions are more the rule than the exception. Providers in a paper-based care delivery environment make decisions on medication selection, dosing and duration without benefit of the latest decision support; and when decision support is utilized, it often resides outside their workflow and may not employ the most appropriate or recent references. High patient volumes can result in clinicians simply not having the time to seek support to make informed diagnostic and treatment decisions.

Redundant Care Delivery

What is a provider to do? The patient sitting before him/her arrives with illegible, incomplete or no information. A complete blood count or chest radiograph may have just been performed for another provider, but the results are not available for the current assessment, necessitating repeat testing to render appropriate care. In addition, the lack of readily available information during specialty referral often results in repeat testing.

Poor Customer Satisfaction

The patient caught in the middle of the inefficiencies and frustrations of the healthcare system is less than enamored with this situation. Family, work and personal time, which are already at a premium, suffer as a result, leading to widespread patient dissatisfaction. As a result, patients may choose to avoid preventive care visits or seek acute care in high-efficiency, limited services care venues such as urgent care clinics.

THE ELECTRONIC HEALTH RECORD TO THE RESCUE

Accessibility and Legibility

The traditional written patient medical record resides in the chart racks of the ambulatory practice, the health information management department of the hospital or, in the case of an active patient, in the stack of paper or the loose-leaf notebook at the patient's bedside. Parts of the patient record may also be located in other venues of care if the patient has, for example, multiple specialists or is provided care in a non-hospital setting, such as rehabilitation or a behavioral health facilities. Accessibility to this record for orders or documentation requires the physical presence of the clinician at the location of the medical record, with one exception, which is the verbal order called in from a remote location by the prescriber to the recipient. Further compounding this inaccessibility, written prescriptions, orders and documents are often illegible, ambiguous, incomplete and devoid of identifying information such as date, time, clinician name and degree. Additionally, paper-based records do not have the benefit of evidence-based practice and/or alerts. Such documents are often associated with adverse events, errors and protocol/policy violations.[1]

Addressing this gap, one of the immediate benefits associated with implementation of the electronic health record (EHR) includes improved accessibility and legibility of the medical record. Patient orders, medications, documents, allergy information, laboratory and radiology results in the EHR are accessible beyond the bedside anywhere within the organization, and, ultimately, even among unaffiliated organizations.

With remote access through virtual private networks, information can be obtained anywhere in the world in a secure and private manner with an appropriate device and Internet connectivity. In addition to accessibility, this information is guaranteed to be complete, legible and unambiguous—with clinician name, degree and entry date/time. Therefore, nursing documentation, testing results and orders can be reviewed and care delivered remotely without the need to return to the clinic, emergency department or inpatient bedside.

Safety Advantages

Multiple studies have demonstrated improvements in medication safety as a result of the effective EHR adoption. Prescription errors are diminished in both the ambulatory and inpatient environments, and this benefit is augmented by combining computerized prescribing with effective clinical decision support (CDS).[12]

Properly designed, implemented and monitored CDS has been associated with significant safety advantages, including avoidance of overdose; prescribing a medication to which the patient is allergic; and recommendations for corollary orders (e.g., an aminoglycoside level check to be ordered with a long course of aminoglycoside therapy).

Turnaround time for STAT services such as critical medications, radiology testing and respiratory therapy have been demonstrated to improve, particularly when the EHR is implemented with process improvement and notification enhancements.[13]

This can be particularly important when appropriate timing of diagnostic bedside tests and treatments are essential to favorable patient outcome (e.g., first dose antibiotic for serious bacterial infection).

The miscommunication, which is considered the root cause of many patient care delivery errors, can improve through the increased legibility of provider documentation that comes with EHR implementation. This improvement has been associated with several advantages, including reduced clarification calls from the pharmacy for illegible prescriptions, clear communication between care providers on therapeutic plans and goals and coherent patient discharge instructions. Disease-, condition- and procedural-based care are often inconsistent between patients and providers. Inconsistency and non-protocolized care likely result in inconsistent outcomes. The EHR allows the adoption or creation of templates, care plans and sets of care orders that are evidence- or consensus-based. These tools allow the prescriber to provide consistent care to every patient, every time.

The Data-Driven Organization and Quality Applications

The traditional approach to quality often begins with a labor-intensive sampling of written patient records, serious event occurrences and consensus meetings. But this approach often leads to education and other interventions, which may not have a sustainable impact on quality. The EHR provides a rich source of granular and comprehensive clinical data, which can be collected, analyzed and disseminated.

Through this process, opportunities for quality improvement are often detected and targeted with focused interventions. The results of these interventions can then be followed sequentially, utilizing the same EHR data. The performance improvement processes of the organization can be made more efficient, comprehensive and effective. Targeted reporting to individual or groups of providers gives them the information needed to support effective quality efforts.

Engaging the Patient, Family and Primary Care Physician

Patients, family members and primary care providers often express concerns regarding their involvement in integrated care delivery. Information gleaned from laboratory and radiology studies, diagnostic and therapeutic procedures, emergency department, clinic and hospital visits are often difficult to obtain in today's complex healthcare environment. The EHR offers these stakeholders the opportunity to not only view and download this information but to contribute to its content and accuracy. Healthcare organizations that choose to adopt patient portal modules for their EHR open the opportunity for these activities, as well as such critical tasks as appointment scheduling, communication with providers, medication refills, retrieval of education materials and important links.

Health Information Exchange

According to the eHealth Initiative, there are now more than 50 active health information exchanges in the United States. These exchanges allow for the secure and private movement of important information, including demographics, medication, laboratory, radiology, problem lists, allergy, immunization, provider documents and other data across large networks, thus facilitating the availability of information to providers with a need to know and a desire to improve care delivery.

The EHR, as a primary source of important health data, represents an important component to the effectiveness and value associated with health information exchange. Though interoperability challenges exist, these will likely be overcome in the near future. Health information exchanges allow for the analysis of regional health data in recognizing trends, patterns, disparities and opportunities for improved healthcare delivery, as well as an infrastructure to introduce region-wide interventions.

CONCLUSION

In subsequent chapters, we will explore the accomplishments of many organizations in realizing the enormous value of implementation, adoption, and meaningful use of the EHR for patients, providers, and organizations. These organizations in many cases represent captains of sailing vessel in open waters. They are charting our route, exploring new environments, and communicating both their successes and challenges as we move toward a new era.

References

1. Kohn LT, Corrigan JM, Donaldson MS, eds. *To Err is Human: Building a Safer Health System.* Institute of Medicine. Committee on Quality of Health Care in America. Washington, DC: National Academy Press; 1999.

2. *National Healthcare Quality Report 2007.* Agency for Healthcare Research and Quality. Available at: www.ahrq.gov/qual/nhqr07/nhqr07.pdf. Accessed January 15, 2010.

3. Institute of Medicine. Value in Health Care: Accounting for Cost, Quality, Safety, Outcomes, and innovation. Workshop Summary: December 16, 2009. Accessed December 22, 2009.

4. Fisher E, Goodman D, Skinner J, et al. *Health Care Spending, Quality and Outcomes: More Isn't Always Better.* The Dartmouth Institute for Health Policy & Clinical Practice. February 27, 2009. Available at: http://dartmouthatlas.org/atlases/Spending_Brief_022709.pdf. Accessed January 17, 2010.

5. Physicians' Use of Information Tools and Performance Data. The Commonwealth Fund. Available at: www.commonwealthfund.org/Content/Performance-Snapshots/Improving-Quality-Using-Systems-Oriented-Strategies/Physicians-Use-of-Information-Tools-and-Performance-Data.aspx. Accessed January 21, 2010.

6. Samaan ZM, Klein MD, Mansour ME, et al. The impact of the electronic health record on an academic pediatric primary care center. *J Ambul Care Manage.* 2009;32(3):180–187.

7. Merenstein D, Daumit GL, Powe NR. Use and costs of non-recommended tests during routine preventive health exams. *Am J Prev Med.* 2006;30:521–527.

8. Mehrotra A, Zaslavsky AM, Ayanian JZ. Preventive health examinations and preventive gynecological examinations in the United States. *Arch Intern Med.* 2007;167:1876–1883.

9. Wang TJ, Mort EA, Nordberg P, et al. A utilization management intervention to reduce unnecessary testing in the coronary care unit. *Arch Intern Med.* 2002;162:1885–1890.

10. Merritt Hawkins & Associates, 2009. Survey of physician appointment wait times. Available at: www.merritthawkins.com/pdf/mha2009waittimesurvey.pdf. Accessed January 20, 2010.

11. McGlynn EA, Asch SM, Adams J, et al. The quality of health care delivered to adults in the United States. *New Engl J Med.* 2003;348:2635–2645.

12. Kaushal R, Shojania KG, Bates DW. Effects of computerized physician order entry and clinical decision support systems on medication safety. *Arch Intern Med.* 2003;163:1409–1416.

13. Mekhjian HS, Kumar RR, Kuehn L, et al. Immediate benefits realized following implementation of physician order entry at an academic medical center. *J Am Med Inform Assoc.* 2002;9:529–539.

CHAPTER 2

Engaged Leadership: The Critical Ingredient for Success

Joan R. Duke, BS, MA, FHIMSS

"Of all the things I've done, the most vital is coordinating those who work with me and aiming their efforts at a certain goal."

—*Walt Disney*

INTRODUCTION

Successful EHR implementations start at the top, with leaders who have a vision of these systems as a means to achieve their organizations' objectives. In fact, leadership is a good indicator of a successful EHR implementation. Healthcare organizations that qualify for the HIMSS Nicolas E. Davies Award of Excellence and other successful organizations are motivated by leaders who are committed to the vision of the EHR and how integrated health information can be used to improve the quality and efficiency of their institutions.

However, it is not sufficient for leaders to just have vision. Leaders need to clearly articulate their vision and the specific results they hope to achieve. They must inspire the organization in a manner that engages the staff to execute that vision. This vision should not focus on technical details; rather, it must articulate how EHR technology is integral to achieving the organization's strategic objectives.

Strategic objectives vary based on the organization, but often include ways to reduce costs, ensure profitability, grow the organization, build new service lines, gain efficiency, maintain staff, deliver quality of care, maximize patient safety and create an environment that is satisfying for patients and staff. Leaders who understand that the EHR is the tool for achieving strategic objectives can often turn a vision into an action plan.

The plan for an EHR project generally begins with board members, executives and medical leadership, who engage the entire organization and medical staff in the project. The next step is to form a steering committee that includes executives, managers, clinicians and other stakeholders who have the responsibility and authority to achieve the expected outcomes. The group's charge is to clearly define the project's goals and objectives in order to determine how outcomes will be measured after implementation and how the EHR will be used to support the structural and process changes that will achieve the desired outcomes.

The role of assembled leaders does not stop with articulation of the vision, goals and objectives, but continues as active program proponents and members of the project. Adopting EHR systems requires continual investment and support. The successful project includes organization leaders, managers, physicians and clinicians who understand that EHR technology is more of a journey than a destination. They are leaders trusted by peers and willing to stay the course as the project confronts inevitable challenges. It is a hallmark of successful EHR projects that leaders do not retreat during difficult times. Leadership participates, sponsors and supports the ongoing efforts of the many project teams that include the operational and clinical managers, physicians, key staff, experts, and, of course, IT staff.

The project team members selected must be well-respected by the staff and must be able to see the big picture—and not just their area of expertise. Their knowledge and their ability to collaborate is critical to successful implementations.

Leaders are the sponsors of the project teams. They support the project manager and ensure that teams are well-organized, adequately staffed, sufficiently funded and motivated throughout the project to achieve the goals and objectives. Leadership moves the project in the right direction by establishing expectations, setting milestones, identifying measures of success and reporting results. The leadership role continues throughout the project and post-implementation, with active involvement and oversight of the operational and system changes, project timing, costs and results.

The EHR helps staff work more efficiently, delivering safe, high-quality care. Success with the EHR is demonstrated by the achievement of clinical and operational initiatives and by a patient-centered approach to providing care.[1] The continued focus is on best practices and the process improvements enabled by the EHR system. It is not only the system and technology that change; the process and the cultural transformation will achieve broad gains in quality of care and revenue.

When visiting successful organizations, such as the Davies Award winners, one is struck by the spirit and enthusiasm of the leadership. When that enthusiasm infuses the organization, each staff member is motivated and committed to the effort and shares responsibility for achieving the objectives. The staff demonstrate system knowledge; understanding of the changes; willingness to work hard to make the changes needed; pride in their achievements; collegiality with each other; and a team spirit that allows them to have fun along the way. Physicians and staff buy into the vision their leadership envisions, seeing the improvements in their jobs, organizational efficiencies, and most importantly, patient care.

The road to the EHR is filled with "potholes," which need to be identified and filled to achieve benefits. The massive changes caused by implementation of the EHR create stress within the organization. Capable leaders guide their organization through the disruption. These leaders and project champions are engaged, hard-working and willing to be the agents of change for the process redesign.

What follows in this chapter is how successful organizations were guided by leadership who could articulate their vision, organize their projects and motivate clinicians and staff to change their practices to achieve the benefits from EHR implementation.

Leadership

As established, leadership is the generator and motivator for the use of EHRs in organizations and, post-implementation, make significant progress using this technology to achieve their vision of patient-centered, efficient and quality care. Support of the executives, managers and supervisors is required to make the changes needed to realize the vision. There are many examples of successful leaders in winners of the Davies Award.

Maimonides Medical Center in Brooklyn, NY, won the 2002 Davies Organizational Award. Maimonides was an early leader in envisioning what technology could do to achieve their organizational objectives. Their EHR story began in 1996, when executives made a commitment to a strong information environment that would improve the quality and effectiveness of patient care, increase patient satisfaction, reduce costs and position the hospital for future growth and initiatives. Their vision was clear: only a system providing real-time access to comprehensive clinical information—wherever and whenever needed—would deliver the objectives.

Three leadership factors were cited as critical to the success of the Maimonides implementation:

1. A focused CEO who was prepared for the expected difficulties—especially with community-based physicians—that typically accompany implementation of a project of this nature.
2. The financial commitment of leaders, not only in purchasing and installing the IT, but also for change management activities and ongoing operations.
3. Remaining undeterred that no other New York City community physician group had ever used hospital-based information systems.

The commitment was plainly expressed by the CEO and COO when they reserved one-third of the medical center's capital budget for IT, thereby enabling Maimonides to become a world-class medical facility in the use of technology. Maimonides recognized that physicians control 90 percent of healthcare expenditures.[2] Having identified that, the CEO took a strong stand by requiring 100 percent physician adoption of computerized provider order entry (CPOE) and supporting changes to processes that would enable improved clinical decisions.

From their vision, Maimonides set out strategic objectives for the health system:

- Improve service efficiency by streamlining healthcare processes and workflow to reduce costs and medical errors.
- Facilitate decision support.
- Improve patient outcomes.
- Provide access to patient records and images at remote locations.
- Improve patient satisfaction.

These objectives fit within a series of strategic imperatives that the institution had defined to fulfill its mission as a major urban medical center and teaching hospital. The objectives also were expressed in measures of return on investment (ROI), quality improvements and other benefits. The board did not merely approve the budget and objectives, but required frequent updates on the status of the project; and once implemented, how well the organization was meeting their objectives. Figure 2-1 shows how the vision was translated into strategic initiatives.

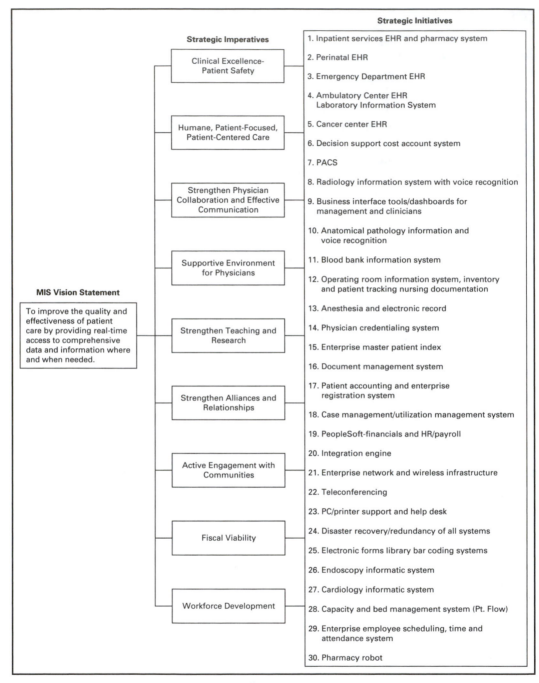

Figure 2-1: Vision Transformed into Strategic Initiatives. (From Maimonides Medical Center, used with permission.)

Alignment of Strategy, Goals and Objectives

Central to Maimonides and the other health system examples that follow is the ability of leadership to communicate the concept of EHR technology as a strategic investment that is critical to achieving the enterprise's goals and objectives, as depicted in Figure 2-2.

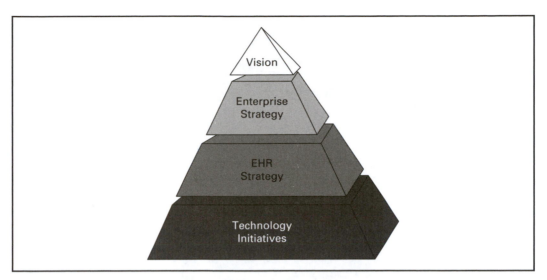

Figure 2-2: Structural Illustration of Goals and Objectives.

The focus is not on the technology but on the business and clinical problems to be solved. Success is measured by achievement of the business and clinical goals and objectives.

Figure 2-3, from the New York City Health and Hospitals Corporation (NYCHHC) Davies Award application in 2009, depicts how their EHR strategy of care redesign, quality of care improvements and revenue enhancements fits into their corporate strategy and how they will measure success.

One of their networks, Generations+/Northern Manhattan Health Network, won a Davies Organizational Award in 2006. Generations+' exemplary medical records implementation, part of an initial effort to install comprehensive clinical systems in each network, is described in more detail.

At NYCHHC, IT governance exists at both the corporate and local level. The goal is to integrate and standardize the systems across the seven networks to take advantage of uniform best practices and standardized reporting.

The move to planning and prioritizing IT at a corporate level began in 2001, with the appointment of a corporate CIO who is a member of the executive team and oversees the network CIOs. Corporate governance also includes a chief medical officer (CMO), who coordinates plans for the clinical information systems. Over time, the structure has fostered an evolution from decentralized development and local implementation to a federated model with greater alignment across the network.

The change has been enabled by continuous communication between the network chief medical information officers (CMIO) to the corporate CMIO, CMIOs and medical and nursing leadership, network CIOs and the corporate CIO and network executive directors to the president of the corporation. They now must agree on resource priorities and implementation of solutions across their organizations. The clinical systems have, through this coordinated leadership, evolved from an individual network focus to one that is increasingly centered on the patient.

Generations+/Northern Manhattan Health Network comprises three hospitals in New York City that care for some of the most medically needy and underserved communities in

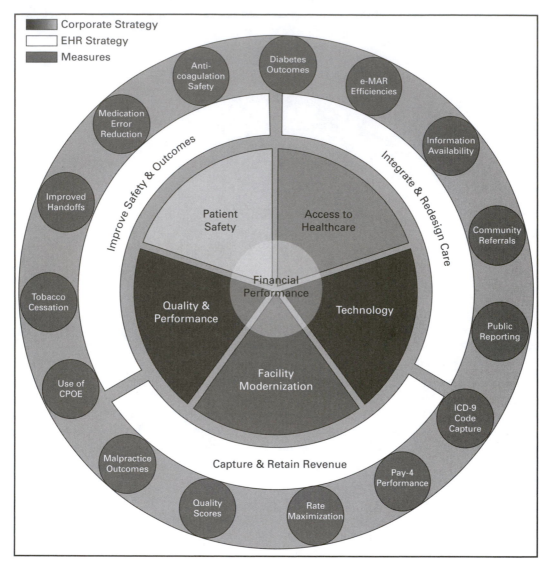

Figure 2-3: NYCHHC Success Model. (**From New York City Health and Hospitals Corporation, used with permission.**)

the nation. The network's vision was to serve as a patient-centered, community-oriented and safety-focused organization to fully support its primary care initiatives. Generations+ is the largest network in the New York City Health and Hospital Corporation; the NYCHHC Board of Directors and the presidents of the corporation were part of the planning process, approved the plan and budget and directed implementation of the EHR. At the local level, the senior vice president and CEO of Generations+ led the implementation, specifically directing the needs assessment and planning activities, establishing priorities, allocating resources, approving policies and monitoring the implementation process. He chaired a steering committee, which included senior staff, medical directors and representatives from information management and information systems. A medical informatics committee also was represented on the committee by the chair of the interdisciplinary group from across the hospitals' functions.

The key with Generations+, as with other Davies Award winners, was leadership's ability to engage top executives and clinical leaders in the vision and the active management of a project supported but not led by IT. This is a proactive role for executives and clinical leaders as technology champions, rather than as mere bystanders in EHR implementation.

Another key role illustrated by Generations+ was leadership's participation in the decision-making process to review program issues and disagreements among departments, so they could be clarified or resolved in a timely fashion. To quote from their application, this role is one in which: "The CEO is a tireless champion of IT both in the network and in the communities we serve; he views the transition to the EHR, enhancement of billing and business systems, electronic communication enhancements and consolidation of services through automation as mission critical initiatives owned by the members of the executive team—not IT alone."

Another Davies Award winner, Citizens Memorial Healthcare (CMH) in Bolivar, MO, demonstrates that it is not just the large population centers or teaching hospitals that can successfully implement an EHR. At the time of its Davies Award application, CMH was a rural, integrated healthcare delivery system comprising a 74-bed acute-care hospital; five long-term care facilities with a total of 476 beds; a residential care facility with 60 beds; home health, hospice, home medical equipment, homemaker services and health transit services; and 16 rural physician clinics.

During the Davies Award site visit to CMH, it was clear that the board, executives, managers and staff were engaged and enthusiastic about the EHR. The hospital used the sign-on page of the system to let everyone know that the HIMSS Davies Committee members had arrived. The enthusiasm was not just about the site visit but also from a staff appreciative of the improved care and operational environment that was enabled by IT. The environment of the project and supportive culture were created and driven by the leadership of the organization. This leadership included the president of the board, CEO, executive management and medical staff members. In addition, the CEO had been the keynote speaker for the project implementation kick-off, expressing confidence in the success of the implementation and the positive impact it would have on patient care, quality and service.

CMH's strategic objectives, which guided the project, were the result of planning and collaboration among strategic planning teams that included administration, management staff, board of directors and medical staff.

The organizational objectives fell into five categories:

1. *Quality of care and service excellence* through master facility expansion, medical staff recruitment and development, clinical program development and quality improvement efforts.
2. *People focus* through recruitment of qualified staff, development of existing staff and retention.
3. *Financial strength* through productivity improvements and medical staff engagement in financial efforts.
4. *Accuracy and completeness* in documentation and coding.
5. *Market development* through the implementation of a comprehensive marketing plan and improved access to care in all areas.

The goals and objectives for the project, named Project Infocare, were formalized during a planning retreat. Infocare's goals and objectives were aligned with and key to achieving CMH's larger organizational objectives. The project goals were:

- Project Infocare will be implemented to enable a patient to enter anywhere into the continuum of care and have a personal identity that is maintained across that continuum.
- Physicians and other caregivers will have access to all of that patient's medical information within the healthcare continuum.
- Healthcare providers will be able to document efficiently and safely within the software system.
- Providers will be supported by CDS that will prevent medical errors and improve adherence to standards of care. Providers will be able to spend more time with patients.
- The community will realize the benefit of the investment of time, talent and money in Project Infocare by enabling the healthcare continuum to become technologically advanced and poised to grow to meet demand, as well as to offer new services to current patients and to the community at large.

One more example of visionary leadership in a large organization was 2004 Davies Organizational Award winner Evanston Northwestern Healthcare in Illinois (now called NorthShore University HealthSystem). The CEO, working with the board of directors, established the organization's number one priority: implementation of a paperless, patient-centric EHR with true CPOE. He believed moving to the EHR "was the right thing to do ... the status quo was unacceptable," and he insisted on 100 percent use of the EHR by staff and physicians.

This one project would impact all of the enterprise's strategic objectives, which, encompassing three hospitals and 68 office locations, were simply stated as:

- Best possible care and clinical outcomes for patients.
- Patient safety.
- Patient satisfaction.
- Retention of talented staff.
- Sound financial performance.

The project goals were articulated by NorthShore's top leadership, including the vision for the new paperless system, which required every physician and clinician to use the system. They understood that only with adoption at 100 percent would the system-wide project meet its goals of:

- Improving patient safety by eliminating problems associated with illegible orders and medication errors.
- Ensuring that physicians, clinicians and administrators have access to the right patient data at the right time.
- Ensuring the accuracy of the information and coded data in the record.
- Simplifying processes and making them consistent across the organization.

Leadership and vision are the same factors that lead to successful EHR implementations in ambulatory care organizations. That said, there is a distinction between the hospital/health system environment and the ambulatory care or physician-practice setting.

In the latter, one or more physicians typically champion the EHR implementation and do so in a much smaller environment. In this situation, if even just one person resists the implementation, the leadership challenge is compounded. Yet that is frequently the case; either a key staff person and/or another physician may oppose the change. Getting everyone onboard and prepared to use the EHR is critical to success. Let's examine how this has played out for a number of Davies Award-winning physician practices.

Oklahoma Arthritis Center's (OAC), PC founder developed a vision for the future to support the growth he saw coming. He believed that "becoming electronic was the only way to go" and that the EHR system was needed to not only support growth, but to also support integration of ancillary services. His vision was much the same as larger healthcare organizations:

- The EHR would increase efficiency.
- The system would reduce the daily cost of a unit of services, leading to increased profitability.
- The electronic chart, with better organized and more complete information about the patient, would lead to improved clinical outcomes.
- The EHR, with better patient scheduling, tracking, prescribing and other features, would make the practice run more efficiently, bringing more satisfaction to patients and providers.

Winner of the 2006 Davies Ambulatory Care Award, Alpenglow Medical, PLLC, is a two-physician primary care practice based in Fort Collins, CO. Founder Daniel Griffin, MD, (author of Chapter 4) cites his early training and personal experience as shaping his view that the practice should value patients' time and need for customer service, while delivering high-quality services. He believed that if the clinic was fully efficient, it would maximize revenue generated per hour, allow physicians better management of their time and reduce malpractice insurance premiums. For him, the structural elements needed were:

- Electronic management of patient and practice information.
- Staff support of seamless information to provide the foundation for customer service.
- The practice, at its inception, opening with electronic health records in place and the involvement of every staff member in ongoing financial and efficiency improvements. The approach engendered by the vision enabled complete and accurate documentation for better care delivery and knowledge management.

At North Fulton Family Medicine in Alpharetta and Cumming, GA, (2004 Davies Ambulatory Care Award), three physicians researched solutions and worked to get buy-in from other practice physicians and staff. They understood that an EHR was needed to recoup the time and money spent on administrative functions and to improve the quality of care, while growing the practices. In particular, the following practice goals were emphasized:

- Save costs associated with clerical full-time employees, supplies and chart storage space.
- Save time spent waiting for lab tests, reporting on lab results and managing patient charts.
- Improve coding of procedures, thereby increasing charges.
- Accommodate the maximum same-day encounters, per patient requests.
- Implement workflow improvements supported by the EHR to meet growth strategy, while reducing overhead and improving patient care.

Their belief in using technology solutions and tools to grow the practice made the growth much less painful and expensive and set the tone for the practice to achieve their objectives and gain value from their EHR.

Implementation Governance and Organizational Structure

As EHR projects move from planning to implementation, the nature of governance and the structure of committees are critical factors in translating goals and objectives into achievement of outcomes and the realization of value. Governance is a process of exercising authority and control over decisions about priorities and resources to achieve objectives. Figure 2-4 demonstrates the following distinctions between enterprise and IT governance roles.

Enterprise governance ensures that technology aligns with enterprise strategy, focuses on clinical and operational problems to be solved and measures performance according to the business goals. It maximizes the use of financial, human and technology resources for overall benefit to the organization. Figure 2-4 demonstrates this idea.

IT governance is an organized framework of roles, responsibilities, policies and methods used to guide, direct and manage IT resources. It is an extension of enterprise governance, not an "island" function delegated to the IT department. IT governance requires executive-level involvement and participation by users and other key stakeholders.

EHR projects must be governed by defined structures and clear oversight from governing board(s), committees and project leadership. Governance includes program management of the operational changes and management of the EHR project. It includes the individual

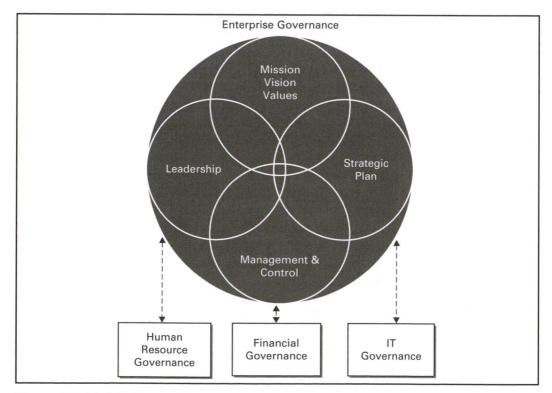

Figure 2-4: Model of Enterprise Governance.

or individuals who can cross medical disciplines, departments and organizational entities to address issues. Organization structure will vary based on size and complexity, but the following is a summary of what is found in a Davies Award-winning organization:

- Regular project reports to the board, executive leadership and medical committees.
- Governing committees that include key stakeholders that provide oversight of the project and address issues across organizations and departments.
- Executive sponsors that ensure the project meets its value objectives by enabling users and the necessary resources and budgets to be available.
- Program management team that is responsible for operational changes, project management and developing action plans for execution and control of all project activities.
- Process transformation teams that include affected clinical and operational management and staff who are involved with process remodeling and implementation of the process changes.
- Cultural change management to include leadership development, policies, procedure revisions and communication vehicles such as letters, newsletters, meetings, rewards/recognition, etc.
- Physician and clinician advisory groups active in charting the implementation of organizational best practices, analysis of clinical results, and continuous quality improvements.
- Competent and well-funded technology teams.

A successful IT governance structure is exemplified in the approach taken by 2007 Davies Organizational Award winner Allina Hospitals & Clinics, Minneapolis, MN. This health system includes 11 hospitals and 65 clinics. The IT initiative began with no project governance in place outside of a steering committee. A new governance structure, which was developed as part of the implementation kick-off, is depicted in Figure 2-5. The key roles include:

- An oversight committee, which is a subgroup of the board of directors. The committee guides the overall strategy of the implementation and reviews project status and budget on a quarterly basis.
- A steering committee that serves as the major approval body, governs the operational aspects of the implementation and assists the Project Management Office in decisions related to implementation. This group approves strategic direction, timeline changes and implementation scope changes.
- A project management office to provide the day-to-day operational leadership of the implementation.
- A physician engagement team to foster physician involvement in the project.
- A CDS team that is accountable for the development and maintenance of clinical content tools in the EHR, including note content documentation, order set content, rules and alerts, protocols, care plans, flowsheets and evidence links, as well as educational materials for patients and family caregivers.
- Detailed advisory groups, comprising subject matter experts from across the organization to help make organization-wide design decisions for the system.
- Hospital, ambulatory, revenue and physician advisory groups—four separate advisory groups comprising experts from across Allina who govern design decisions for their respective areas.

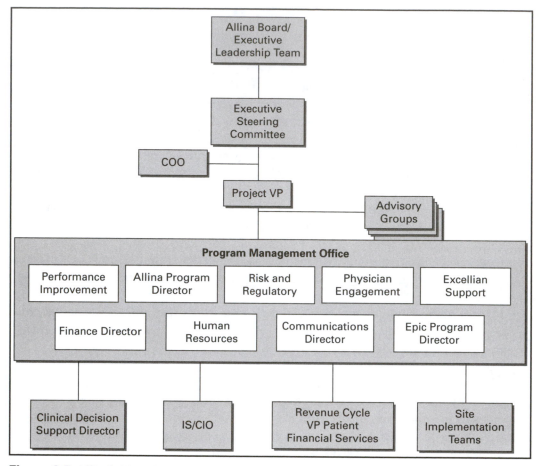

Figure 2-5: Allina's New Governance Structure. (From Allina Hospitals & Clinics, used with permission.)

The IT governance structure at 2004 Davies Organizational Award-winner NorthShore, in Evanston, IL, engaged not only their leaders but also included executives and medical staff leaders. The organization's structure was unique at the time in that it included a medical informatics department. This department served as the link for operations, clinicians and the IS department. The informatics department also was key to the operational re-design and implementation process, and today, continues to provide guidance to the IS department on clinical process issues and assists clinicians in the effective utilization of the EHR.

2008 Davies Organizational Award winner Eastern Maine Medical Center's (EMMC) governance structure evolved during the first years of design and implementation to add a program management office for overall business case analysis and project management.

In addition to transformation of care teams that remodeled key processes, Bangor-based EMMC has another support team that deals with cultural changes. This team works to develop leadership, accountability, consistent application of policies, employee/staff satisfaction, internal communication, change management and educational alignment. The development of the teams and stakeholder involvement is described in the next section of this chapter.

IT Leadership in the Physician Practice

Leadership is equally vital to the success of EHR implementation in the physician's practice. While in this environment, fewer people may be involved in leading and championing the implementation, the role of the physician leaders is all the more visible and must be equally persistent. If the physicians are not fully engaged, the staff will not give the implementation the priority it needs to become in their day-to-day work.

What follows are a few examples of strong leadership and how that leadership guided their practice to an award-winning EHR.

At Georgia-based Roswell Pediatric Center, winner of the 2003 Davies Ambulatory Care Award, one of the managing partners served as the project executive sponsor and administrative lead. The planning team included the client services manager, the project manager from the vendor who worked with a team of superusers, and key staff.

The practice administrator was the project manager and the implementation lead, providing day-to-day operational leadership. She was supported by the vendor's client service manager. The implementation team included a senior project manager, a clinical project manager, an administrative lead, a medical knowledge author, a clinical trainer, an engineering services specialist and a technical lead.

One of the main factors Roswell cited that contributed to their success was the project charter that outlined every detail and every person's responsibility in the implementation. This document provided a clear understanding of what to expect and when to expect it. The process of creating the charter required the practice to establish their expectations at the beginning of the project, which led them to define "success" in meeting their objectives.

Georgia-based Piedmont Physicians Group (PPG 775), winner of the 2006 Davies Ambulatory Care Award, comprises eight internal medicine physicians who provide both primary care and rheumatology. The project was coordinated by an executive steering committee composed of key decision-makers from the practice and from Piedmont Hospital. This governance group included the senior physician, the practice's office manager and the hospital's CIO. The implementation team also was multidisciplinary, comprising representatives from the practice and the hospital.

Critical factors cited for their success included technical support, decision-making and commitment from Piedmont Hospital. More important for the practice was the commitment from practice physicians and staff. The senior level sponsorship included the three most senior physicians who "led the charge" and were the first to drop the paper chart. This major change demonstrated their commitment and encouraged others to adopt the EHR.

Engaging Physicians, Stakeholders and Staff

Engaged leadership is the forerunner of engaged participants within the entire enterprise. In particular, engaging physicians on staff, associated or attending, is one of the key challenges.

2003 Davies Organizational Award winner Cincinnati Children's Hospital Medical Center (CCHMC) thought one of their greatest risks was that the clinicians would not buy into the new clinical system and into the process changes that would be needed. CCHMC, a relatively early adopter of EHR, is a 324-bed tertiary care hospital serving primary areas in southern Ohio, northern Kentucky, eastern Indiana and West Virginia. They were the first healthcare system to combine technological innovation with an industry-standard process improvement approach in addressing strategic institutional goals. They achieved rapid implementation of a clinical information system that provides physicians, nurses and allied health professional staff with advanced, pediatrics-specific CDS to meet the unique needs of safely caring for children.

Understanding the need to engage physicians and clinical staff, CCHMC included clinical leaders during the planning, design and implementation phases. These efforts culminated in the appointment of an associate professor of radiology as Medical Director of Information Services and an associate professor of pediatrics as the Clinical Order Entry Project Director. They formed their CPOE design team with a group primarily composed of physicians. The physicians received compensatory pay for the time invested in this team. Multidisciplinary users also were invited to join design teams. The clinical documentation team was primarily composed of nursing and included affected ancillary personnel. Specific resources were invited as necessary; for example, allergy physicians attended the design team meetings related to the allergy data collection screens. The process CCHMC leadership followed recognized that clinical support would be needed to ensure success during the implementation and to sustain ongoing operations.

EMMC's strategy was to identify stakeholders to be involved with design decisions, planning and implementation. The leadership employed the following methods to engage physician leaders in planning the EHR:

- They engaged a range of physicians in the project, which included private, community-based, regional and hospital employees.
- The physicians participated in the development of disease-specific order set content.
- They developed specialty event sets by working with the project team on setting up their view of EHR to incorporate only the specific data elements needed by the specialty.
- They developed a shared regional oncology record available 24/7 for EMMC and rural hospitals to reduce visits and duplicate testing.
- They discussed EHR and CPOE at section and service meetings.
- They conducted provider surveys.
- They sponsored active participation, a project whereby private orthopedic surgeons reviewed data, participated in process re-design and continually reviewed performance against goals.
- They held a vote for the mandatory medical by-law changes, including CPOE.
- Some physicians also became members of the issues/recommendations, clinical informatics committee and operations council. They were recruited to champion the vision of the EHR.
- Clinical coordinators reporting to EMMC's CMIO were hired to round with physician groups to help spread the vision and bring suggestions from the providers to the transformation of care teams.
- A 15-member clinical performing group (CPG) for CPOE representing various clinical service areas in the hospital (including project sponsors) was formed to assist the project team in the solution design, testing/validation and overall championing of the project.

- Stakeholder involvement included not just physicians, but also subject matter experts in nursing, pharmacy and other ancillary areas. The project management methodology continues to ensure the consensus of the clinical stakeholders through a clear definition of stakeholder involvement during each phase of the project's lifecycle, as shown in Figure 2-6.

EMMC used a structured methodology to manage and execute the organization's strategic projects. It included a Project Management Office (PMO), using process improvement techniques and standard project management methodology from the Project Management Institute's Project Management Body of Knowledge (PMBOK®) and LEAN management methods. Their process clearly defined stakeholder involvement during each phase of the project lifecycle. Stakeholder involvement and consensus began with initiation and planning of the project and continued through implementation, education and deployment. The clinical system team participated in system design, scripts preparation, testing and accepting of the systems. Their involvement did not stop with implementation, but carried through into post-implementation, with continuous improvement of the deployed systems based on feedback and regular communications with providers and other system users.

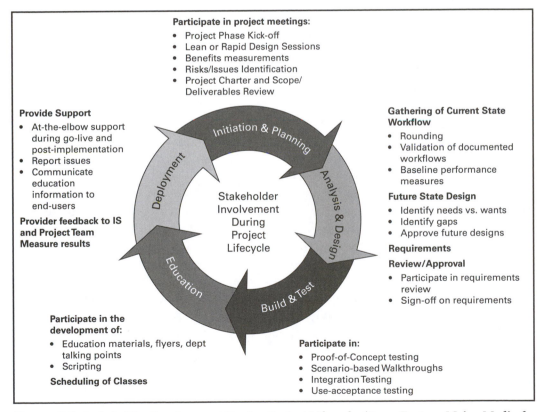

Figure 2-6: Stakeholder Involvement During Project Lifecycle. (From Eastern Maine Medical Center, used with permission.)

Oklahoma-based Cardiology of Tulsa, 2006 Davies Ambulatory Care Award winner, is a full-service cardiology practice that offers comprehensive, noninvasive diagnostic and therapeutic care, ranging from disease prevention and testing to interventional cardiology and electrophysiology.

Their business objectives recognized physicians' needs by providing full access to each patient's medical record from every location where care was provided, including the physician's office, satellite location, hospital, home or on the road.

Cardiology of Tulsa employed a "pull" strategy—rather than a "push" strategy—with physicians. In other words, they discovered that physicians were less resistant to change because leadership kept physician needs in mind throughout the selection of the EHR, the design of the templates and the deployment of the system. The EHR team worked closely with the physicians to explain the capabilities of the EHR and listened as the physicians explained how they wanted it to mirror their work habits.

The business objectives of Beaumont-based Southeast Texas Medical Associates (SETMA), a 2005 Davies Ambulatory Care Award-winner, mirror those of the other winners. They saw the need for EHR in dealing with the complexities of 21st century medicine. SETMA realized that the ability to measure provider performance and the outcomes of medical decision-making was only possible with the EHR. Additionally, they wanted to establish a national standard of care and best practices, regardless of setting, which included outpatient, inpatient, long-term residential facilities and home.

The leaders were "sold" on an EHR system, but to proceed, they needed to sell the idea to several groups, including physicians and staff. They nurtured a physician champion respected by providers who was totally committed to the project. There was collaboration between the technical team and healthcare providers to ensure the system would work in the clinical settings. The collaboration was driven by mutual respect and trust. Building consensus among providers allowed for standardization of care, standardization of documentation and comparison of care and comparison of documentation. This consensus was cited as the most important decision that directly impacted their success.

The 2007 Davies Ambulatory Care Award-winning Valdez Family Clinic in San Antonio, TX, is a single-location, single-physician family practice serving an economically disadvantaged and medically underserved community. It can act as a model for a target audience of a single-physician practice's success with EHR. The same leadership and clarity of vision, goals and objectives were determining factors for the practice's success.

Alicia Valdez, MD, owner and operator, cites attitude as making the difference at the Valdez Family Clinic. As a leader, she inspired group commitment to the transition to an EHR. She made everyone in the clinic part of the selection and implementation process, so the EHR was not something imposed on the staff. Dr. Valdez's belief that people would support their own decisions and commitment to the transformation made possible with EHR resulted in their transformation and in never looking back. Moving the practice from paper would have been impossible without this right attitude.

One last organization to reference and drive home this point is 2008 Davies Ambulatory Care Award-winner Palm Beach Obstetrics & Gynecology PA in Lake Worth, FL. It is a full-service obstetrics and gynecology practice comprising six providers working in two offices and four hospitals.

A quote from Palm Beach sums up the theme of leadership: "Leadership is the most important asset. The ability to recognize talent and place it in its appropriate department is critical. … Change is difficult for everyone, and discipline and encouragement from the leadership team was essential for success."

CONCLUSION

Leaders are visionaries, translators of the goals, guides to the right path, champions, mentors, active project participants, overseers and communicators of the process. They build the right culture of passion and enthusiasm. They set the goals, guide the execution, resolve problems and celebrate success. Leadership for the implementation of EHRs is about creating a way for people to do the right things. EHR success is due to many factors, but one of the most important drivers on the road to success is the visionary leader.

References

1. Chen C, Garrido T, Chock D, et al. The Kaiser Permanente electronic health record: transforming and streamlining modalities of care. *Health Aff.* 2009;28(2):323–333.
2. Drazen EL, Metzger JB, Ritter IL, Schneider MK, eds. *Patient Care Information Systems: Successful Design and Implementation.* New York, NY: The Free Press; 1995:20–21.

CHAPTER 3

Readiness Assessment: You Know You're Ready When…

Susan Heichert, BSN, MA, FHIMSS; Barbara M. Drury, FHIMSS; and Patricia B. Wise, MA, MS, RN, FHIMSS

"By failing to prepare, you are preparing to fail."

—*Benjamin Franklin*

INTRODUCTION

By Patricia B. Wise, MA, MS, RN, FHIMSS

The Davies Awards have repeatedly revealed a shared conviction that from the top of the organization down through all levels, healthcare is an information business. As noted in Chapter 2, successful EHR implementations are the result of focused strategic planning, vision, leadership and daily, tactical, hands-on guidance. Proactive implementation management drives widespread organizational support and promotes staff involvement. It starts with a readiness assessment of the organization.

Assessing the readiness of a healthcare organization is not an easy task. Regardless of whether the implementation will occur in a large, complex, multi-departmental hospital or a single-site ambulatory practice, it is essential to understand the impact the EHR will create on the culture, people, resources and key stakeholders in the organization.

Readiness is a term that can be used in a variety of ways to apply to an EHR deployment. One might consider technical readiness, workflow readiness, training readiness and so on, but the most critical factor for success, as demonstrated by Davies Award winners, is cultural readiness. If your organization is not culturally ready for an EHR, you will quickly find that planning for and enabling the culture change that are needed is a critical success factor.

One method of assisting in the cultural change is to identify the specific areas of preparation that must be addressed prior to the transition. Understanding and planning for these preparations engages the organization and starts to move staff into a proactive ownership role in the change process. This chapter will highlight the readiness process and provide examples of how Davies Award recipients paved the path for successful implementations.

ASSESSING READINESS IN THE HOSPITAL OR HEALTH SYSTEM

By Susan Heichert, BSN, MA, FHIMSS

Many organizations are taking a closer look at implementing EHRs, especially now that mature implementations are beginning to demonstrate the capability to support achievement of such strategic goals as improving patient outcomes, qualifying for federal incentives and providing data to respond to continually increasing reporting needs.

Although some organizations by-passed the readiness assessment phase in their EHR implementation and jumped right into the system selection process, many of the Davies Award winners deliberately assessed the organization's readiness from a leadership perspective as their first step.

They knew that, "You know you're ready for an EHR when leadership is committed to a strategic plan that highlights the EHR." Their assessment started with assessment of leadership and resource needs. They assessed the "people" element: executive commitment, resource commitment and the identification of key stakeholders.

"People" was the common theme for the first stage of assessment for EHR readiness. Although EHRs and CPOE are increasingly accepted by the medical community, the commitment required to see these projects through is substantial. A transition of this magnitude requires certain key people elements to be in place. An assessment tool used by Bangor-based Eastern Maine Medical Center (EMMC) (2008 Davies Organizational Award) highlights a number of elements that should be in place before deciding to move to the EHR (see Appendix 3-1).

The EHR needs to be part of the organization's strategic plan and linked to the organization's goals. For Davies Award-winning organizations, a clear understanding of what each hoped to achieve via the EHR implementation was necessary to create common understanding needed to move such a complex project forward.

For example, the Bloomington, IN-based Center for Behavioral Health (CBH) (2006 Davies Organizational Award) created a strategic planning team that developed concise objectives for their EHR. An IT assessment and planning process was initiated, and a formal needs-assessment with a consulting company was undertaken, followed by a year-long series of steps to ensure IS efforts would support organizational strategies. Top issues were identified, resulting in the identification of a need for an EHR and adoption of guiding principles. The assessment and planning team eventually became the ongoing IS steering committee.

Executive Commitment Is Understood

Every Davies Award winner cited the need for leadership to be crystal clear about the organization's commitment to the EHR and firm on the decision to move forward (see Chapter 2).

Evanston, IL-based NorthShore University HealthSystem (2004 Davies Organizational Award) (formerly Evanston Northwestern Healthcare) noted that it is easier to build and sustain enthusiasm for a project that staff is sure will come to fruition. A track record of successful technology rollouts for physicians (e.g., imaging) was also cited by NorthShore and EMMC as a way to create trust in the ability of the organization to deploy an EHR.

All leaders must be ready to consistently communicate and adhere to the underlying reasons for moving to an EHR. Challenges will arise from every area in the organization, demanding that the decision to implement an EHR needs to be reviewed, re-thought or rescinded. If the leadership team is not solid enough to withstand those challenges, work first must be undertaken to strengthen the team.

CBH cites the example of a leadership challenge that developed when they moved to centralized online scheduling and away from the traditional "black book."

"Clinicians perceived this change as a loss of control, as schedules also became more standardized. Many of these clinicians continued to surreptitiously use their black books. It wasn't until the CEO declared that the only pertinent schedule was the electronic schedule that this behavior waned."

Tacoma, WA-based MultiCare (2009 Davies Organizational Award) took the approach of holding attitude and environment change seminars, which were hosted by top leaders in the organization. This tactic gave them the opportunity to have potential end-users raise issues early, while at the same time gain some understanding of the cultural readiness of the organization for change.

Some Davies Organizational Award winners were moving from automation to automation, rather than from paper to automation. 2005 Davies Organizational Award winner Citizens Memorial Healthcare (CMH), Bolivar, MO, found that change to a new system may be resisted even when end-users already have automation in their department. They noted on occasion that functionality was lessened or lost, but that the overall benefits from the new system outweighed the negative impact of the loss.

Certain key stakeholders who may have been champions of the "old" system may not immediately agree with a decision to implement a new system and may be a challenge to the leadership team. Other challenges the executive team will face are determining how much time the physician leader will have allocated to the project and how he or she will be paid for undertaking the leadership role.

A best practice among Davies Award winners was to have adequate physician time dedicated to the project, especially in the areas of CPOE and documentation. In most cases, this required the commitment of a full-time physician.

Reimbursing end-user physicians for their participation in the EHR implementation and training also needs to be addressed and was frequently cited by the Davies Award winners as a challenge for top leadership. Organizations differed on their approach— some paying for participation, but not for training, and others paying for all physician involvement.

Resource Commitment Is Understood

Financial and staff resources, including opportunity costs that are incurred as other projects are put on hold to implement the EHR, must be well understood before deciding to embark on the EHR journey. The commitment of financial and human resources is often of a greater scope than that demanded by any other project the organization has ever undertaken.

The CEO of 2007 Davies Organizational Award winner Allina Hospitals & Clinics, Minneapolis, referred to the decision to move to an EHR as a "bet the company" decision, due to the substantial organizational resources required. Most of the organizations made reference to putting other projects on hold, as the EHR project not only consumed a substantial percentage of available capital, but also involved such a large cross-section of staff.

Key Stakeholders Are Identified and On Board

Another key to success cited was the involvement of both formal and informal leaders of stakeholder groups in the process of assessing the organizations' readiness for the transition. Their attitudes and beliefs influenced key staff groups—positively for those appropriately engaged and negatively for the organizations that did not engage the leaders ahead of time. These leaders, whether administrative or clinical, will bear the brunt of overcoming the cultural change. They need to be part of the process and adequately supported throughout it.

Assessing Readiness Prior to Vendor Selection

You know you're ready for an EHR when… key success factors are defined. Once the organizations were comfortable that the leaders and key stakeholders shared a common commitment to the long-term EHR project, key organizational criteria for success were elaborated. These criteria shaped the scope of the EHR implementation.

Among the Davies Award winners, criteria included measures such as: 100 percent of physicians will use CPOE, no paper records will be maintained, all patients will have the opportunity to interact with their EHR. MultiCare took the approach of setting an overarching goal of achieving the ideal patient experience and developing success criteria from there. Critical success factors were then reviewed and approved by the medical staff. They also conducted an analysis of the medical staff and segmented the providers based on their likelihood to adopt or resist new technology. Strategies were then put in place to assist staff as needed.

You know you're ready for an EHR when… your end-users have assessed the level of standardization of processes. Once the high-level direction is in place, the next step involves a more detailed assessment. All of the Davies Award-winning health systems took the time to assess their organizational processes to determine their readiness for transition. This stage is all about *process*. Assessing processes provides a good idea of how much prep work, such as standardizing processes; order sets; and terminology and creating crosswalks from current to future processes will be required prior to implementation.

Additionally, organizations noted that this kind of work is generally time-consuming and should be started immediately, even prior to vendor selection and contracting. Following are key areas that were assessed by the Davies Award winners.

Although some care processes varied based on the type of clinical unit, standardization of certain core processes was seen as essential to recognition of benefits, as well as a smoother implementation.

NorthShore used surveys, observation and engagement of end-users to understand current processes, to identify those that should be consistent but were not and to develop a plan to close the gap. They spent an entire year on process review and redesign, all of which was driven by end-users. This in-depth, grass roots methodology paid off in high levels of adoption because of the extensive degree of ownership assumed by end-users who felt that EHR adoption was critical to achieving their patient safety goals. End-users who help create and are invested in a process are less likely to look for workarounds that subvert the reasons for the standardization.

Examples of key processes reviewed for standardization included physician ordering, nursing documentation (flow sheets and care plans) and pharmacy formulary (for organizations with multiple sites). CBH engaged end-users in creating a map of every process and standardized any processes that varied between departments.

Another common practice among Davies Award winners was to collect all forms— not only to identify and minimize variation but to ensure that all existing processes were reviewed and plans were made for users to transition from their existing process to the new process.

One clear lesson is that end-users must also be involved in this part of the assessment, as they are the only ones who know what forms or parts of forms are actually used. This collection activity was helpful in engaging them in the culture change as well. CMH developed a "chart of the chart" to ease transition to a paperless environment. Each chart form was identified, and the plan for the transition of that form to electronic format, the timeline for transition and the action plan for transition were all developed.

An important element of standardization that is critical for decision support and reporting is standard data information models and terminology. 2006 Davies Organizational Award winner Generations+/Northern Manhattan Health Network, New York, NY, is an example of an organization that successfully implemented standard data information models shared across disciplines within and across facilities. These models incorporated standard definitions and terms, including minimum data sets. Other organizations utilized standard terminology sets—a decision that is best made prior to building the EHR system.

Having standardized physician order sets and preferred orders lists in place prior to CPOE is one of the most essential elements for a successful transition. Most Davies Award-winning organizations had customized paper order sets for each particular physician prior to implementation. In some cases, these order sets had existed for years and were ingrained in the culture. Each organization made the decision whether standardization of the order sets was required before implementation, shortly after or ever.

CPOE can be implemented with non-standardized order sets, but the opportunity for assisting physicians to achieve best practices will not be realized until best practice sets are created. Many organizations choose to implement standardized orders sets, incorporating what the organization and the physicians agree are best practices, which physicians can then customize. CMH developed a report to determine each physician's most commonly ordered tests and then set up their commonly ordered test lists prior to their training. Not only did the physicians feel that they were ready to transition to the new system, but they had very positive opinions of the training.

Developing standardized order sets was seen as one of the first tests of physician readiness for an EHR. A common Davies Award-winning practice was to approach leaders of each medical specialty to chair committees to review all existing order sets and develop the new sets. Whether or not physician leaders agreed to step up to take on this challenge and the participation of physicians in each specialty was an early indication of whether the physician community supported the organization's EHR goals. The support varied depending on the type of setting—academic vs. community hospital and multi-site vs. single site. Generally, support was highest in academic settings and single sites where the physician community was more heavily engaged with hospital operations prior to the EHR decision.

You know you're ready for an EHR when… you have a consistent value message, clear communication channels and a solid marketing strategy. Understanding the gap in organizational standardization provided substantial background for developing the value proposition or "the case for the EHR."

In completion of the first stage of readiness, the creation of a consistent supported message for all leaders to use when engaging staff seemed to be a common indicator among Davies Award winners. Often, standardization of clinical processes had implications to business processes, such as registration and billing.

NorthShore cited the importance of considering all of the potential impacts and not having too narrow a focus. Another process that was assessed at this stage was whether adequate communication channels existed within the organization. EHR implementation requires solid, consistent and reliable channels. Physician communication in particular was seen as challenging, especially for cases in which many of the physicians were not employed by the hospital.

CMH notes that the organization needs people capable of developing a marketing strategy that will be used throughout implementation. They had a unique method of preparing by utilizing "Franklin Covey's 4 Roles of Leadership Model," which includes pathfinding, aligning, modeling and empowering.

In *pathfinding*, they developed and publicly expressed their vision statement and statement of confidence. In *aligning*, they positively engaged resistors, and marketed the product to end-users. In *modeling*, they served as cheerleaders, established scope, removed obstacles and served as communication liaisons; and in *empowering* they selected implementation team leaders who were trusted, respected, had enthusiasm and communication skills and were motivated.

You know you're ready for an EHR when… you know how big your hardware investment will be. A final consideration by most organizations before deciding to move to an EHR was an assessment of their underlying technology platform. This assessment was undertaken to ascertain what currently exists and to obtain a high-level estimate of what new technology would be necessary. Once an EHR vendor was selected, a more detailed and specific assessment of technology needed to be completed. The first level was seen as necessary to better understand the financial commitment that was required. Following are some of the areas taken into consideration:

- Wireless. Does the organization plan to incorporate wireless into their technology platform? What currently exists and where does it need to be expanded?
- End-user hardware. This category was a big contributor to system expense in many cases. Obtaining a high-level understanding of the magnitude of increases in end-user hardware contributed to a more accurate financial estimate. Items considered included WOWs (workstations on wheels), bar-coding equipment, auto paging and handheld devices.

- Network readiness. Is the organization experiencing the kind of uptime it will need to support an EHR? Is redundancy in place to create the nearly 100-percent uptime end-users will demand? Are experienced resources available in-house or will the organization look to external resources? Does the network extend to all areas that require coverage?

Generations+ only focused on network connectivity in the clinical areas at first and learned that they needed to consider non-clinical areas as well. Physician offices, administrative suites and conference rooms were not included initially, and the demand for access in these areas quickly became obvious after go-live.

Another lesson from Generations+ relates to the change in how PCs are perceived in relation to other medical equipment. They relate the story of how it took a major New York City power outage for them to discover a vulnerability in their power source strategy. The computer room was on emergency power supply, which maintained the application, but the user desktops were *not* on emergency power supply. The system was up, but no PCs could access it because in the pre-EHR world, PCs were not considered direct patient-care devices. Today, however, a good percentage of the workstations are connected to the emergency supply and identified with a red outlet.

- Does the network have the ability to transmit large data files (e.g., images) as needed? Can the network handle the volume of traffic that is anticipated? Allina developed a system response team and process. This team included vendor representatives, as well as various technical members, and would immediately be called into action when a trend in slow system response calls to the help desk developed or in reaction to monitoring tools indicating system response issues.
- EHRs generate lots of data that need to be maintained somewhere, but must remain available for retrieval. Does the organization have the necessary storage architecture in place to meet the demands of an EHR?

Assessing Readiness after Vendor Selection and Before Implementation

You know you're ready for an EHR when... you've defined the scope of your EHR project. What's in the EHR? Once the EHR vendor is selected, the readiness assessment takes on a different focus and a more detailed scope definition needs to be developed. For example, one organization focused on selecting their EHR vendor first and then looked at what other technologies would be necessary to achieve the organization success factors outlined earlier. This organization determined that in order to achieve their vision, they would need to develop interfaces to several of their existing ancillary vendors, as well as select a new imaging vendor.

Creating a plan from the outset that packages various smaller projects together to achieve a unified EHR appears is a common theme among the Davies Award winners. Some organizations chose to do this in stages, while others orchestrated all of the projects to go-live at the same time. Understanding the organization's culture, including its appetite for risk and ability to absorb change, influences which path each healthcare system chooses. Other influences included the financial impact of rolling out multiple sites in a short period, which drove the Phased Approach vs. the Big Bang decision.

Almost all organizations experienced changes to the original scope at some point in the project. Some of the organizations were able to phase-in CPOE—mostly related to the fact that their providers and caregivers did not cross units. Again, this type of decision was site specific.

NorthShore originally planned for a Big Bang go-live in their first site, but the pharmacy system was not ready for physician ordering. They decided to modify their approach and went live with documentation in the first phase, with clerical staff entering the physician orders from paper. CPOE then went live in the second phase. A benefit of this approach was to identify any issues with orders being correctly transmitted to the ancillary departments before the physicians started using the system.

Additionally, physicians were able to gain familiarity with the overall conventions of the system before taking on the order entry component. Some Davies Award winners used formal tools to determine cultural capacity for change; others relied on knowledge from their tenure within the organization to inform their strategic choices.

You know you're ready for an EHR when... you have formal management and governance structures in place. Many organizations have never deployed a project with as many ramifications to the business as an EHR. Often formal management processes including project management, change control and testing were not as structured or as extensive as the Davies Award winners found necessary for an EHR rollout. The extent of discipline required for these processes was among the lessons learned verbalized by many of the winners.

Another question asked was whether the organization had the proper structures and discipline in place to manage such an extensive project. An EHR was often among the largest project that each site had ever undertaken. Most of the Davies Award winners employed some type of formalized project management structure—usually in the form of a project management organization (PMO). The PMO generally comprised senior leaders who could remove roadblocks related to such factors as lack of staff and financial resources or who represented important constituents of the end-user community.

EMMC experienced the consequences from the lack of these structures, which included inefficient tracking and reporting of activities and decision-making, scope creep and an ineffective change control process. They established a strong governance structure and created clear processes with checks and balances built in. Sub-groups that reported up through the PMO were also identified, as well as their scope and decision rights. For example, all awardees developed some type of provider governance group, which often became the start of their physician user group. These groups generally were given decision rights for provider training, support and adoption activities.

Other processes used by Davies Award winners included a more formalized IT change control process than what had previously existed. Due to the integrated nature of the EHR—whether from single vendor or best of breed—a change in one area can have unintended consequences in other areas. Creating a process whereby changes are tested in non-production environments, reviewed by a group representing all modules before moving the change to a production environment and then moving changes to a production environment in a scheduled and planned manner was cited as a requirement before moving forward with the EHR.

Testing can also be viewed as a form of determining readiness. Again, many organizations moved to a deeper level of testing for the EHR implementation than what they had undertaken in the past. One of the areas of testing that is cited as essential by several of the awardees is user acceptance testing (UAT).

Allina skipped the UAT step with early deployments due to time constraints, but learned of the critical nature of this when physicians had difficulty using the order sets as built. Order sets had been built in the order that they appeared on the paper order set, with the assumption that users would be accustomed to that presentation. However, automation of the order flow meant that the paper layout no longer was intuitive in the "new world."

For the subsequent implementations, selected physician leaders were involved in order design and implementation of UAT, which allowed fine-tuning of the order sets prior to go-live. This also created more familiarity with the potential pitfalls for the physicians who would be assisting others within their specialty. Another benefit of UAT was the identification of device issues with workstaion on wheels (WOWs), such as screen size, battery life, storage space on the care unit, and even the ability to fit the WOW through the door of a patient's room. Almost every Davies Award winner mentioned finding these types of issues either before or after their go-live. Those who found them after would have preferred to find them before!

You know you're ready for an EHR when… you have an adequate training structure and strategy. Readiness for large-scale training was addressed by every Davies Award winner. Many utilized a formal tool to assess basic computer skills among the end-users. CBH initially used a self-reporting tool, but found that users often overestimated their basic computer skills. They then implemented a skills test approach and were able to better determine basic Windows training needs and provide remedial training.

Other areas of assessing for training readiness cited by Davies Award winners included determining whether the organization would be using an e-learning approach exclusively or in conjunction with other types of training. For multi-site systems, a determination of whether training would be centralized or decentralized was made, and then the organization's readiness to deploy either of those strategies was assessed.

For example, several of the multi-site winners selected the centralized option, which then created a need to develop a physical site for the centralized training. Other organizations selected a mobile option and created a "training center on wheels" to bring the training to each site. Physical distance, number of available trainers and the organization's culture will all impact the strategy selected for training.

You know you're ready for an EHR when… your managers and staff are ready. Several of the organizations devoted time to the preparation of the management staff. MultiCare developed specific content for management staff to assist them with communicating a consistent message about the change and to prepare for the issues their staff may raise at various phases of the project.

Conducting dress rehearsals or regular scripted practice sessions was another common theme of awardees. These rehearsals would be held on the unit with the various end-users who would be going live, usually three or four weeks before the actual go-live.

One of the important lessons learned was the critical nature of transitions of care, or hand-offs, in any process. These transitions are the areas that were focused on during the dress rehearsal, as they were the most problem prone. An example of a complex transition that was cited is the medication reconciliation function, which required handoffs between the patient and various caregivers, as well as between various units.

Another type of dress rehearsal utilized to assess readiness was a practice run through of how end-user calls would be triaged. Especially important was preparing a methodology for responding to potential patient safety issues. For example, a user may call in with a problem related to the system that is causing erroneous information to be entered into the record. This type of call may have previously been handled by a safety report or phone call to the risk department. Involving the stakeholders in developing a new process ahead of a go-live ensures that safety issues will be handled appropriately.

You know you're ready for an EHR when... you have a strategy to get data out of your EHR. A common theme among award winners was the recognition that some type of data warehouse or repository is needed to generate the outcomes data that demonstrate achievement of the strategic goals. The organization may already have a data warehouse in place, but, as CBH noted, it may be necessary to review and dramatically revise your business intelligence strategy.

A final area that deserves mention is analyzing processes for outside people or groups that currently access the paper medical record to obtain data from the EHR. Some of these groups include surveyors, patients and third-party billing agencies. Several organizations mentioned that this process was initially a low consideration on the priority list, and some had to scramble to accommodate those types of users.

Assessing Readiness before Final Go-Live

Several of the Davies Award winners used various tools and methods to assess their readiness for going live with a system or a module. Tools were used to determine end-user, site and project team readiness. Data from the assessment were then used for the "go/no-go" decision points. Pilots were also frequently initiated to test readiness for a larger scale rollout.

You know you're ready for an EHR when... you can measure and demonstrate your readiness for go-live objectively. Keeping each hospital unit on track with the tasks they must complete prior to go-live was cited as another readiness challenge. Allina developed a tool to assess the progress toward readiness of each unit throughout the implementation, affectionately known as the department readiness assessment tool (DRAT).

Goals were set at regular intervals for various criteria including basic computer skills readiness, scheduling of super-users, understanding of new reports, unit device readiness and completion of staff training. At each checkpoint, the unit leader completed a survey, which then fed into the overall hospital readiness assessment.

The progress against the goals was reviewed at the PMO, as depicted in Figure 3-1. Units falling significantly behind in an area were addressed on an individual basis with additional resources or relevant assistance.

For example, 90 days before go-live, training needs for the department should be identified. At 60 days prior, all users should be scheduled for training. At 30 days prior, all users should be trained. Allina found the DRAT tool useful to keep implementations on track and assess the overall state of readiness of the site for the Big Bang implementation.

MultiCare utilized a similar survey (see Table 3-1) prior to and after go-live, which helped identify staff preparedness, system stability and gauge awareness of the technology being implemented, as well as end-user perceptions and concerns, which changed as the project progressed.

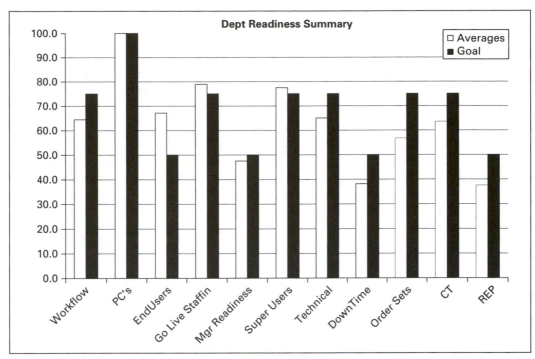

Figure 3-1: Department Readiness Graph. (From Allina Hospitals & Clinics, used with permission.)

Table 3-1: MultiCare Readiness Assessment. (From MultiCare, used with permission.)

	90 days	**60 days**	**30 days**
Workflows	My staff & I have attended the following workflow-related events: • Workflow Walkthrough event at _____ on June 3-4, 2008 • Tunnel Tour at TG/MB in _____ • Hallway Huddle at Allenmore in _____ • Operational Leadership Review of departmental workflows • Clinical Director review of workflows as part of weekly Clinical Director meeting	I have participated in detailed key workflow reviews within my department	I have resolved any workflow-related issues and questions
		I have identified processes needing redesign within my department as a result of workflow changes	I have updated department-specific documentation to reflect any changes
		I am working with project team members on issues and questions related to key workflow changes so that I may make changes to my department's processes where needed	I have educated my department staff on the new key workflows and processes
	I am aware of the _____ key workflow changes that I need to prepare my staff for: (attach to cover later)	I have initiated communications with my staff regarding the key workflow changes that impact departmental processes	Updated procedural and workflow documentation is complete and will be available in my department for reference at Go-Live

(Continued)

Table 3-1: (Continued)

	90 days	60 days	30 days
Management Education	I am aware of application education requirements for myself and my staff	My management team and I plan to attend application education requirements that are specific to my area	My management team and I have completed appropriate application education sessions
Staff Education	I understand the education offerings required for my staff	(>50% or <50%) of my staff members have been scheduled for education	Most of my staff members have completed education
			Scheduling of all remaining staff is complete
			Staff members have review their access codes and practiced logging into the system

Piloting

A commonly utilized approach to assess readiness is the "pilot." For Davies Award-winning organizations, a pilot was a small-scale deployment of all or a portion of a system to determine how it operated in a "real world" environment with real end-users." Pilots took a variety of forms. Most Davies awardees utilized a unit-based pilot for either portions of, or the entire EHR. Some multi-site organizations utilized one of the smaller sites as a pilot.

Winners found that pilots were useful in identifying inadequate numbers of super-users, missed workflow steps or challenging workflows, functionality issues, adoption risks, failure to identify reporting needs and inadequate staff preparation. Obviously, the earlier a pilot was conducted, the more time the site had to remedy the findings. EMMC also found the pilot useful to practice and refine go-live processes, such as the process flow for user call triage and resolution.

CONCLUSION

Common themes for assessing readiness for the EHR are evident throughout these Organizational Award winners' sites, as well as some valuable lessons learned, which can be summarized in three categories: leadership and governance, standardization and preparation.

Leadership and governance. Common purpose and ability to focus for both the administrative and the clinical leadership are key. Decision-making structures must be in place to prevent scope creep, flexibly deploy resources and provide a platform for creative solutions to take shape.

Standardization. How standard are the organization's processes, and how much work should be done before focusing on the build of the EHR? Many activities can precede the EHR deployment and will provide immediate benefit to the organization. These include workflow mapping, process review and standardization, terminology standardization and business and clinical standardization (including formularies, care plans, etc.).

Preparation. Is the organization equipped to staff the necessary preparation steps, especially in regards to backfilling of clinical staff, so that they can be engaged in the

EHR implementation? Many activities will pull unit staff away from their usual duties, including testing, training, practice sessions and dress rehearsals.

What these Davies Award winners consistently demonstrate is that a thoughtful assessment of their readiness allowed them to mitigate the areas in which they were less ready as an organization to successfully deploy and support an EHR. By paralleling the implementation of the readiness mitigation strategies with the actual EHR implementation, they were successful in meeting their strategic objectives.

These organizations value the readiness assessment step and feel that the effort expended pays off in a successful implementation. Each time they add additional pieces of functionality to their EHR they go through the necessary steps to assess their readiness, which will improve the success of their outcome.

READINESS ASSESSMENT IN THE AMBULATORY SETTING OR PHYSICIAN'S OFFICE

By Barbara M. Drury, FHIMSS

Although an ambulatory practice might not have the multimillion dollar EHR implementation budget of a large healthcare enterprise, the diligence in addressing a readiness assessment is equally important. In a small practice environment, a successful implementation can become derailed if just one or two practitioners resist the change. Leadership is crucial and must reach out to include all of the staff in planning. Workflow is of paramount importance and must be considered throughout the planning process. Keeping an eye to the future in your readiness planning pays big dividends in future flexibility. Is your ambulatory practice ready?

Introduction

During the period in which the 19 Davies Ambulatory Care Award winners of 2003–2009 selected and implemented EHRs, there were far fewer resources available to assist a physician office in assessing the office's readiness to move to an EHR than are available today.

In all cases, someone in the office identified pain points and thought an EHR would alleviate some of the issues. However, while some pain points or needs are common among the winners and others were unique, nearly all of these winners share organizational attributes that helped them look to the EHR as a potential solution and helped them weather the many issues encountered along the way. These organizational attributes can be inferred to be readiness indicators for other physician offices as they consider their own readiness to become users of this technology.

None of the winners used a formal readiness assessment; that is, none worked with staff to identify skills and change issues, and none of the applications reference an assessment of facility or technical readiness. And yet, all became very successful users of an EHR, largely due to pre-existing organizational attributes, which are described in the following sections of their applications: leadership environment; budget and funding capacity; clinician with business or technology training or prior EHR experience; experience with computerized billing and scheduling; willingness to look at workflows; willingness to change courses; willingness to accept local responsibility; recognition that care delivery is also a business;

recognition of the value of data above digitized documents; culture of patient/population management prompted by initiatives from payors, national groups and/or research efforts; and miscellaneous organizational attributes.

Leadership Environment

As in the hospital, and as discussed at length in Chapter 2, leadership is critical to a successful implementation. This section would not be complete if the importance of leadership commitment was not again emphasized. Most offices have regular staff meetings that include both business-operational staff as well as clinical staff. These regular forums facilitate a formal and regular process in which different departments can participate in discussions to achieve the mutual goals of the practice.

Specifically, here are examples of how leadership got engaged in the practices of Davies Ambulatory Care Award winners:

Roswell Pediatric Center, Alpharetta and Cummings, GA (2003): "Our managing partner works with me on the day-to-day decisions. We have an executive committee, which meets with me monthly, along with a monthly partner's meeting. The best thing about our practice is our staff, starting with the owners. They make decisions based on what is the 'right or fair thing to do,' taking into account fiscal responsibility. This sets a great example and tone for the rest of the decisions made in our practice by all employees."

Old Harding Pediatric Associates, Nashville, TN (2004): "The decision to move forward with an EHR came in three phases. A campaign called Compassionate Care 2000 was launched in the office in March 2000. 'Compassionate' stood for providing quality service focused on kindness, understanding, and accessibility. 'Care' meant we were committed to excellent pediatric medical care, education, prevention, and to providing a nurturing workplace. '2000' signified that our future was focused on technology, quality assurance, research and dedication to education for future physicians. The second phase started in August 2001 when a strategic planning committee was formed by representatives from every aspect of our office, including patients. The annual Director's Retreat in October 2001 was the third phase of the decision-making process."

Budget and Funding Capacity

All of these Davies Ambulatory Care Award winners had expected a temporary surge in expenses, but all of them experienced additional costs that were either not anticipated at all or exceeded the original estimates.

This required re-direction of available funds for: increased staff efforts; new staff or consulting services; and additional modules, interfaces or equipment.

Without the financial capacity to acquire and pay for these additional services (in-house or outsourced) the practices would not have succeeded. While it takes excruciating effort to identify 95 percent of all expenses, there will always be unanticipated expenses during the selection, implementation, on-going use and growth of an EHR system.

A good example of the on-going financial requirement will be fine-tuning software and users in order to demonstrate the increasingly complex meaningful use criteria being developed by the U.S. Department of Health & Human Services. While not all-encompassing, here are some of the "extras" that required additional funding among the Davies Ambulatory Care Award winners:

Virginia Women's Center, Richmond (2009): "We also established an EHR Helpdesk for application support. The staff EHR director role developed into the Clinical Applications Directorship, with responsibility for interfaces, new form development, application support, content development and ongoing application training and retraining."

Cardiology Consultants of Philadelphia (2008): "We undertook a six-month project to develop our own fully customized content. IT support was obtained by hiring full-time staff to develop our IT infrastructure, as well as to implement EHR deployment. Hundreds of PCs had to have software upgrades. All computers were updated to Windows XP professional; those that could not were replaced. Friday afternoon: EHR pizza parties!"

Palm Beach Obstetrics & Gynecology PA, Lake Worth, FL (2008): "Before installation, we obtained the T-1 lines and VPN configurations needed for adequate connectivity between both offices. One week before go-live, we stopped seeing most patients in the office and started the training process. The initial surge in data entry meant the temporary addition of one employee and an increase in overtime."

Piedmont Physicians Group (PPG 775), Atlanta (2006): "Prior to go-live, temporary workers were hired to enter problem and medication lists for patients scheduled for the following week."

Village Health Partners (formerly Family Medical Specialists of Texas), Plano, TX (2007): "We hired a network consultant to install the hardware and network. First, in order to limit patient inconvenience and to the extent possible, we did not schedule follow-ups in our go-live month. Secondly, we planned for a 20 percent drop in revenue for two months. Both ended up being very appropriate."

Alpenglow Medical, PLLC, Fort Collins, CO (2006): "The practice closes several days per year to allow full participation in update trainings."

Cardiology of Tulsa, Oklahoma (2006): "The practice hired temporary employees as the scanning team and scheduled crews to provide coverage from 7 a.m. to midnight, five days a week. It took three years to complete the task, and it cost the practice $200,000. The benefits greatly outweighed the costs, however, because physicians had complete access to electronic histories and records."

Offices considering implementation of an EHR should make note that in spite of these additional expenses, these practices were and continue to be successful businesses, as well as exemplary EHR users.

Clinician with Business/Technology Training or Prior EHR Experience

While not a requirement, one-third of the Davies Award winners had a clinician with broad and relevant training or experience outside the realm of patient care, either in academic preparation or previous electronic record experience. Cardiology of Tulsa, Village Health Partners and Virginia Women's each had physicians with a Master's in Business Administration. The managing partner for Palm Beach Obstetrics & Gynecology has a Bachelor of Science degree in computer science, and the group's office administrator had previously implemented an EHR in another office.

Prior to opening the practice, the lead physician for Valdez Family Clinic, San Antonio, TX, (2007 Davies Ambulatory Care Award) had managed research in a chemistry lab. Alpenglow Medical's lead physician completed a certificate program in "The Business of Medicine" through the Harvard Schools of Medicine and Business.

The lead physician for Pittsford, NY-based Pediatrics @ the Basin (2004 Davies Ambulatory Care Award) was on the University of Rochester Medical Center's Ambulatory Information Services Committee. The lead physicians for Georgia-based Evans Medical Group (2003 Davies Ambulatory Care Award) and also Village Health Partners had previously used electronic record systems in training programs.

Cardiology of Tulsa in Oklahoma, had experienced a previously failed EHR implementation. The presence of prior experience in business and technology or with previous EHR implementation before tackling the winning EHR implementation undoubtedly supported the decisions necessary for such a significant project as EHR implementation.

Experience with Computerized Billing and Scheduling

All 19 winners had already implemented an electronic practice management system before implementation of an EHR. All were client/server technology-based (none Web-based). This initial step into the responsibilities of using and maintaining a computer system is an essential readiness indicator.

All the lessons learned from the implementation of a practice management system are readiness indicators for moving to a more complex system with implications far beyond a patient financial balance. One-third had previously implemented a practice management system, which was sold or developed by the same company that also offered the EHR that the practice eventually selected.

These practices enjoyed the benefit of bi-directional information via programming code that was developed and maintained by the same vendor. The integration of practice management functions and electronic record functions increases opportunity for efficiencies in two major areas: single entry and maintenance of patient demographics, and all billing codes are a derivative of the charting process—reducing duplicate entry efforts as well as aligning claim data with documentation data.

However, two-thirds of the Davies Award winners elected to retain their existing practice management system and pay for the development and maintenance of an interface between their existing practice management system and the unrelated EHR that was selected (see Figure 3-2).

This is a high percentage (66 percent among Davies Ambulatory Care Award winners) and likely a reflection of the time period when these winners were making their EHR selections. At the time, most single-vendor solutions were actually two products integrated via acquisitions (by analogy, the two products now had the same foster parent, but each has different technical DNA), as there were fewer than five choices of a truly single-data base solution available to these practices at the time of their EHR decision.

Of the 66 percent that retained an unrelated practice management system, minimizing double entry between the practice management and the electronic record system had to be addressed. One of the winners has no interface between the practice management and EHR systems. That requires the practice staff to enter patient demographics and insurance information twice—into both the practice management system and the electronic record system.

In addition, billing codes generated by the electronic record are printed to a "super bill" or charge ticket for later entry by the billing staff after the patient visit. Seven of the

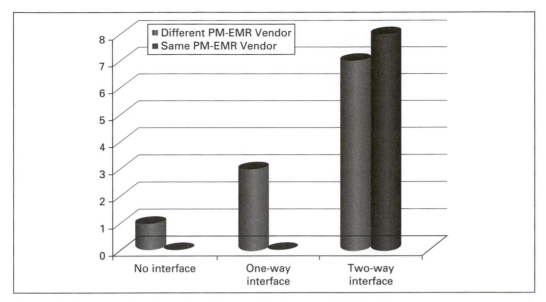

Figure 3-2: Approach to Interfaces Between Business and Clinical Systems.

winners developed and maintained a bi-directional interface between different practice management and electronic records systems. Three of the winners opted to develop and maintain a uni-directional interface out of the practice management system and continue using super bills or charge tickets to check billing codes for later entry by billing staff.

Whether the practice management system and EHR are from the same or different vendors, clearly the majority of these Davies Ambulatory Care Award recipients found value in the initial investment in an interface plus ongoing software maintenance fees, while reducing duplicate data entry and data maintenance for business and clinical users.

Interfaces require initial payment to each of the sending and receiving software vendors, as well as annual maintenance fees to maintain the code written by each of the sending and receiving software vendors. These interface maintenance fees usually accommodate updates from one party or the other.

Willingness to Look at Workflows

This group of Davies Ambulatory Care Award winners all articulated an approach to workflow that said "there are no 'sacred cows'—let's take this opportunity to look at how everything in our practice works."

In some of these offices, the new workflows came first and the EHR came second. In others, the EHR tools came first and the new workflows followed. Both approaches resulted in successful users of the technology in their setting. Here are some of the commitments to workflow design that were addressed by these winners.

Before: "Our EHR team worked with each department to make sure we knew how their workflows should be set up." Edmond-based, 2008 Davies Ambulatory Care Award-winner Oklahoma Arthritis Center (OAC) P.C. measures the success of the EHR through the improvement of the day-to-day workflow of the practice. "We are constantly looking at our workflows to figure out how we can enhance them."

Before: "Many of my processes were easily engineered into the EHR, so my staff and I were able to conduct business without tossing out the efficient processes that we had developed." —Riverpoint Pediatrics, Chicago; 2004 Davies Ambulatory Care Award.

Before: "We developed workflows for the most common visits. These workflows were integrated into forms and protocols." —Valdez Family Clinic.

Before: "We included all the staff in every workflow discussion from the beginning. We based training around workflows. It was done all together because in a small office basically all common workflows involve all members of the staff. We would map out our current workflows, then spend time looking at ways it could be done in the EHR. Once a new workflow was decided, it was documented and we practiced with test patients until everyone felt comfortable. This was accomplished by analyzing the workflows of our most common tasks in the office and automating them as much as possible. Our staff is now keenly aware of the importance of workflow and process improvement." —Village Health Partners.

Before: "The practice realized significant benefits through process improvements— not necessarily because physicians worked faster, but because the installation of the system required that workflow throughout the organization be evaluated. Implementation of an EHR represents a complete reengineering of workflow and of the way all individuals view their jobs, their responsibilities, and how they interact with their colleagues. Each step must be carefully planned, ramifications of the change must be carefully considered." —Cardiology of Tulsa (COT).

Before: "Design began with an intensive workflow improvement effort. The practice hired an industrial engineering consulting group to complete a series of time motion studies related to workflow throughout the office. These studies identified key areas for improvement, and the in-house work group used them to develop future state workflows. The EHR implementation was an opportunity for process improvement. The EHR would not be implemented around existing processes. Instead, the practice would identify optimal processes for the flow of information and the delivery of care and then build the EHR around those processes." —Piedmont Physicians Group (PPG 775).

Before: "The process redesign was dictated by the design of the workflow." —Southeast Texas Medical Associates, Beaumont; 2005 Davies Ambulatory Care Award.

Before: "Early on, our implementation administrative lead began introducing non-clinical staff to the product and discussing how the EHR would affect their workflow. We discovered ways to improve efficiency, create new workflows and design transition plans for staff." —Old Harding Pediatric Associates.

After: "Almost every workflow was transformed by the implementation of the EHR." —Palm Beach Obstetrics & Gynecology, PA.

After: "Additionally, our EHR support team continually rotates from site to site to ensure that workflows are being followed." —Cardiology Consultants of Philadelphia.

After: "We have had significant changes in workflow that positively impact our face-to-face patient time." —Pediatrics @ the Basin.

After: "The practice has taken advantage of customizable features, which allow the practice to design workflow based on its preferences." —North Fulton Family Medicine, Alpharetta and Cummings, GA; 2004 Davies Ambulatory Care Award.

After: "By instituting EHR, we gained more uniform clinical workflows. We were able to audit these workflows, which would have been essentially impossible with paper charts." —Virginia Women's Center.

Willingness to Change Course

This attribute was evidenced by these Davies Ambulatory Care Award winners' ability to have a plan; assess how the plan was working from a process, a people (patients and staff) and a technology perspective; develop an alternative plan based on information, and actually change course in the middle of a process. Not just flexibility within the practice but informed decision making around the original plan and the optional plan.

Here are some examples from the winners that not only demonstrate the change in direction but also illustrate some take-aways on what didn't always work as each expected:

Evans Medical Group: "The forms made by the software developer to input the data were not to our liking, as they did not fit into our workflow, so we paid them to make a form that would help us get the data where we wanted. Changes that may seem small often have a large 'trickle down' effect. When I used to change forms without consulting others, it would often have much bigger changes to the workflow than expected. Changing a form may result in a different person inputting data and may significantly change that person's job description. We now do not allow changes to happen unless we have discussed them and tried them in a smaller part of the practice to make sure there is not too great of an effect."

Roswell Pediatric Center: "After a few months on the system and several power blips, we purchased and installed 15-minute UPS for the clinical workstations."

Virginia Women's Center: "It was difficult to accept failure and the financial burden of the unused technology (bubble-sheets and scanners). Knowing when to quit was a challenge. As the EHR was implemented, it became clear that when providers utilized the developed tools correctly, very little keyboard entry was needed. Voice recognition became less important and was ultimately discarded. We quickly learned that durability is a major factor with tablet PCs. We abandoned the initial tablets for much sturdier models and equipped them with wireless cards to allow universal access to the network regardless of nationwide location."

Cardiology Consultants of Philadelphia: "We quickly realized that the clinical content was inadequate to support our cardiology practice. We then undertook a six-month project to develop our own fully customized content, during which time no further providers went live. Initially, we scanned many existing patient documents into the EHR. This was both inefficient and costly. Subsequently, we minimized the amount of existing document scanning during subsequent office go-live."

Sports Medicine & Orthopedic Specialists, Birmingham, AL; 2005 Davies Ambulatory Care Award: "[For go-live] we should have reduced our patient numbers by one half. After a day without a lunch break, the staff regrouped to assess our progress and plan. The decision was made to limit patient visits for the following two weeks."

Following approval from its board of directors, Cardiology of Tulsa identified a task force that would direct preparation for and implementation of the system. After a trial run revealed substantial hurdles during implementation, the project was tabled. In the process, COT developed the capacity to be a "learning organization," incorporating and integrating new approaches as it recycled lessons learned.

Village Health Partners: "Starting in early July, we began to develop our plan to transition our paper records into the EHR. The initial plan was to transfer it all. After a short discussion with our project manager regarding time; resources; and cost of this path, we quickly changed our minds. After a few days, our second plan was scratched. At that point, we determined that the most accurate and efficient way was for it to become the responsibility of the physician. However, this quickly proved to be problematic in many instances because the information we had in the paper chart was either incorrect or outdated. Once we went to our current system of 'just in time' input, we really progressed."

Alpenglow Medical: "Reception staff reported waiting several seconds for needed information due to slow printing and all information printing to one central printer. We purchased new printers."

Oklahoma Arthritis Center: "We planned for battery backups on all of our equipment, but we did not do an electrical survey of the server room. A few months after the instillation, some of our fuses for the servers started tripping unexpectedly. The battery backups did a good job of keeping everything up, but we ended up having to have an electrician run a dedicated circuit to the server room."

Willingness to Accept Local Responsibility

Selecting and implementing an electronic record is definitely not a passive experience. These Davies Ambulatory Care Award winners jumped into the process with both feet: local team, local expectations, local user needs, local customization and staying engaged with the vendor. They owned the whole process and accepted responsibility for doing what was necessary without blame.

Local team. Smaller practices had less formal "team" structure, but could take advantage of including everyone. In others, teams were formed: For example, at the Virginia Women's Center the EHR and IT teams joined together to ensure completion of responsibilities. Roswell Pediatric Center set up a team of super-users that included the original search/selection team and several other key staff members.

Pediatrics @ the Basin, on the other hand, had an excellent IT person as part of the team and felt lucky to have a good team to select, implement and make the most of their system. From the start of this process, "we recognized the need for a dedicated team to lead the search for and help coordinate the implementation of an EHR."

The team at Old Harding Pediatrics had a physician, nurse, executive administrator, and an assistant administrator. They divided their duties—project manager, implementation lead, implementation administrative lead, implementation clinical lead—and used an outside source for implementation technical lead.

At Southeast Texas Medical Associates, an informatics committee was organized to design an implementation strategy and decide what the goals and objectives were for going forward with an EHR and EPM. Once a vendor was selected, a template committee was established to guide the building of the templates, which, as was discussed earlier, is an important part of the transition to the EHR.

Local expectations. While EHR vendors and trainers often guided the implementation process, the Davies Award winners all set expectations for individuals in the practice, as well as their own overall practice metrics. Within their practices, they decided upon how they would go-live, their expectations for training, and their timing for transitioning to a paperless environment.

In the Virginia Women's Center, every provider was expected to function on a full schedule within two months. The paper chart was available for the first visit, so the provider could review it and determine if any additional paper documents needed to be scanned.

Southeast Texas Medical Associates decided to use a Phased Approach and "go live" with one "pod"—a subunit of their clinical staff, which is a self-contained team of physicians, nurses, nurse practitioners and unit clerks—at a time. Each month thereafter, they took an additional "pod" live on the EHR. Within one month, they were seeing all their patients using the EHR.

Piedmont Physicians Group (PPG 775) became completely chartless within six months. Each physician and staff member at Piedmont was required to take four-hour classroom sessions with a trainer and was given an open book proficiency test with case studies at each phase of training. Only those who passed the exam proceeded to the next stage of training.

Alpenglow's implementation team determined that, at go-live, they could see six patients per day successfully without falling behind on the day's schedule, thus the team scheduled six patients per day for the first week. Re-assessment at the end of that week indicated that they could see 12 patients per day the second week and were up to 20 by the third week.

Local customization. Nearly all of these Davies Ambulatory Care Award winners recognized that the selected EHR content, out-of-the-box, was close but required work to make the EHR "fit" part of their care process, their users and their workflow. In some cases, these winners actually became subject matter experts for their vendor.

For example, Cardiology Consultants of Philadelphia undertook a six-month project to develop their own fully customized content. At Palm Beach Obstetrics & Gynecology, stock clinical templates provided by the company were customized by the physician super-user to fit most of the clinical situations encountered by their practitioners. Many templates were created from scratch to describe even infrequent clinical conditions, and at Alpenglow, the lead physician was responsible for customizing the clinical content of the EHR.

For Piedmont Physicians Group, clinical content was developed and customized by an in-house team. Early in the process, four super-users were trained by the vendor, who were then responsible for translating the future workflows and physician requirements into clinical content.

Stayed engaged with the vendor. One of the themes of taking local responsibility, for better or worse, was that the practice "made noise" and stayed engaged with the vendor. That means articulating, confronting and acknowledging that it takes both parties at the table to make a successful EHR implementation.

In some cases, that meant not complaining but articulating a problem, or developing content, or serving on user groups, or acting as a reference site, or pushing the vendor to include priority items in research and development. It meant that these practices had the attention of their vendor; they were "known" by name by their vendors, and each practice actively demonstrated increasing use of the vendor's product. The message? Be brave and speak up!

Recognition That Care Delivery Is Also a Service Business

Attention to patient customer service throughout the go-live is essential; communication with them is critical. Two practices even notified patients about plans for implementation of the EHR and how patients might expect some adjustments to schedules or changes in procedures in the office during that time.

Cardiology Consultants of Philadelphia posted signs in each office informing patients of the transition to an EHR, and called patients scheduled to be seen in the early days of each physician's adoption to alert them to the possibility of delays. At Cardiology of Tulsa staff explained the transition to EHR to each patient, and informed them of the benefits that would result from the change. Both from a business perspective and a quality of care perspective, the importance of customer service was mentioned by many of the winners:

Cooper Pediatrics, Duluth, GA; 2003 Davies Ambulatory Care Award: "I have always been very customer service oriented, and the EHR allows me to offer better service than my competitors without raising my prices."

Wayne Obstetrics and Gynecology, Jesup, GA; 2005 Davies Ambulatory Care Award: "Staff can focus on patient-friendly service."

Piedmont Physicians Group: "We have two groups of customers—our patients and physicians who refer patients to us. Our stated goal of improving customer service extends to both groups of customers."

Alpenglow Medical: "Alpenglow was constructed around the business principle of superior customer service, with the primary goal of achieving 100-percent patient satisfaction."

Village Health Partners: "The mission of Village Health Partners (VHP) (formerly Family Medical Specialists of Texas) has always been to provide unsurpassed customer service and clinical quality. We have a great understanding of what patients value most—access, convenience, and communication."

Oklahoma Arthritis Center: "Both teams can begin to process the patient's request at once, thus creating a more efficient work environment and superior customer service."

Virginia Women's Center: "Practice decisions have always been strictly guided by the question, 'What is best for the patient?'"

Recognition of the Value of Data Above Digitized Documents

Davies Award winners frequently mentioned the use of discrete data, rather than simply using a computerized document. Some had the foresight to plan for the use of data, while others grew, some painfully, into understanding the significance of data in the local practice, as well as with other entities. In the current and future environment, the use of data to report meaningful use and to achieve process improvement and improved outcomes is and will become even more critical. Here are some of their findings:

Features of the Virginia Women's Center's database enable the practice to maximize success of their clinical research program. Internal quality assurance reports allow monthly reporting of adherence to universal best practices. Their persistence in achieving consistency in entering data per field ultimately enhanced reporting capabilities. They were able to increase clinical visualization and safety by designing specific disease-oriented flow sheets that allowed at-a-glance review of discrete data fields, which also helped avoid the trap of "much electronic data, but difficult to see."

Evans Medical Group: Getting the clinical information in the exam room in a form that would allow it to effect real-time decisions was a major step toward becoming truly computerized. It was this process that taught them that the real impact of EHR would not be as a record-keeping device but as an interactive database. They began to imagine having 100 percent immunization rates, top-quality disease management, and being able to share that information with both payors and patients. They now regularly search the database for patients who are overdue for shots. An example search would be: "Show me all of the patients who are three-month-olds who have not had their first DTaP and do not have a scheduled appointment."

The work groups at the **Piedmont Physicians Group (PPG 775)** spent significant time establishing standards for what data and how much should be completed. The key for them was to understand what data are required for insurance, quality measurement, etc. Their practice allowed numerous individuals to enter data, which resulted in issues with data accuracy and consistency. They found that cleanup routines should be instituted immediately after implementation and performed on a regular basis to keep the data integrity high.

Cardiology Consultants of Philadelphia: "Now that all CCP providers have been on EHR for more than one year, we have begun to collect aggregate quality data, grouped by provider, for use in internal quality improvement and, eventually, for pay-for-performance contracts."

Cardiology of Tulsa wanted to move from a "document management" to a "data management" model, which would allow the practice to mine the data available and use them to improve operational efficiency and clinical effectiveness. At **Southeast Texas**, the expectations in deciding to implement an EHR and the principles which guided the choice included the realization that the complexities of 21st-century medicine required "data management" rather than "document management."

Alpenglow determined that they wanted a system that could serve as a database for knowledge management of ideal clinical care.

Culture of Patient/Population Management Prompted by Initiatives from Payors, National Groups and/or Research Efforts

While all applications make reference to improvements in patient health and care processes, more significantly, many of the winners were well aware of national and payor guidelines and metrics for proving that evidence-based guidelines were used at the point of care, as well as retrospectively monitoring through lists or registries for patients in need of clinical attention. It is important to have the capacity to achieve rapid progress toward compliance with emerging national outcomes standards. Following are telling statements from their award applications:

Evans Medical Group: "Our chart audits by insurance companies have consistently gotten the highest grades possible and often effusive praise from the reviewer."

Roswell Pediatric Center: "We are able to customize decision support to meet our specific needs. For example, wellness checking is based on both our clinic and national guidelines."

Virginia Women's Center: "We are members of a Medical Quality Improvement Consortium and are members of the Women's Health Best Practices Group, working diligently on development of quality assurance indicators for obstetrics and gynecology."

Riverpoint Pediatrics: "I have been able to provide better and faster service to each family and have seen a 100 percent increase in the number of patients in my panel due to compliance with the PHO regulations."

Pediatrics @ the Basin: "They provide communitywide clinical guideline initiatives. We used the provided guidelines to create templates for the initial evaluation and follow-up care of patients with asthma. We can show how our assessment is supported by our history and physical and how our treatment is directed in accordance with national guidelines."

Piedmont Physicians Group (PPG 775): "A significant component of the quality care program is the increasing use of the EHR to measure and improve clinical performance, based upon HEDIS (Healthcare Effectiveness Data and Information Set) and NCQI (Nursing Care Quality Initiative) standards. The practice currently bases a portion of physician compensation on their ability to meet clinical quality standards, which are annually set."

Cardiology Center of Philadelphia: "It was clear that quality improvement initiatives were becoming the general trend in medicine and would likely become mandated in the future."

Cardiology of Tulsa: "EHR functionality would allow us to adopt and respond to all types of performance measures, focusing clinical efforts on improved patient care and allowing it to take advantage of pay-for-performance initiatives as they become available. We hired a physician to head practice efforts to maximize data mining. This physician combines her medical background with computer programming expertise to allow the practice to use the database as effectively as possible. In addition, she will continue our efforts to facilitate data sharing among researchers and to identify national standards for optimal disease management and health maintenance programs."

Southeast Texas Medical Associates: "Through the electronic medical record, our practice, in collaboration with the Physician Consortium for Performance Improvement, a national organization of the American Medical Association (AMA), Centers for Medicare and Medicaid Services (CMS), the National Committee for Quality Assurance (NCQA), other professional organizations and all specialty societies of the AMA, has created a treatment and educational plan for helping patients avoid CHF (congestive heart failure). Additionally, the practice has implemented the Physician Consortium for Performance Improvement data sets for chronic conditions."

Village Health Partners: "These data are then compared with millions of other patient records. It uses guidelines from NCQA and Doctor's Office Quality Information Technology (DOQ-IT) to provide benchmarks and comparison for many evidence-based measures for diseases and preventive care. We can measure ourselves individually, as a practice or against the consortium."

Alpenglow Medical: "The latest upgrade of the EHR system is being used to run disease-specific reports on specific patient populations to identify patients missing recommended services, or responding inadequately to treatment."

Miscellaneous Practice Attributes

While not every Davies Ambulatory Care Award winner mentioned the following, several applications included these other practice dynamics that are worth noting:

- The existing practice management system was evaluated for its ability to continue to meet the practice's requirements, as well as its business and technical impact on a new electronic medical record.

- Leadership interpreted complex information, such as costs into clear and understandable metrics, such as "one extra patient per day" to help peers put the information into perspective.
- Recognized that implementation of an electronic medical record would never end—a journey with new tools, new processes, new costs, new rewards—that continuously challenges the practice.

CONCLUSION

Since the world of ambulatory EHR products includes a few highly successful, many average, and more than a few disastrous implementations, perhaps these organizational attributes highlight why these specific practices became Davies Ambulatory Care Award Recipients. The goal must be to increase highly successful implementations and decrease or eliminate the disastrous implementations. As these practices have succeeded by using a wide variety of products, technology and truly doing it "their way", maybe it's not always about whether the car has wheels, seatbelts and airbags and more about the driver (the abilities of the EHR user) and the road conditions (organizational attributes).

APPENDIX 3-1
EASTERN MAINE MEDICAL CENTER: CPOE CHECKLIST

Project

1. Target date is established for beginning CPOE pilot.
2. IT budget includes CPOE.
3. CPOE vendor selected.
4. Project team identified.
5. Lead physician identified with dedicated paid time.
6. Decision made on reimbursing physicians for CPOE committee work and training.
7. Nurse dedicated to CPOE project.
8. Multidisciplinary committee identified to oversee the project with physicians from at least two clinical specialties.

Leadership

1. Decision to move forward and CPOE plan have been endorsed by the board and Medical Executive Committee.
2. Representatives of community physicians have been involved and support the decision to move forward.
3. Pharmacy and nursing execs have been involved and support the decision to move forward.
4. Hospital executive other than the CIO has been charged with accountability for success of the CPOE project.
5. Physician exec has accountability for the success of the CPOE project.
6. Hospital sets a formal Quality Improvement/Safety agenda each year to identify improvement targets and CPOE is on it.
7. Set of objectives that outline success criteria is developed.

Structure and Process

1. A formal process exists for providing information to physicians about changes that affect them.
2. A formal process exists for physicians to provide feedback about changes that affect them.
3. Pharmacists regularly participate in the role of clinical pharmacist on the inpatient units, or clinical pharmacists conduct rounds on inpatient units.
4. The hospital undertakes clinical quality improvements that cut across disciplines and departments.
5. The hospital has an interdisciplinary group that meets regularly to identify and address patient safety issues.
6. The hospital periodically adopts new quality/safety metrics when new gaps in care are identified and need to be addressed.
7. The board or a sub-committee receives patient safety reports, including metrics on a regular basis.
8. The hospital has staff resources with skill and experience in working with clinical and operational staff to improve high-risk or inefficient processes.
9. Pharmacy, nursing, and medical staff have successfully worked together to address a process with an identified quality or safety gap.

Culture

1. The hospital has one or more committees through which administration and community physicians meet regularly to address hospital issues.
2. Active physician participation on hospital committees is part of what is expected to maintain privileges.
3. Most physicians believe the hospital is able to deploy IT that improves care.
4. The hospital is involved in a patient safety or quality collaboration with an external organization (e.g., Institute for Healthcare Improvement (IHI), Veterans Health Administration (VA), Premier and other hospitals in health system or state).
5. Patient safety is a regular agenda item at medical staff meetings.
6. Patient safety is a regular agenda item at nursing staff meetings.
7. Physicians chair some improvement projects addressing care processes in the hospital.
8. Representatives of community physicians are currently involved in at least one improvement project addressing care processes in the hospital.
9. The hospital Medical Executive Committee has set a policy regarding expectations for physician use of CPOE.

Care Standardization

1. To what extent are medication administration times standardized across acute care units in the hospital?
2. To what extent is documentation of medication administration standardized in care units in the hospital?
3. To what extent is medical record information on patient weight reliably updated for patients' post-admission to the hospital?

4. The hospital has a process in place for developing, approving, and encouraging the use of standardized order sets and clinical protocols. The department of medicine has a process in place to develop and encourage the use of standardized order sets and clinical protocols. To what extent are diagnosis-specific order sets for hospital care (e.g., pneumonia, knee replacement) routinely used by physicians?
5. Physician compliance with the hospital policy for signing verbal and telephone orders is greater than 90 percent.
6. The percentage of medications ordered that are not included in the hospital's standard formulary is less than 5 percent.
7. The hospital's pharmacy and therapeutics committee (or equivalent) regularly develops drug protocols for high-risk medications.

IT Management

1. The hospital has an Information Systems Steering Committee with decision-making authority, which includes representatives of the medical staff and nursing.
2. A process is in place to monitor use of clinical computer systems and target physicians and nurses for additional training as needed.
3. A training team is in place that includes nurses and others who understand the needs and workflow of the clinicians.

Chapter 4

EHR Selection and Implementation: 'How To' Considerations

Daniel Griffin, MD
With Addendum by Denni McColm, MBA

"Let our advance worrying become advance thinking and planning."

—*Winston Churchill*

INTRODUCTION

The goal of this chapter is to provide guidance for EHR selection and implementation, using lessons learned and perspectives gained from Davies Award applicants and winners. If you have read many Davies Award applications, you may think, "I won't find much information about choosing an EHR." That information is a rather brief section of the applications.

Often, applicants simply state, "We chose Acme EHR because it does x, y and z." They don't spell out the selection process because the award is for implementation; it goes to the organization that is best able to implement whichever software they chose.

However, I believe successful implementation to be unattainable without the best possible EHR selection. Therefore, I will expand on the knowledge gleaned from the applications by including advice from discussions with contenders during site visits and conversations with fellow Davies Award winners.

The second section of this chapter will take you through the steps of EHR implementation. The Davies Award applications are a rich source of material in compiling this section of the chapter. I will include, as many of the applicants do, critical components of success, as well as potential mistakes.

SELECTION

Choosing the EHR software for your practice or hospital group is an exciting process, opening the door to a world of new possibilities. Although this task can initially appear daunting, as you move through the process you will learn a tremendous amount about the available options on the market. This first part of the chapter will be divided into the following eight sections:

1. Assembling the selection team.
2. Evaluating the current workflow.
3. Planning for the new EHR workflow.
4. Generating a wish list of features.
5. Making the initial list of products to evaluate.
6. Eliminating products, leaving a very short list or a limited number of finalists.
7. Submitting an RFP and getting bids.
8. Performing due diligence and signing the contract.

Assembling the Selection Team

Ask the brave pioneers who chose an EHR for their workplace this question: "If you could do one thing differently, what would it be?" The most likely answer would be, "Everyone who's going to use the EHR should have a say in its selection."

An EHR is a tool. If you are looking for a tool to uncork a bottle of wine, a corkscrew is clearly the winner. But you probably wouldn't choose a corkscrew to remove a splinter, cut string or whittle. In light of this concept of having a tool that performs on many levels, for those who don't want to be stuck with a screwdriver for all occasions, there is the multi-faceted Swiss Army knife. In this way, your EHR needs to be useful not only to doctors, but to nurses, receptionists, administrators, billers and laboratory staff. You want to find the Swiss Army knife of EHRs.

We've established that many different types of workers will need your EHR to serve as an effective tool. If you delegate EHR selection to an office manager, you may end up with a tool that makes office management easier but everyone else's job harder. If you delegate selection to a senior physician with limited clinical hours, you may end up with an EHR that clashes with the way your practice works today.

The best selection method, according to multiple Davies Award winners, is to assemble a selection team. Of course, it is impractical to include every worker who will use the system on the team, so I recommend organizing your employees into user groups and choosing one or more representatives from each group to serve on the team.

A user group is made up of employees with similar job responsibilities. You could group billers, for example, and refer to this as the billing user group. You could group nursing staff, including RNs, LPNs and MAs in the nursing user group. Your provider user group could contain MDs, DOs, PAs and various therapists. If an individual does not fit into one of these groups, include him or her on the team to evaluate the products for their individual needs.

Once you have defined the user groups for your organization, you need to decide who will advocate for the specific requirements of each group during the selection process. Choose your representatives carefully. For example, large organizations often make the mistake of thinking that everyone who has an MD after their name is a practicing physician. Choose a representative provider who spends most of his or her day seeing patients. Likewise, choose an actual receptionist, not a reception supervisor, and a nurse who provides care, rather than an RN who works mainly in administration.

A good delegate for the team will be typical of their user group but will also communicate with their user group to bring each individual's priorities to the table. Make sure physician representatives aren't overlooking the needs of the physician extenders and therapists in their user group; or include a PA and a physical therapist on the selection team. No one should feel they are too busy to serve on the team. They will be a lot busier if they don't get involved and the product chosen upends their routines and complicates their jobs.

Since many will be using this book as a "how to" guide, I will describe each of the four most common user groups and highlight the importance of including them in the selection process. I suggest you start with these four groups, but add more, depending on the complexity of your organization.

The first of these four core user groups is the *provider user group*. Providers who get involved in selection are getting a good EHR education; any provider with limited or no experience with an EHR will need to spend time studying the products before starting to understand the capabilities of EHR technology. Dictation is a common request of providers who hope to gain the benefits of an EHR without any significant impact on how they are accustomed to practicing. Many providers gravitate toward systems that use tablet computers because they can hold a tablet the way they have held paper charts.

In fact, in the beginning of the process, providers tend to visualize the way they currently interact with patients and use this vision as a model for the ideal EHR. During selection, you can help providers focus on looking for an EHR that makes their jobs easier, not on preserving the trappings of the old system. We know efficiency, quality of care and patient satisfaction improve with the introduction of an EHR. If providers come to understand how and why this happens, they will embrace it as positive change.

The second core user group is *nursing*. Nursing staff perform unique tasks in every organization, and will need to continue working efficiently when the EHR is introduced. The number of varied tasks that are performed by nursing staff in an average day is impressive.

For the nursing staff, it is essential that the system not just be great at generating progress notes but also allow quick and easy access to patient information, such as medication lists. Nurses will need functionality to renew medications, triage telephone calls and enter vitals and clinical history. Further, there must be recognition that the nursing staff spends considerable time working with patients in person, as well as over the phone. Unless a nursing user group representative is included on the selection team, you run the risk of choosing a system that will frustrate these individuals in the performance of their complex and varied job.

Reception is the third user group. They will perform a list of tasks differently with the advent of EHR: scheduling patients, calling with reminders, checking in arriving patients and wrapping up the visit before patients leave. You don't want the EHR to encumber this group.

For one thing, you want a smiling face meeting patients and a friendly voice on the phone. Secondly, if reception is hindered or complicated by the introduction of the EHR, patients will no longer be entering and exiting smoothly, and all user groups will be negatively affected. With the wrong EHR in place, patients could be standing at the counter for long periods while the reception staff enters required information on multiple, slowly advancing screens.

When considering the choice of EHR, receptionists also will want to pay attention to potential problems during check out and bill paying. The receptionist group is the public face of your organization. They will often be the individuals who set the tone for how your transition to an EHR is perceived by patients and the community. Having the receptionist user group represented on your selection team will help in choosing a system that allows these individuals to accomplish their jobs smoothly and efficiently.

Billing staff members form the fourth core user group that must be involved in the selection process. Even in the most recent applications, it is clear that this is an area in which the software is still improving, and billers will need to be able to evaluate new features. Organizations have repeatedly requested the introduction of a hold feature that allows them to review all the bills before they are exported to electronic clearinghouses. Providers often do not prioritize coding and billing until *after* patients have been cared for. On this, even excellent clinicians may need guidance from the billing department; billers need a chance to give providers reminders and ask them questions. The EHR needs to put the bills on hold while all this happens. Your billing staff will be invaluable when it comes to critiquing scrubbing holds and other billing features.

Now that we have reviewed the main user groups, the central lesson of EHR selection bears repeating: No one person has the time or expertise to understand the needs of every different employee at the level necessary to make the best choice. It takes a team to select an EHR.

After defining the user groups to be represented on this selection team, you should start building this team by finding out who the actual leaders are in the various areas, rather than just rounding up the usual suspects. The individuals who have the time to sit on various committees are rarely the individuals with the most patient contact. The people doing the bulk of patient care will be most impacted by implementation. The individuals who will use the EHR to perform their primary job have a large stake in EHR selection. These individuals understand the basic daily work of the organization and are the people you want on your selection team.

When choosing their EHR, 2006 Davies Organizational Award-winner Generations+/Northern Manhattan Health Network in New York City had leading the effort a CEO who was described as a tireless champion of IT. Yet, they formed a committee of active users to make the decision: clinicians, nurses, social workers, pharmacists, dieticians, radiology and laboratory technicians, and respiratory, physical and occupational therapists.

Evaluating the Current Workflow

Although we should be continuously evaluating our workflow and making improvements, this is usually not the case. We often think, "Don't fix what isn't broken."

I assert that if you are not using an EHR, your system is broken. You will not realize how broken your system is until you finish your transition to the EHR. We are by nature critical of change. This is the step in the selection process where I am asking you to be critical of the familiar. Even if you never implement an EHR, performing the following exercise will greatly improve your organization's efficiency.

One advantage of evaluating workflow after the creation of your selection team is that part of this task can and should be delegated. The members of your selection team can be responsible for evaluating the current workflow of the user group they represent.

Have each member of the selection team ask a number of the individuals in their user group to keep a diary for several days of everything they do at work. The team members should record their work days as well. Once these diaries are compiled, go through them and create a list of tasks for each user group. I will use the nursing user group as an example here. This list might include: prepare the exam rooms for the different visits by looking at the schedule to see which supplies need to be available, check phone messages, refill medications, record vitals, room patients, triage for appointments, administer injections, assist patient to bathroom, collect urine from patient, run rapid strept assay, receive critical lab values and alert provider. Any nurse who reads this list will realize that we are just getting started. The list should be comprehensive, and it is important to include not only the tasks each individual will perform but also the mechanics of these tasks.

If the listed task is refilling of medications by nursing staff detail all the steps in the process such as; listen to phone message of request and record patient name and requested medications on message pad, request patient chart retrieval by medical record staff, review requested chart for medication dosage verification, call pharmacy to leave message on automated phone system, document finished task and leave chart in outgoing chart rack for re-filing by medical record staff.

Some offices have even employed consultants to analyze their current workflow prior to EHR selection.

Do not let the quick "little" tasks get excluded from this list. For example, a nurse might put a sticky note on a door, knowing that the provider will have to notice it before entering to see the next patient. How will an electronic system deliver this message in a way that the provider cannot ignore? If a nurse quickly reads a section of the chart to remind herself/himself of a few personal details before greeting a patient, then this needs to be noted and kept in mind for the future.

The physicians need an exhaustive list too. The common practice of looking through the chart before entering a patient room becomes difficult when the EHR can only be accessed after the provider enters the room. Many providers describe the loss of the pre-entry chart flip as walking into the exam room "blind," and are not excited about a system that forces such a workflow on them.

The physician's workflow list needs to include the quick conversation with the nurse authorizing a refill or a short prescription to last until the next appointment. In a paper system the nurse takes care of the rest. In an EHR, will these prescriptions sit in an electronic inbox until the physician addresses them or will the same rapid response be maintained?

Historically, practices left their nurses and medical assistants with a pad of pre-signed blank prescriptions that were filled out based on protocol or verbal direction. For example, the nurse refills prescriptions on non-controlled substances as long as the patient has a scheduled return. Some providers may have grown accustomed to having a nurse or assistant write many of their prescriptions. If the electronic systems require providers to individually sign off on each prescription, this may not be done until day's end. More significant delays are likely if the providers are not dutiful in checking their electronic inboxes before leaving for the day or weekend.

If the organization wants to maintain their current workflow, they need to find an EHR that will enable providers to define protocols permitting nurses to refill certain prescriptions. Also, the EHR should allow the nurse to fill a medication on the basis of a verbal order from the physician.

You need to have a good handle on the sequence of operations in all areas of your organization before choosing and introducing the EHR. Many current workflows have sprung up in an ad hoc manner over time and are most likely not as streamlined as they could be. EHR adoption has repeatedly proven to allow advances in coordination between employees and efficiency of job processes. I have always been surprised at the variability in a single practice between, for example, how different providers work with their nursing staff to accomplish ordinary tasks. An EHR will bring a certain amount of standardization. As long as this standardization improves productivity, it will be embraced by all but the most stubborn of individuals. Step 2 will require the selection team to do their homework: synthesizing the task lists, considering the habits and patterns of the workplace, and acknowledging the order and disorder of daily operations.

Planning for the New EHR Workflow

Once you understand the current workflow in your facility, start imagining the new, post-paper dynamic. People approach this step differently. The goal for many is to re-create the paper environment using EHRs. They expect the EHR to simplify and accelerate tasks, while workplace conventions stay in place. Other organizations are ready to break the mold. They use this opportunity to scrutinize current patterns and arrange them into something better. You might choose the former approach, the latter or perhaps some hybrid. Although there is no wrong choice here, there is definitely a best choice. The most successful implementations happen when EHRs are viewed as avenues for positive change. EHRs don't just save paper, they save lives. The introduction of an EHR is the perfect time for workflow redesign. We will look at a few of the opportunities for such advancements.

One of the workflow challenges when you go electronic is the generation of lab orders and prescriptions. Most of the original EHRs required providers to finish a note prior to sending out a lab order or prescription. This created a problem for the many providers who were in the habit of polishing their notes at day's end. You may want your EHR to allow test orders and prescriptions to go out at any time.

It is not universal for the software to alert providers when a test result is available. In the paper world, a critical lab result is usually called to the office and acknowledged by a nurse. The nurse then writes down the result, often on a sticky note. The dynamic at this point might involve putting this sticky note in a prominent place such as the provider's desk. Some nurses will speak directly to the provider and respond to the test result based on the direction of the provider.

When you implement your EHR, will urgent messages regarding critical labs sit in an electronic inbox until the end of the day? Will the sender of the message be alerted if the message is not read after a specific period of time? Merely marking a message as urgent does not guarantee that it will be read by the recipient in a timely manner.

In the current paper-based workflow, all these issues have been addressed and a functioning solution is, hopefully, in place. The EHR should get prescriptions to patients and lab results to providers even more simply and swiftly.

Another example of an issue for workflow can be the challenge of getting results to the provider in the electronic form that allows the EHR to make the greatest improvement to workflow. A result on a sticky note does not give you ready access to how this result is trending over time. The sticky note method does not give you a list of the patient's current medications, current diagnosis or even the reason the test was ordered.

The EHR can do all these things if the result is brought into the system properly. Ideally, when a result is brought to the attention of a provider, this result should be in the subject patient's electronic chart. This way the provider can reference other relevant data, such as trends of this result. This also will allow the provider to use the EHR to modify medication regimens or document how this result will be handled. Although many systems allow in-house or outside lab and test results to be put into a patient's chart, these do not often work with the speed and timeliness desired for an efficient workflow. One should run through the dynamic of a simple visit such as pharyngitis requiring a rapid strept test, dysuria requiring a urinalysis, a possible fracture requiring x-rays or some other scenario suitable to your practice or organization.

I also suggest that you thoroughly explore the process of prescription writing and prescription refills. Imagine: A provider sees a new patient during a busy afternoon at the clinic. The patient needs a prescription for the acute issue that prompted the visit, plus, she wants her 10 long-term medications refilled by mail order, and a 15-day local supply of each. In addition, she takes one of the medications in two different pill strengths. Run through how the staff would handle this situation today, and then plan how you would handle it with an EHR.

Ask questions: How will you enter medications with unknown doses into the chart? Will there be a way of tracking whom it was that entered the information in the chart? Will you be able to refill a medication if you don't know the appropriate diagnosis for Coreg? Is it migraine prophylaxis or situational anxiety induced by EHR selection team membership?

Create other imaginary patient scenarios, throw in complications and ask more questions: If the EHR allows you to chart telephone calls, will you choose to document all calls? Will each exchange between the receptionist and the patient, the patient and the nurse, and the nurse and the provider be filed as part of one conversation or will the chart quickly fill with each reply filed separately? What will happen to electronic messages sent to an absent employee? (It is easy in a paper environment to look through the paper inbox and take care of any urgent messages.)

The EHR is not only a replacement for the paper chart. The EHR is a replacement for an outdated, inefficient paper-based workflow.

When Bangor-based Eastern Maine Medical Center (2008 Davies Organizational Award) appreciated that the transition to an EHR would affect everything from specific processes to institutional culture, they listed the various areas that would be affected: patient access, care management, cardiac care management, emergency department, medication administration and distribution, surgical services and standardization. Then they created a Transformation of Care Team to make sure the transition to an EHR would improve the efficiency in all these areas.

Generating a Wish List of Features

The next step is often more difficult than it seems: writing down your wish list of EHR features. Your selection team already constructed the foundation of this list as they planned for the new workflow, but the question is: Do they know everything EHRs can do?

For example, let's say "order radiology exams" is one of the tasks performed regularly in your practice. Looking ahead to life with an EHR, you envision a provider in the exam room, deciding to order a chest x-ray. Instead of calling for a nurse who pulls a form from a file folder and fills it out by hand, the provider will use the EHR to populate a radiology request form with the patient's name, insurance information, diagnosis, etc., which then will be printed and given to the patient.

This new workflow saves time and improves accuracy, so you should include that EHR feature on your wish list, right? Maybe.

First, your selection team needs to research other possibilities for this scenario. As they demo EHRs online, or visit fully electronic practices, they should ask how various EHRs handle radiology request forms.

What if your EHR could send the completed form to the radiology center's system electronically? Then the patient calls for an appointment, further expediting the process. The more exposure your selection team has to EHRs and EHR users, the more likely they will put the right things on the wish list and leave the wrong things off.

The expression, "Be careful what you wish for" is particularly relevant for EHR selection teams. For example, it is common for people selecting an EHR to view voice recognition as a significant—even requisite—feature. Davies Award applicants often rule out systems without voice recognition capability, but it isn't until implementation that they realize the difficulties inherent in using this software.

2008 Davies Ambulatory Care Award-winner Cardiology Consultants of Philadelphia wrote: "The limitations of using voice recognition software as a uniform dictation solution for such a large and diverse group of users were not apparent to us at the early stages of implementation. Although amazingly accurate for most users, speech recognition software can be prohibitively frustrating for some. Current speech recognition software has not advanced enough to accommodate users with strong accents, atypical speech patterns, or speakers with unusual tone; timber; or cadence."

These thoughts were echoed by 2009 Davies Ambulatory Care Award-winner Virginia Women's Center: "Because of the providers' previous comfort with dictation, we assumed that voice recognition would be the preferred data entry mechanism and purchased hardware and software to that end. Despite having trained the providers, only a few were able to adapt to the new system. The time required to train the software to users' voices was prohibitive for many. As the EHR was implemented, it became clear that when providers utilized the developed tools correctly, very little keyboard entry was needed. Voice recognition became less important and was ultimately discarded."

Voice recognition is certainly valuable to the right person in the right setting. Its limited benefit with EHRs is a compliment to the software's data entry methods. Have your selection team try out current EHR entry systems; they may find keyboard entry so user-friendly that voice recognition gets crossed off the wish list.

Leave plenty of time for your wish list to evolve with the selection team's growing understanding of EHR details. A single exposure to smart templates and artificial intelligence software will not be enough. Set up practice patient visits, and have team members at the keyboard, documenting. You'll also need to get familiar with functionalities you may not have known about, such as interaction alerts, clinical decision support, quality measurement tracking and equipment and laboratory interfaces.

It is interesting to note that we did not have these features in the paper-based office. We are already demanding more from the EHR than we demanded from traditional, paper-based systems. (This is true for security as well as for features that improve quality of care. Since correspondence being sent or received still involves paper, scanning and paper consultant note generation need to be on the list.)

Take care that you do not become so focused on the bells and whistles that your basic bread-and-butter needs get left off the list. If you purchase a system that can perform comparisons of your diabetic care to both HEDIS and Regional Interoperability Organization data, but creates such inefficiency that a visit for pharyngitis takes 90 minutes, your organization will not be using the system long enough to make use of clinical care comparisons.

Making the Initial List of Products to Evaluate

It's time to start looking at particular products. You're aiming at a moving target, as the market is continually changing. In the early days of EHRs, people believed that as we moved forward, market pressures would limit the number of available software products. The common wisdom was that by this time only a dozen or so products would remain on the market, so early adopters tried to choose a product and company that would stand the test of time. This was a good strategy since most of the 1990s products are no longer on the market; however, they've been replaced by far more than a dozen new EHRs. With the amount of federal stimulus money available, there may even be more products to choose from in the years ahead.

Where can you find a starter list of decent EHR systems? There won't be one in a Healthcare Information and Management Systems Society (HIMSS) publication because HIMSS is vendor neutral. You could look at the products certified by the Certification Commission for Health Information Technology (CCHIT), which are available on their Web site (www.cchit.org). This certification does not narrow the field appreciably, and there is significant disagreement about whether CCHIT certification is a guarantee of quality or usability. However, it does provide a long list of starting candidates. If your selection team finds this list too long, look at publications generated by your providers' specialty groups.

The American Academy of Family Practice (AAFP) publishes an annual review of EHR software being used by their members. The review contains a list of EHRs, along with user reviews and rankings. A number of other organizations also list available EHRs with reviews. Groups such as KLAS (www.klasresearch.com) make a business out of providing rankings and reviews of EHR software. Some of these reviews are free, while others are available for purchase. Other options for getting acquainted with the available products are to visit vendor booths at specialty meetings, or attend vendor shows meetings focused on EHR solutions, such as the annual Toward an Electronic Patient Record (TEPR) or the HIMSS Annual Conference & Exhibition. At these meetings, vendors give demonstrations of their EHRs.

A final recommended option is to join a group that encourages the implementation of EHRs, and use your membership for networking opportunities. This membership will continue to be a source of assistance long after the EHR is selected and implemented.

HIMSS (www.himss.org) is currently the largest health IT organization in the United States, and provides many opportunities for networking and education. The HIMSS Annual Conference & Exhibition is a chance to listen to and talk with individuals recognized for best-practice implementations of electronic health systems in myriad areas, including community health, ambulatory settings and organizations. The Annual Conference also has many vendors who demonstrate their systems. Most states also have active local HIMSS chapters with regularly scheduled meetings.

Once you have compiled a list, you will need to pare it to a more manageable number. Three criteria can be applied at this point and then re-applied more rigorously later. First, narrow your list to products that have been successfully implemented in similar practice settings; second, make sure all EHRs on the list can interface with your equipment and labs; and third, go with a capable vendor.

Fortunately, you have an advantage over your predecessors as you implement the first of the three criteria. Early adopters have paved the way with many successes and failures. Not only will evidence of successful implementation in a similar practice or organization suggest that the product can be used in your practice, but it often means that many problems have already been noted and resolved.

Another advantage to choosing a product widely used in your type of practice setting is the common need for certain features. If you're a psychiatrist, but choose an EHR targeted to primary care, don't be surprised when your vendor won't implement DSM diagnosis support. It's far better to be one of many psychiatrists who use the same software and are likely to advocate for the same improvements.

The second benchmark you want to look for is the EHR's ability to interface with the equipment and labs used by your practice or organization. Having an EHR capable of bringing results into the system directly is far superior to scanning results by hand. This issue is becoming more significant because the data for quality reporting, disease management trending and progress note generation can *only* be drawn from electronic test results.

To earn incentives based on meaningful use and quality reporting, you need a system that enables you to produce these reports easily. Let me use HgbA1c results as an example of the importance of functioning interfaces for reporting, as well as for good patient care.

If the HgbA1c result is brought in electronically the provider or nurse is alerted when the result is critically high. Some systems even issue an alert if the value has changed dramatically from prior levels based on defined parameters. (An HgbA1c of eight is encouraging if the level was 9.5 three months ago, but an eight is a red flag if the level was 6.5 a month ago.)

Another helpful aspect of electronic importation is that you can link directly from a lab result in your inbox to the patient's chart, allowing you to comment, forward for triage or provide quick access to relevant patient history and patient contact information.

When the patient comes in, many systems will trend these results and allow such information to automatically populate the note. A scanned image loses most of this functionality and can be missed as users become accustomed to finding results in the electronic lab section. These scanned test results are also not entered into the appropriate fields for quality reporting.

Now we have arrived at the third criteria—vendor quality. Unfortunately, a great product is not always enough if the company standing behind the product is indifferent to customers or promises more than it can deliver.

You need to choose not only a great product but also a company that can support the constant improvements demanded by users, certification bodies and government. With the rapid advances in EHRs, it is essential that the vendor put a high priority on responding effectively to users. While I'm touting continual EHR upgrades after purchase, let me clarify that it is essential that the EHRs on your list already have all your required features in the current version, an issue we will return to before signing a contract. Look for stable companies that make producing and supporting an EHR their main focus. Most importantly, talk to people at organizations that use your EHR candidates to find out how they are treated by the vendor. You are going to enter into a relationship with one of these companies, and you want it to be a long and pleasant one.

Eliminating Products, Leaving a Very Short List or a Limited Number of Finalists

We see the light at the end of the tunnel. If you have done your work properly, that light is coming from the sun and not an oncoming train. You have already had to apply some criteria to limit your list to qualified candidates. Now, I advise you to stop for a reality check. You want the best EHR available, but you also need to consider your organization's style and the costs. You need a wise decision for your organization's culture, purpose and budget. I have wanted a Ferrari Testarossa since the days of *Miami Vice*, but where would my three kids sit? How harmonious would life be when my wife found out I spent that much money on a car? I hate to admit it, but the Testarossa is not the car for me. Similarly, you don't need the perfect EHR; just the right EHR for you. Software that is designed for a solo practitioner may work poorly in a large group. The opposite is true too; a full-featured program that helps a large group thrive may be cumbersome and difficult to navigate for a small practice. It is not just important that the system works well for your specialty area, but also that it work well for your practice's size. Size may also be relevant to the cost of the system—both up front and in recurring costs. A large group or organization could leverage features for capturing patients into higher revenue centers such as imaging, procedures or laboratory services, while small practices may only be swamped by the continuing outlay of funds for features that are attractive, but not cost-effective.

It is a challenge when the EHR must work well in multiple healthcare settings. This can be the case if an organization, such as a hospital system, is looking for a system that works well in an inpatient setting and also has an outpatient module.

There are plenty of examples of hospitals with large budgets purchasing systems that work very well in the inpatient setting, but have a negative impact on the workflow in the ambulatory setting. Some outpatient modules are so inefficient that implementation may not even be viable for the ambulatory sites. If a hospital offers to give your clinic an EHR, that free software may wind up being the most expensive choice for your practice. It is better to borrow money from a lender to purchase a system that improves efficiency and quality than to accept a free system that decreases the number of patients you can see, reduces profitability and introduces frustration and complexity.

From the hospital or large organization perspective, it may be worthwhile to consider buying two different systems and creating an interface to allow information to move between the systems, rather than compromising quality on the inpatient or outpatient side.

Also, if the hospital plans to offer EHR software to groups in the community, it would be constructive to include representatives from those groups on your selection team. It is essential to use the same process described earlier: Assembling the selection team and assemble two separate teams if you are planning on choosing systems for two such different settings as inpatient and outpatient care.

Getting advice from a group of senior physicians with no prior EHR experience and more duties in administration than patient care will not lead to an EHR choice that meets outpatient clinic needs. Since a hospital- or large organization-driven EHR implementation with community extensions have great potential, the selection of the outpatient product deserves as much attention as selection for inpatient care and should have its own selection team.

Once we recover from the realization that we will be commuting to work in a minivan rather than a high-end sports car, it is time to generate a checklist to evaluate EHRs. Several checklists are available and can be downloaded. The Doctor's Office Quality-Information Technology group (DOQ-IT) and organizations such as HIMSS provide these checklists, some for free and others for purchase. I recommend customizing these lists to represent the unique needs of your practice or organization. It is essential that the members of the selection team understand their workflow and verify that the checklist includes EHR functions for all their needs.

However, it is not enough that the EHR is able to perform the desired tasks. The tasks must be accomplished in a way that doesn't impede workflow. Products have achieved CCHIT certification despite requiring multiple mouse clicks, screen changes and long waits just to check-in a patient. If you want patient check-in to be smooth and quick, put that on the checklist, too. If you send out many consultation letters you need a system that does this in a way that will not increase workload. Get all these needs on your checklist. You need to see that the EHR can do these tasks—and do them well. My kids can do the dishes, but it will take an hour, glasses will be broken and the kitchen will be covered with suds and puddles.

There will be several ways to learn about software and evaluate functionality. When you reach this stage, you should be talking directly to EHR vendors. Caution: there is a tremendous difference between what software demos can do and how an actual software product works once implemented in a practice setting.

As you select your final candidates, take the time, effort and expense of actually visiting locations where the software is being used. You should be talking to vendors, but also to actual users via site visits. Most of our colleagues are willing to give an honest appraisal of the EHR they use. The entire selection team should be included in these visits and discussions. Since travel is expensive, plan on only a few site visits. Limit the number of products which are worth site visits, but do not limit the number of people who go on the trips. Each team member will need to sign off on the selection, and they will not be able to do this if they have not used the EHR in a working environment and asked questions of the users in their job roles. The expense of site visits pales in comparison to the expense of the wrong EHR decision.

When planning site visits, look for implementations in practice environments that are similar to your own. If this means a large hospital system, find a similarly-sized organization that uses the EHR of interest. A group practice or solo practice should look for a site similar in size, patient demographics and specialty. There are many products customized and optimized for primary care that have been difficult to customize to a specialty, such as cardiology. It is always necessary to verify that all the features required are available in the current version of the software. The only way to do this with certainty is to actually see the program working in the real world. The best way to judge the system's abilities is to use it yourself. Beware of the promised upgrade that may never come. You need to know that your team's checklist features are already up and running. As with all purchases, you lose bargaining power once the money has changed hands.

Submitting an RFP and Getting Bids

To reach this stage your organization has applied stringent standards, eliminating most candidates. The fewer products left at this point, the more attention you can give to each finalist. Do not, however, limit yourself to one product at this stage. I encourage people not to fall in love with a single product. This needs to remain an objective business decision. Every year the committees selecting the Davies Award winners evaluate excellent implementations in similar practice settings using different EHRs. More than one EHR can be a great match for your organization.

The advantage to considering more than one product at this stage is that you will be submitting a request for a proposal (RFP) to vendors. RFPs list all the features that you expect to be available in the purchased software. It also is time to negotiate purchase price, support fees, training costs and, in some instances, hardware purchase costs. Having multiple options prevents you from overpaying for software services or hardware. Repeat this mantra: "There are several excellent software packages available on the market that can allow a successful implementation in a variety of practice environments."

The RFP will be a modified form of the checklist you have generated. This is a good time to address an important aspect of the decision process—cost. The costs of selecting and implementing an EHR can be complicated and difficult to identify when evaluating another organization's experience. One large variable is the cost of hardware. If an organization already has a computer network for the purposes of billing or practice management, then the computer hardware cost may be limited to the addition of computers, scanners and printers. If nothing is currently in place, you will be purchasing servers, installing wired or wireless networks and, in some cases, performing physical renovations to accommodate new systems. Software expenses take two forms: upfront purchase prices that are often adjusted based on user licenses and recurring costs that cover upgrades and continued use of the systems. In addition to software expenses, there will be expenses for hiring IT support personnel to maintain these systems, assist in any modifications and upgrades and set up and monitor security to protect against data loss or theft. Training costs can be considerable, but necessary for successful implementation. Training will start before the EHR is implemented and will continue post-implementation. The RFP should include all the relevant financial aspects of the selection and implementation so that this can be brought into the decision process.

Performing Due Diligence and Signing the Contract

Before you take the plunge, double-check your work. Although possible, it is difficult—and prohibitively expensive—to change electronic systems once the implementation has begun. Unfortunately, there are a number of examples of group practices splintering because of a failed EHR implementation, even among Davies Award applicants. Stay focused and be meticulous.

Verify that all EHR functions in your RFP are present in the current version of the selected software. If you need a system that can scan outside consultant notes, for instance, validate the scanning claim by actually scanning a note and seeing it in the chart. It is disastrous to purchase a product and then postpone your implementation while waiting for the promised upgrade that will finally deliver the program you need. I have known many users who spent money on an EHR they never used in their practice because they paid for an empty promise.

Entering the final run-off, you should be down to two vendor candidates. This will give you leverage during your last negotiations. Make sure that both vender proposals contain a clear agreement covering all expectations and outlining the specific costs. In addition to the purchase of the software, hardware and interfaces, you may also be working with the vendor with regard to implementation. It is essential to negotiate training and support fees along with the purchase. There will be many options for training: Web-based, telephone, in-person or training centers. The pros and cons of these methods will be discussed in the next section, but it is essential to realize that training and implementation are ongoing processes, not one-time expenses.

Key points that also should be in the contract include: functioning interfaces, ongoing fees and permissible increases, training and required functionality. All the commitments should be clearly spelled out in writing and include financial repercussions if they are not fulfilled. It goes without saying that a lawyer and accountant review the contract before it is signed. Do this after each revision—even if the revisions seem small. Never sign anything unless your lawyer reads it first.

IMPLEMENTATION

Selection of an excellent and appropriate EHR is not sufficient for success. Practices have purchased the identical EHRs that Davies Award winners used, only to mishandle the implementation, give up and return to paper charts. Skillful implementation is just as crucial as selecting the most suitable EHR.

The second part of this chapter will be divided into eight key steps for skillfully introducing your new EHR.

Assemble the Implementation Team

Asking one person to lead implementation would be like expecting a one-man band to play a symphony. You need a team. Members of your selection team may be ready to sign up for phase two, bringing along the experience and knowledge gained during selection. In fact, for small practices, the implementation team may be the selection team, even the entire office staff. In large organizations, the selection team is often the core of a larger implementation team.

According to successful implementers, you need to include two types of people on the implementation team: EHR advocates and EHR experts, known in the industry as champions and super-users. An EHR champion promotes the transition to the EHR. A champion is 100 percent committed and will be ever vigilant against backsliding toward paper-based systems. Their positive energy will be contagious.

Champions can and should come from every user group—provider, nursing, reception and billing. In fact, it is ideal to have a champion in each group. I have visited many practices that identified a particular physician as their EHR champion. After a little time onsite, it would become clear that there were actually a number of champions spread throughout the organization, driving the implementation. The transition to an EHR will certainly bring initial frustrations for many users. There will be times when future benefits are not readily apparent. These are the points at which the champions will step up to remind their colleagues of the importance of the mission and of maintaining the vision. This is an example of management responsibility distributed to individuals not necessarily in management. You will want to give the EHR champions support, as there will usually be a few self-appointed champions of the status quo.

A super-user is a staff member with a level of training and expertise in using the system that allows him or her to serve as a resource for co-workers. Super-users started out with proficiency in computer basics, then spent the extended time in EHR training. Now they are competent, confident and ready to share their tips and strategies.

Usually, individuals in healthcare easily accept a coworker in a teaching role; such a dynamic is already in place for other workplace tasks. Super-users are natural problem-solvers for their department, and will e-mail vendors with requests for new features and modifications. While demanding, this role can be very satisfying. People who want to help others are rarely in short supply in healthcare organizations, but do keep in mind the extra time super-users will need for training.

Don't assume that the most senior person or supervisor will make a good super-user. You want to select people who are easily approached. The last person to whom employees want to admit difficulties is a boss or supervisor. Having an accessible peer creates a favorable and non-threatening dynamic.

To summarize, super-users need to have these qualities: experience with computers, time for advanced training and a helpful the-door-is-always-open attitude. Often these super-users only become apparent after implementation has begun. You should be flexible and observant enough to identify them, and enable them to step into the role. Larger organizations should plan to have super-users available at all office locations during all shifts for at least the initial period of implementation.

Choose an Implementation Approach

Now that you have selected the people who will help lead the transition, it's time to choose your style. There are two basic styles that have been used successfully: the Phased Approach and the Big Bang.

The Phased Approach can be further divided into two methods. The first method is a step-by-step introduction of various modules, beginning with one feature of the EHR. For example, the software module which allows nurses to record vitals. Once the nursing staff is comfortable recording vitals, you bring in the next module, such as recording and prescribing medications. Introducing the medication module gets the clinicians in on the act. More sophisticated modules that trigger vaccination alerts or clinical practice guidelines can be brought on board after all users are comfortable with medication recording and prescribing.

With the second form of the Phased Approach, you transition departments, clinics or providers one at a time in a staggered start. Some clinics transition one provider and assistant pair at a time; some hospitals make the emergency department the first phase of implementation. With any form of the Phased Approach, you will find that everything learned during first phase allows future phases to run more smoothly.

The Big Bang is exactly what it sounds like. You schedule a specific go-live date and from the moment your doors open that day, all employees use the EHR for all encounters. This method requires more advance preparation and education than the Phased Approach. Users must be trained in every system feature, or the whole organization will grind to a halt on go-live day.

Ultimately, the Phased Approach will require the same amount of training, but it will be spread out over a long period. The first hours and days after the Big Bang will reveal many challenges that must be met quickly, so as not to derail patient care. On the positive side, the Big Bang makes it easier to enforce the transition to the EHR. The approaching deadline is motivating. When the starter blows the whistle, you know you have to jump into the pool. Then, it's sink or swim.

The crucial factor in scheduling your implementation is not whether you choose the Phased Approach or the Big Bang—both methods have yielded favorable outcomes. The crucial factor is a plan to leave paper-based systems behind permanently. Unless a specific date is put in place for retirement of the paper charts, a certain percentage of the staff and providers will continue to use the old systems long after other providers have transitioned. A hybrid environment complicates everyone's job. Providers and staff who are onboard with the EHR expect it to be a complete and accurate source of patient information. Meanwhile, their change-resistant co-workers are continuing to record things in the paper charts. It's a good idea to physically move the paper charts offsite to finalize the new order. Once the paper chart habit is broken, efficiency will increase, even for those individuals who were reluctant at the start.

2007 Davies Ambulatory Care Award-winner Village Health Partners (formerly Family Medical Specialists of Texas), Plano, orchestrated a Big Bang, but felt that they would have had a better experience if they had used the Phased Approach. In their lessons learned section of the Davies Award application they state, "We did go-live with all functionality but given more time, a staged approach would have been more appropriate. The Big Bang approach puts a lot of pressure on users to master a large amount of features and information at one time. Staging would have flattened the learning curve and especially helped the stress level of some of the slower users."

When Eastern Maine Medical Center moved to an EHR, they report that they "rolled out the EHR functionalities in a Phased Approach to accommodate the readiness and maturity of the clinical system to support the care model and the gradual introduction of cultural change to EMMC staff."

Undertake Pre-Implementation Training

There are various training options. On-site training is that training done when vendors send instructors to your facility. The vendors may also offer off-site training at their central or regional training facility. Training also can be accomplished remotely, with the trainer and trainee talking over the phone or Internet and sharing the computer screen. Remote training can be both cost-effective and very helpful.

The following advice may seem obvious to you, having included all user groups every step of the way, but make sure that every employee in your organization gets first-rate training. There are organizations that budget hours of one-on-one training for physicians and expect a one-hour group lesson to suffice for the rest of the staff.

Although providers must be completely fluent and comfortable with the use of the EHR, it is also important that all the support staff have a similar comfort level. An efficiently run office has a lot to do with the staff that supports the providers and not just the actions and efficiency of the individual providers.

There are two distinct phases to training: pre-implementation and post-implementation. It is standard to spend a considerable amount of time on pre-implementation training, but successful implementation examples also incorporate ongoing training. Post-implementation training increases fluency with the software and keeps everyone up to date as the vendor introduces periodic upgrades. EHR software is far from static; the constant advancements make practicing with one both demanding and exciting.

Create Plan for Transition of Paper-Based Charts to Electronic

The system has been selected, an implementation team is in place and your staff is being trained on the use of the EHR software. Before the first patient is seen using the new system, there is still work to be done.

One of the most problematic and controversial processes is the conversion of the existing paper records to electronic form. This is a pivotal point in the implementation process, with vast potential for mistakes and unnecessary expenditures. In the future, there will certainly be instances in which practices are converting from one electronic format to another, but currently, most practices have existing paper records that require incorporation into the EHR.

It is important to pause and make a few distinctions regarding importing of information into the EHR. I will define four forms of import into the EHR: electronic import, data-entry, indexed scanning and bulk scanning.

There is a hierarchy to the usefulness of this information, depending on how it is brought into the chart. Ideally, all information in an EHR is brought in electronically or through data-entry, allowing labs, problem lists, medications and allergies to be recognized as identifiable entities, with links to databases that provide interaction and dosing guidance. Lab results are brought in as numerical entries, with reference to normal and abnormal values and trending. Information that is brought in through electronic import and data-entry represents the most useful form of information to populate the patient record in the EHR. Most forms of scanning are bringing in photo images of patient information that are not properly linked to any identifiable data field. If you scan in an allergy list that includes penicillin, the EHR will have no means of recognizing that and alerting you when you try to prescribe ampicillin.

There definitely will be things that you will want to scan into the EHR. This is true initially and will be true for some time going forward as the rest of the healthcare world transitions to electronic systems.

As mentioned, there are two basic approaches to scanning: indexed scanning and bulk scanning. In indexed scanning you scan all the pages of the old paper charts into matching sections of the new electronic chart. For example, you would scan old progress notes into the EHR progress note section; all the radiology reports into a radiology report section; and so on. Now if you need to review an old mammogram you can go to the radiology report section of the electronic chart and find the report; it will be there whether it was done since the introduction of the EHR or 10 years ago. Although medication and allergy lists might be scanned in under such sections, these would be better brought in through data entry. Some implementations may involve scanning, then performing data-entry while looking at the scanned image.

Although the indexed scanning method may seem a perfect complement to electronic import and data entry, it can be costly and time-consuming. Newer approaches being offered by vendors are pre-population services and on-demand scanning of off-site records. Some of these options utilize offshore personnel to perform these functions to control costs.

Bulk scanning represents the least desirable approach to getting the information in a paper chart into the EHR. Do not bulk scan every paper chart into the EHR. First, it would be an incredible expense in terms of time and money. Second, it would be money poorly spent as it makes it burdensome to find the scanned information in the electronic system. Third, unnecessary information would be scanned: charts of deceased patients, decades-old physical exams, a long string of normal EKGs and other material irrelevant to patient care today.

Although bulk scanning will cost you less than indexed scanning, it will create a chart with the important information buried somewhere deep in the scanned pages. Scanning in bulk creates a chart without sections; all the pages are under one heading, and it becomes incredibly tedious to page through hundreds of scanned pages searching for that one important lab result or brain CT.

For many practices, indexed scanning of the entire old chart is just too costly and time intensive. One helpful realization of Davies Award winners and applicants is that only a certain amount of material in the paper chart needs to be brought into the EHR. There is a large amount of information in an old paper chart that does not need to be available immediately at the point of care. The EHR is primarily designed to improve patient care and provide information relevant at the point of care. It is not an electronic filing cabinet to clear your medical record shelves.

This realization can lead to a much more selective approach to scanning. Your organization should decide what information the provider requires at the point of care. Many practices have found it advantageous to make a checklist of items that must end up in the electronic chart. This checklist can contain two subsets: information to be scanned under specific headings and information to be typed into the appropriate fields. If you are in primary care, you may want the most recent EKGs, colonoscopy reports and radiology reports, including mammograms, scanned into the EHR. Current medications, allergies, vaccinations and diagnosis will need to be brought in through data entry. The checklist may vary for different specialties or for an outpatient versus an inpatient record.

It is critical that qualified clinical staff is enlisted for any portion that involves data entry. Although index scanning of one paper chart section into the matching section of the

EHR is a basic task, data entry of information such as medications, allergies and medical diagnosis is not. This is not the time to hire a college or medical student. If you use staff members who do not have an understanding of medical terminology and are not familiar with current medications, you'll increase the risk for confusion and mistakes. Misfiling is annoying when EKGs have been scanned under radiology, but could compromise patient care when methotrexate is substituted for metatolazone in a medication list.

After data entry is complete, it is recommended that there is verification that high-priority items such as previous EKGs, recent mammograms, colonoscopy reports, vaccination records, laboratory results, radiology reports and pathology reports are present in the electronic chart and that the information entered is accurate. Many systems are starting to allow tagging of the entries with levels of verification to assure an understanding of the level of confidence regarding the entries. Paper charts are often incomplete or inaccurate. This mandates a face-to-face review, with the patient, of medication lists, allergies, past medical history, past surgical history and other information.

Many practices start with an attempt to scan entire charts and then, over time, convert to the selective, checklist approach. Cardiology Consultants of Tulsa, an 18-physician practice and one of the 2006 Davies Ambulatory Care Award winners, reported, "The practice hired temporary employees as the scanning team and scheduled crews to provide coverage from 7 a.m. to midnight, five days a week. It took three years to complete the task, and it cost the practice $200,000."

2008 Davies Ambulatory Care Award-winner Cardiology Consultants of Philadelphia, which used a different approach to minimize scanning, reported, "Our model for transition to EHR involved keeping paper charts available until the third EHR return visit of each patient. This dual active chart approach ensured that our providers had access to complete patient records, while minimizing the amount of scanning and data entry required during transition. Physicians were encouraged not to request documents be scanned into a patient chart until the third EHR visit, at which point most patients have almost a year of records in their electronic chart." At that point, they felt that most charts were complete. This method requires very little scanning, but does have the downside of perpetuating a hybrid practice until the whole patient population has been in three times.

All these approaches will need to incorporate some system and timeline for the removal of paper charts from the premises. Some organizations have allowed providers only one visit after implementation with the paper chart being available. Some have picked three visits as the magic number. Although there may be variability in when the paper charts are moved off-site, it is essential that a date be set.

Generation of Timeline for Full Implementation

Even with the Big Bang approach, you probably won't use all the advanced functions of your new system on day one. Functionality above the basic features will be called for in time. Implementations may not use performance-tracking systems at first. You may want to wait to implement clinical decision support until users are comfortable with the fundamentals. (Since these decisions tend to complement a solid initial implementation, it is not even essential to include their introduction in this timeline prior to starting the implementation.) I encourage you to first focus on the basics and only introduce advanced features onto a solid foundation.

As I mentioned in "Choosing the Implementation Approach," there must be a mark on your timeline for retirement of the paper charts. Do not leave this to the discretion of the clinicians. Such a decision inevitably creates a potentially permanent hybrid environment. Removing the paper charts from the premises is vital to becoming an EHR-based organization.

One of the Davies Award applicants likened this to Cortez having his men burn their ships when they arrived in the Americas. Old habits may die hard, but the resounding conclusion of those who have arrived at their paperless destination is: "I would never go back." Don't compromise the mission by allowing lingering access to paper charts. (Most states require providers to keep charts for a specified period of time, so despite the story of Cortez burning his ships, resist the urge!)

Begin Your Implementation

It is time for the actual implementation. During the implementation, there should be some means of monitoring progress, and getting feedback to decision-makers. Most organizations have no prior experience implementing an EHR, and common wisdom tells us that the best-laid plans may not survive the battlefield. Open lines of communication between those using the system and those able to assist in training and modification of the system will help the plan survive.

In organizations that have undergone the most successful implementations, there are frequent meetings to consult, debrief, vent and exchange recommendations. Often, meetings lead to modifications of the implementation style or schedule.

There should always be a meeting at the end of the first implementation day, and I will leave beverage choice to the discretion of the readers. As a member or leader of the implementation team, listen to your co-workers and be responsive. Problems such as workflow modification or training will require responses that may spell the difference between a smooth ride and derailment.

Since it is rare to have someone in the organization that has been through an EHR implementation, help from the EHR vendor can be central. These vendors have assisted multiple practices through the process. In addition to the vendors, there are consultants with experience in implementation, as well as product and hardware selection. If you are considering a consultant, it is preferable to start well before the implementation rather than waiting until you are struggling. Although every organization or practice is unique, there will be challenges facing your organization that the vendor or consultant has seen before.

Continue the Implementation

At this stage, you may feel as though all the important aspects of a successful implementation have been addressed. Your EHR is the most appropriate software product for your situation. You have reviewed workflow and visualized how the transition will improve it. The implementation team chose your approach, hammered out a timeline, got everyone through pre-implementation training and put ongoing training in place. Your paper charts' days are numbered. The electronic system is up and running and the first patients are being seen. But don't assume that that the system will function well under a *laissez-faire* policy.

Look for complications and mistakes—almost anything can still be remedied. Even this late in the game, Davies Award winners have regrouped from a poor start and modified their strategies to achieve an exemplary implementation. 2009 Davies Ambulatory Care Award winner Virginia Women's Center reports that they began their implementation by asking patients to record their histories by filling out a No. 2 pencil bubble sheet.

"This exercise slowed registration, causing massive delays in the providers' schedule. Additionally, the patient-entered data was often inaccurate and required more time to correct than when simply entered by trained medical assistants. We abandoned further development of the questionnaires, although not soon enough after the problem was identified. It was difficult to accept failure and financial burden of the unused technology. Knowing when to quit was a challenge."

The early days of implementation may be the steepest portion of the learning curve, and problems should be viewed as opportunities to set off on a better path. At this stage, groups attempting to scan every item in every chart have thrown up their hands and made a checklist of pertinent items to transfer. Inadequacy of training now becomes obvious, and should be brought to the attention of the organization. You may realize that an essential software feature is missing. Davies Award-winning applications provide many examples of how obstacles were successfully surmounted and disasters averted.

CONCLUSION

It is great to reach a time when the basics are all in place and things are functioning smoothly. Now, you can start thinking about the future. In the world of EHRs, the future gets brighter every day. Initially, many groups chose to implement an electronic record primarily for financial benefits. Now, they are looking for opportunities to improve patient care. EHRs are giving providers greater flexibility with access from home or a mobile device. You can make it home for dinner with the family, knowing you can finish off your work after the kids have been tucked in bed. A call from the emergency department can be better managed when the relevant patient information, medications and a recent EKG are available to guide you. An after-hours call from a patient can be turned into a scheduled visit the next morning due to access to the scheduling module from a remote computer or smart phone. Performance reports can be generated from your home, and claims can be scrubbed remotely. You may have implemented an EHR to mitigate a lack of storage space for paper records, but now you realize that the EHR makes it easier to communicate with consultants, colleagues, hospital staff, nursing homes and other individuals and institutions involved in the care of your patients.

Initially, people worried that the technology would come between healthcare workers and patients, but you realize that the EHR quickly facilitates tedious jobs, freeing time to connect with patients. As EHR systems improve, the applications become more numerous and more impressive. The ability to look into the future and follow new and promising pathways will set off the most exciting and exemplary examples of EHR implementation in the coming years. Once you have selected your system and implemented it, the improvements in efficiency, financial success and patient care will just be beginning.

ADDENDUM 4-1: A HOW-TO-GO-PAPERLESS GUIDE

By Denni McColm, MBA

Once you have an EHR system, you would think that the paper chart would simply disappear. Unfortunately, it isn't that easy. You will probably have to take some deliberate steps to eliminate the paper chart to gain the full clinical and financial benefits of the EHR you invested in. Here's how:

1. **Decide that the elimination of the paper chart is the end point of your EHR implementation.** Know that if you keep even a partial paper chart, you will significantly diminish the clinical and financial benefits of the EHR. Discuss it with everyone who will listen. Hear their concerns. Publish, promote and discuss the various steps. Show a timeline of progress. Wear people out talking about each step!

2. **Set a target go-live/paperless date within one year.**

3. **Convene a team (nursing, physicians, IS, medical records) that is small, but representative of your practice/organization.** Designating a project manager tasked with keeping it all moving is helpful. This is your "paperless team," "save a tree team" or "clinical care enhancement team." They will be the drivers of the process within their area, but it will take many people configuring, implementing and changing processes throughout the organization.

4. **Take an inventory of the documents in paper charts. Use some current, recently discharged paper charts. (See Addendum Table 4-1.)**
   - Category 1: Documents that are already in the EHR, but are still being printed out.
   - Category 2: Documents that could be electronic. Be creative and resourceful.
   - Category 3: Documents that cannot reasonably be electronic by the go-live date. Minimize this category as much as possible—that is the goal. Examples of these items are patient signed documents and clinical test results not interfaced.

   With each document, discuss how it will be printed and how a full chart will be compiled when requested by an outside party.

Addendum Table 4-1: Inventory of Documents.

Document	Plan	How	Date
Lab Results	1. Already electronic.	Train physicians to view online and stop printing.	1/1/2008
Nursing Flowsheet	2. Could be electronic.	Configure and test nursing flowsheet in nursing software module, train nurses, implement, train physicians to view and stop printing.	6/1/2008
Patient Consent Form	3. Cannot be electronic by go live (no patient signature interface or software available).	Create indexing, workflow and processes for scanning and retrieving, train user to scan and view.	8/1/2008
Physician Order Sheet	2. Could be electronic.	Configure and test CPOE software and workflows, train physicians, stop printing.	7/1/2008
Etc.			

5. **Evaluate the go-live date, based on inventory.** Move it closer if you can, but don't push it out unless you absolutely must.

6. **Start with Category 1: Documents that are already electronic.** Train users (physicians, nurses, medical records, billing, radiology, etc.) to access the information. Pay attention to workflow and people using paper to drive their daily work. Replace any paper "prompts" with reports or other methods. Then, stop printing. You will have a hybrid chart starting at this point and continuing until you are paperless. This will serve as incentive to the other phases, as it is awkward to manage a partial electronic/partial paper chart.

    Make sure your medical records department is fully aware of the plan. Don't let them print the "full" chart upon discharge. When requested for outside parties, copy the paper, print the online portions and send both. Define this as your legal medical record in your policies, including the dates for each phase.

7. **Attack Category 2: Documents that can be electronic.** Implement the electronic systems in phases with set dates. For example, you may need to implement nursing documentation and flowsheets, ancillary documentation, radiology, lab, etc. then CPOE and physician documentation.

    Note regarding physician documentation: One of the hoped for benefits of an electronic record is the elimination of dictation, but one of the most difficult transitions for physicians is the use of templates. You may want to confer with your physicians to determine the best approach—either dictation or templates or a combination. Be prepared to assure quick turnaround times if you allow dictation. Do not allow handwritten notes that will be scanned.

8. **Get ready to scan Category 3.** Prepare your document management/scanning system. This may involve establishing the indexing method to "connect" documents to the electronic record. Creating and defining categories for documents so they can be located and searched may vary depending on your software; the goal is to make sure scanned documents are accessible to the physicians who will be using them during patient care visits.

9. **Scan Category 3 documents.** Scan Category 3 documents over a weekend and be paperless on Monday morning. Have staff available to support physicians. Then—celebrate!

ADDENDUM 4-2: SUPER-USERS: A BEST PRACTICE

By Denni McColm, MBA

One best practice at Citizens Memorial Healthcare (CMH), winner of the 2005 Davies Organizational Award, has been in the area of super-users. In addition to information systems staff dedicated to supporting users, CMH has more than 50 designated super-users throughout the organization.

Each super-user assists with one or more software applications or departments. The super-users were initially identified because they were the "superstars" during each application implementation. Super-users receive a super-user stipend of $40 per two-week pay period in addition to their regular pay for serving in the role, or $1,040 per year. Prior to inviting a super-user to fill a role, CMH obtains a commitment from the super-user's direct manager that he or she supports the super-user in the role.

Super-users act as liaisons between information services and end-users. They help innovate and recommend new approaches, processes and enhancements. Although super-users serve as support all of the time while in their regular role, they also float to the information services department for dedicated time to do testing and training. Floating time, paying a stipend and obtaining manager commitment have all been keys to the success of the super-user program at CMH.

The following is an Invitation to become a super-user at CMH and the Super-user Agreement:

SUPER-USER AGREEMENT

Because Information Technology Matters: An Invitation to be a Super-User

We spend a good portion of our lives at work. Here at CMH, that's a good thing— we have opportunities to work with great people, a worthy mission, and a great environment.

Still, there are things that we might want to change. While we may not be able to knock out that wall for our own "park view;" get the thermostat set correctly; or offload the monthly reporting, we can make changes to the virtual workplace of Meditech. The processes, rules and dictionaries are, in large part, created and maintained by us. We would like your help in making our Meditech workplace more efficient, more integrated and more comfortable.

Because of your experience, your work with Meditech and your commitment to CMH, we would like to invite you to become a Meditech Super-user. The Super-user is a formal agreement between you and CMH, which will allow CMH to compensate you for your work in creating the Meditech environment. The details of this agreement are in a separate document that you will sign. Your supervisor and the executive team for CMH have already approved this arrangement for you.

If making a difference matters to you, please join us as a Super-user.

SUPER-USER AGREEMENT TEMPLATE

Infocare Super-User Agreement

Super-user Name: _____

Module/Department/Facility: _____

Super-User Qualifications

- Currently working in the assigned department or module.
- Thorough knowledge of policies and procedures and the inter-relationship among departments
- Respected and trusted by end-users and managers.
- Interest and enthusiasm for the Infocare project.
- Good communication skills. Ability to listen well.
- Organized. Ability to manage projects and timelines.
- Ability to positively motivate non-subordinate co-workers.

Responsibilities

Assist IS Specialist in testing new functionality, DTS's, upgrades, new versions and changes in procedures in the Meditech system to assure they function as designed and intended.

Assist IS Specialist in training and supporting end-users in the use of Meditech and related software, including new employee training and retraining on new or changed functionality.

Act as a liaison between end-users and IS in order to expedite identification and clear communication of issues within the software or procedures.

Assist IS in the resolution of issues that may arise within the module or area relating to the satisfactory operation of the module.

Participate in interdepartmental meetings that provide a forum for raising and resolving issues.

Be a positive peer resource for other end-users during daily operations.

Assist IS with hosting other organizations for site visits to CMH, showcasing the positive impact of the system on the organization.

Assist with the development, review and maintenance of training materials and downtime procedures for end-users.

Module-Specific Responsibilities

I understand that:
- I will receive a stipend of $40 per pay period for fulfilling these responsibilities.
- This agreement is valid only as long as I am able and willing to fulfill these responsibilities.
- This agreement can be ended by either the IS Department or by me at any time.
- This agreement may cease if grant funding is ended or discontinued.

Super-user Signature:_____
Date:_____

Supervisor's Agreement

I support the above-named employee in the fulfillment of these responsibilities as super-user. I understand that this employee will float to the IS Department when fulfilling some of the above responsibilities as specified by his or her IS Specialist.

Supervisor Signature:_____
Date:_____

CHAPTER 5

Making the Business Case for EHR: Getting to ROI

David Collins, MHA, CPHQ, CPHIMS, FHIMSS, and Nancy R. Babbitt, FACMPE

"When I am getting ready to reason with a man, I spend one third of my time thinking about myself and what I am going to say and two-thirds about him and what he is going to say."

—Abraham Lincoln

INTRODUCTION

The best purpose statements are often five to seven words that precisely describe an organization's primary objective—its focus, its purpose, its intent—all pinpointing what it produces or what service it provides. Implementing an EHR is so all-encompassing that it naturally moves the organization to embrace with seriousness its purpose statement or to create a new one with a developed business case that will speak to this new way of doing business—one in which workflows are redesigned, and extensive training is required to facilitate new ways of practicing medicine to achieve new operational, clinical and financial objectives. This roadmap to success must be built at the beginning of the EHR journey.

With the appropriate training, strong leadership, executive commitment and perseverance not only can implementation of a system successfully break even financially, but may also result in revenue gains, new efficiencies and improved performance in patient safety and quality outcomes. To measure success, every member of the organization needs to be on the same page, and success must be defined at the beginning of the project.

What executive management considers a successful implementation in a health system and a physician considers in an office practice may be different from those of other clinicians, administrative staff, billing staff, medical records staff and others. Developing the business case and defining success upfront are very crucial steps in this career-defining decision.

JOURNEY TO THE EHR: THE FIVE RIGHTS

Analogous to the five rights of medication administration—the right medicine to the right patient at the right time using the right dose with the right method of administration—building the business case for the EHR requires similar elements.

These rights have been discussed in previous chapters, but let's review them briefly, as they are so important to the ability to make a successful business case: First, having the right leadership; second, having the right vision and business objectives; third, having the right buy-in; fourth, having the right workflow redesign and necessary training; and fifth, having the tenacity, flexibility and ongoing commitment to achieve new objectives and leveraging this technology for maximum efficiencies.

Right 1: Leadership

Leadership is key for success. No leadership, no success. It is truly that plain and simple. (This was discussed at length in Chapter 2.) Leadership can also be one of the biggest challenges you will face. It can be nerve-racking to stick your neck out for something you believe in when the costs and risk are so high.

Analyzing and establishing the business case up front is an important function of leadership. Relying on the data you have compiled for your business case, and using the advice in this book to navigate your project are important steps that will lead you to successful implementation. The optimal business case will demonstrate improvements in patient care, along with increasing revenue and decreasing costs.

Right 2: Vision and Objectives

Having the vision of "why" to implement, and setting the primary objectives of the EHR, will ultimately justify the investment. When it comes to making tough decisions, improved patient care is our first criterion. Answer the question or dilemma, "What is the better choice for patient care?" Then ask, "Is it a reasonable choice relative to cost and benefit calculations?"

For example, if faced with the choice and extra cost of a patient portal—do you need one for your system? If your health system or practice would benefit from online communication with patients, improving their care and creating the capability to schedule appointments, collect payments and provide other functionality online, it would be reasonable to compare the additional cost of the patient portal to the savings of reduced cost in staff time, postage, printing and increased collections.

2003 Davies Ambulatory Care Award-winner Roswell Pediatric Center in Georgia uses a patient portal in many patient care areas. Triage questions are answered online in a secure format, and e-mails about important clinical information are routinely sent. Through the portal, prescriptions are refilled, payments are taken, appointments are scheduled and referrals to specialists are provided. All of these functions help to provide excellent care with optimal customer service. Additionally, staff is more efficient and the number of phone calls is reduced. Compared with the cost of the portal, Roswell Pediatric Center has achieved a positive return on investment (ROI) and meets its business case objectives of providing better care, increasing revenue and decreasing costs.

Right 3: Buy-In

The shift in doing business as usual, the change in culture and the way medicine is practiced will not automatically transition seamlessly with the new EHR system. Hand in hand with leadership, buy-in must be achieved at the clinical and business levels. If buy-in is not achieved, then "build it and they will come" will ultimately become "build it and they will creatively develop workarounds." Chapters 7 and 8 in this book specifically address how to get your physicians and staff involved and garner their buy-in into this process. The fear of failure needs to be replaced with gaining clinical, operational and financial efficiencies.

Right 4: Workflow Redesign and Training

The goal of EHR implementation is not to "electrify paper." If the same workflow is maintained with the EHR as it currently exists with paper, then its true power and value will not be realized.

Although it adds time upfront, it is important to assess the way you do things now and keep an open mind for better ways to accomplish the same tasks with an EHR. Part of your business plan should be the improvements or changes that will need to be made in workflow. Once these new processes are implemented, training—followed by ongoing training—is essential to developing the new comfort zone users need to integrate this new way of doing business and practicing medicine into their everyday routine.

Right 5: Tenacity, Flexibility and Ongoing Commitment

The implementation journey is truly never-ending. Objectives will be achieved; however, the most successful systems realize that this is a process of relentless discovery. As objectives are achieved, new benefits are realized and new goals are set, leading to additional efficiencies. This process will not be smooth and flawless. It will require the ability to absorb a few punches, duck to avoid a few others and keep going even after the wind has been knocked out of you.

ESTABLISHING THE BUSINESS CASE

Defining goals and objectives, including a process to measure the success of milestones, is the first step in developing the business case. From this, an organization can measure and compare progress as it moves forward. Modifying the approach as appropriate and revisiting alignment to the organization's mission once efficiencies are realized, are all critical components of success.

2007 Davies Ambulatory Care Award-winner Valdez Family Clinic, San Antonio, TX, mapped out the transition from paper to digital with very specific business goals in mind:
- Return to pre-implementation patient flow capacity within 90 days.
- See the same number of patients in a four-day rather than 4.5-day work week.
- Improve office processes efficiency.
- Increase the accuracy of coding.
- Move billing in-house without adding staff.

These business objectives were targeted to improve care, to create improvements in operational efficiencies, and to achieve financial sustainability. Successful achievement of these goals will be detailed in the section "Justifying the Business Case: Measuring Return on Investment."

Bloomington, IN-based Center for Behavioral Health, a 2006 Davies Organizational Award-winner, shared several key lessons learned as it developed its business case and set its objectives. The center provided important advice for those who make the decision to implement an EHR. They suggest:

- Work processes should be mapped and revised before starting the EHR implementation. If you wait until you are underway, it is too late.
- Computer proficiency of each physician and staff member should be evaluated early by using an objective system. Asking people to assess their own computer skills is a waste of time.
- Support for end-users should be varied with different types and intensities offered. Some need handholding and some want a list of FAQs.
- For training, a good microphone should be implemented before using video files with sound for training.
- Assign one or two people to the EHR for 100 percent of the time. No matter how motivated employees are, there are still only 24 hours in a day, and employees assigned part-time still have other jobs to do. Alternatively, have blocks of time committed to this purpose.
- Finally, if you are ever in doubt how to reward or placate users—give them chocolate.

Case Study 5-1

THE HOSPITAL-ALIGNED PIEDMONT PHYSICIANS GROUP

2006 Davies Ambulatory Care Award winner Piedmont Physicians Group (PPG 775), was formed as a way to broaden Piedmont Hospital's ability to serve patients throughout the Atlanta market. Faced with challenges unique to hospital-aligned physician groups, the PPG 775 executive sponsor collaborated with system executives and physicians to develop a core set of business objectives:

- To improve the safety and quality of patient care through disease management, improved medication management and improved preventive measures.
- To increase the satisfaction of patients and physicians by improving productivity, creating efficiencies, reducing redundant work effort and reducing turnaround times for refills and referrals.
- To improve the operational and financial condition of the practice by increasing productivity and optimizing the efficiency of staff workflow.

A series of metrics—clinical, performance and financial—were developed for each of these objectives. For example, as measured by physician use of the EHR, the group achieved significant financial results. They report physician use as falling into three categories, with each achieving specific annual savings:

- Fundamental users: $14,500.
- Average users: $56,000.
- Power users: $62,000.

2006 Davies Organizational Award-winner Generations+/Northern Manhattan Health Network in New York, set several very specific business objectives, with a 10-year expected ROI of more than $360 million. This project was designed with the objective of implementing the EHR throughout New York City Health and Hospitals Corporation (NYCHHC). The expected savings were:

- Reduction in ancillary tests by 21 percent.
- Reduction in drug costs by 4.9 percent.
- Reduction of medical records staff (pilot hospital reduced 11 full-time employees [FTE]).
- Reduction in malpractice costs by 6 percent.
- Reduction in data entry costs (eight FTEs at pilot site).
- Elimination of departmental systems and reduction in maintenance costs (50 percent of departmental systems converted).
- Reduction in costs of meals by eliminating tray wastage by 2.3 percent.
- Reduction in cost of forms by 30 percent.
- Facilitation of laboratory consolidation not quantified initially.

JUSTIFYING THE BUSINESS CASE: MEASURING RETURN ON INVESTMENT

Traditionally, cost has been the number one barrier to health IT adoption. Providers are often skeptical of whether costs can be reduced and revenue generated. They are concerned that the ROI will be too slow in coming and may not exceed the initial investment outlay, and that the loss of productivity in transitioning from paper to digital will be too high.

Valdez Family Clinic provides a counter argument to each of these perceived barriers. The total cost of their EHR implementation in the practice, including hardware and training, was $56,810. ROI was better than anticipated, with an average billing increase of $21.93 per patient visit. Based on 9,600 yearly visits, 2007 billing increased by $210,528. Further, cost avoidance of $33,400, resulting from the elimination of outside billing, offset the cost of the software, and a $2,400 decrease in staff overtime brought total financial improvement to $243,928. This provided a projected net revenue increase of $187,118 in the first year, a return of more than 325 percent.

Additional efficiencies included the fact that at no time during the Web-based or on-site training was it necessary to close the office.

2008 Davies Ambulatory Care Award-winner Oklahoma Arthritis Center (OAC), P.C., Edmond, discovered that the transition from paper to digital workflow for charge entry required additional resources to optimize the process. The new workflow required charges to be captured in the EHR, which would be automatically entered into the practice management system. The billing team established "report cards" for providers to review what services were charged and what had been missed, as depicted in Figure 5-1. The amount of charges not captured electronically by each provider reflected the amount providers would have lost in revenue. This gave each provider an incentive to bill correctly to ensure proper reimbursement. Once the providers and billing team were comfortable with the provider's ability to charge electronically, paper charge forms were removed, and replaced by an electronic audit.

They also approached their business case slightly differently by focusing on productivity and measuring their financial value based on revenue per unit. OAC considers a "unit" to

Weekly Report Card			
Provider	Error	Times Missed	Lost Income
Dr. Carson	More than 1 dx attached	2	$100
	25 modifier not added to OV w/infusion	2	$166
	Office visit billed under nurse	2	$166
	25 modifier not added to OV w/90772	1	$83
	Office visit not entered 99214	1	$83
	25 modifier not added to OV w/20610	1	$83
	Total Lost Income:		**$681**

Figure 5-1: Physician Weekly Report Card. (From Oklahoma Arthritis Center, used with permission.)

be either a service offered or an employee. The per-employee productivity is measured by dividing the total charges for a given month by the total number of employees on staff that month (including administrative). They found that, as a result of the EHR they had implemented, their productivity increased an average of $13,000 per employee/per month, based on gross income. This does not show additional profit per employee, but does show additional billed services per employee. In addition, per their ROI table, they are able to add providers and increase yearly income without significantly increasing their technology expense, as the initial install and interface costs (the majority of the cost) have been completely paid for. Similarly, they are now able to expand their office square footage by reducing the cost for each additional unit of capacity.

Citizens Memorial Healthcare (CMH) (2005 Davies Organizational Award), Bolivar, MO, named its EHR implementation Project Infocare and identified many of its key goals as process improvements. They also completed a financial ROI analysis and projected that they would experience a positive return within five years of the initial investment, based on the following:
- Growth of admissions.
- Increase in revenue due to the use of standard protocols.
- Increase in net revenue by more accurate coding made possible by improved availability of information to substantiate diagnoses.
- Elimination of five positions.
- A decrease in transcription costs.
- Elimination of medical records scanning and microfilming costs.

At CMH, hardware costs were particularly significant because of the lack of information systems infrastructure within the organization. Local, metropolitan and wide area networks had to be established along with the acquisition of the servers and devices to support the system. Surveys were conducted and a walk-through in each department and facility was conducted to help in estimating the number of devices that would be required for the project. Employees were challenged to decide: "If the patient chart was on a computer—how many computers would you need in your department?"

Personnel costs were budgeted, and time was floated during the implementation to a Project Infocare department to allow for accurate capture of these costs. Personnel costs were estimated using a document provided by the vendor for each application. These estimates were quite accurate.

Travel and training costs were significant, but were minimized as much as possible. During travel to the vendor's training site in Massachusetts, a corporate apartment was rented, which significantly reduced hotel costs, and a leased car was maintained to reduce car rental costs. During vendor travel to the hospital, the vendor was requested and agreed to stay at a local hotel in Bolivar where the hospital has a reduced rate.

At $5 million, the size of the initial budget was large for a rural hospital and community. The funds were financed with tax-exempt bonds. An additional amount of $1 million was approved and financed one year later to complete the full EHR in CMH long-term care facilities and physician clinics.

The commitment of Tacoma, WA-based MultiCare (2009 Davies Organizational Award) to achieving the expected benefits from implementing MultiCare Connect resulted in the development of a Benefits Realization Program to articulate the total cost of ownership and the ROI, and to inform the organization's ongoing MultiCare Connect Optimization efforts.

The total cost of ownership was determined by quantifying the costs for the following categories over a 10-year period:

- Hardware.
- Software.
- Implementation operating expenditures.
- Implementation personnel costs.
- Facilities.
- Ongoing capital expenditure.
- Ongoing operating expenditures.

The model included incremental increases for items such as salary, maintenance contracts and volume licensing. The results showed a 10-year total cost of ownership of $126 million ($58.4 million for implementation expenses and $67.4 in ongoing expenses). The ROI projections were determined based on targeted process improvements, as well as efficiencies created simply by automating processes. The analysis included the determination of whether the returns were expected over a multi-year period or as a one-time benefit. MultiCare has measured an initial net benefit in excess of $42.6 million since June 2007. Given MultiCare's continued commitment to optimize MultiCare Connect, their ROI projections indicate they will break even in 2012.

In their financial performance, MultiCare reported achievements of:

- $12 million in net benefit as a result of improved patient responsibility collections.
- More than $1 million in avoidable write-offs.
- $20 million in improved cash collections.

MultiCare also reported other ways they achieved performance improvement in both clinical quality and business functions—more than we can relay to you here. They are certainly a harbinger of ongoing benefit that EHR implementations have in store.

Having taken a brief look at how MultiCare achieved benefit, it's appropriate to briefly review the report of value from the most recent Davies Ambulatory Care Award winner: Virginia Women's Center in Richmond.

At the beginning they, "braced for a 10 percent to 15 percent decrease in productivity as a consequence of implementation. The value proposition turned out to tell a story of fantastic ROI for us. Most notable is the marked profitability growth post-implementation. Average profits per shareholder physician stayed level during implementation, and the year post-implementation resulted in a 19 percent increase!"

"The expected immediate $300,000 elimination of transcription costs proved to be true. However the anticipated reduction in FTEs did not occur. In fact, the staff to provider ratio rose from 4.01 to 4.41 during the implementation and fell to 4.33 the year post-implementation. [Their] business model has always included a higher than average staffing complement to allow productivity and patient services that result in higher than average revenue production.... Workflow efficiencies and enhanced revenue cycle management contributed to favorable profitability. The volume of patient throughput was increased. Pre-EHR, the average number of annual patient visits per provider was 5,314. Post-implementation, it rose 11 percent to 5,629."

The average number of annual relative value units (RVU) per provider jumped over 13 percent with the EHR. On the cost side of the financial report, operating costs, as a percentage of revenue, decreased from 61 percent to 59 percent and staffing costs, as a percentage of revenue fell from 29 percent to 26 percent.

SETTING OBJECTIVES: LEARNING FROM EXAMPLE

In making their business case for the EHR, 2008 Davies Organizational Award-winner Eastern Maine Medical Center (EMMC), Bangor, looked first to their strategic vision for the project:

> "All EMMC providers will be able to treat a patient using one shared electronic record system, no matter where in EMMC the patient seeks care. Information will be instantly available, improving patient safety, enhancing outcomes, and saving money."

From that vision, they began making their business case by developing goals and measurable objectives that aligned directly with the organization's overall goals.

Table 5-1 presents those project's goals aligned against EMMC's strategic "pillar" goals and specifies the measurements that will be used to assess the project's success in meeting those goals.

Table 5-1: Pillar and Project Goals. (From Eastern Maine Medical Center, used with permission.)

Quality Pillar Goal: Improve Patient Safety and Quality of Care	Service Pillar Goal: Improve Provider and Staff Satisfaction	Growth & Finance Pillar Goals: Increase Volume and Market Share, Improve Financial Results
Project Goals Aligned to this Pillar Goal: • Standardize and stream-line Patient Care and Documentation. • Improve Orders and Order Management Processes that promote patient safety and high quality of care. • Transition Medical Care toward Best Practice Models. • 100-percent compliance with CMS Core Measures. Measures of Success Against These Goals: • Use of CPOE. • Risk management reporting of medication incidents and pharmacy interventions. • Compliance rate with Core Measures (CMS) and other industry-based goals. • Compliance with nursing documentation requirements.	Project Goals Aligned to this Pillar Goal: • Improve clinicians' work-flows through the use of the clinical information system. • Provide a technology infrastructure that meets the care delivery needs of EMMC. • Automation of data collection and reporting of quality measures for CMS and other regulation. Measures of Success Against These Goals: • Use of EHR. • Efficiencies gained in data collection. • Time-savings in optimiza-tion of clinicians work-flows. • Dependability, stability and performance of EHR systems.	Project Goals Aligned to this Pillar Goal: • Improve patient throughput. • Contribute to revenue growth, cost savings and cost reductions through the use of clinical information systems. Measures of Success Against These Goals: • Benefits gained from clinical systems serv-ices available to other organizations. • Decrease in length of stay and cost per case.

CONCLUSION

No matter the size or demographics of these Davies Award winners, developing and achieving their business plan objectives was key to their effective implementation. Their stories offer inspiration for EHR project management and the planning part of the process. They all had the five rights in their business plans: leadership, vision and key objectives, buy-in, workflow redesign, and having the tenacity, flexibility and ongoing commitment to achieve new objectives and leveraging technology for maximum efficiencies. All of these key areas are an integral part of making your business case for success a reality.

CHAPTER 6

Process Improvement: Toward More Efficient Workflow

Margaret Schulte, DBA, FACHE, CPHIMS

"We cannot solve our problems with the same thinking we used when we created them."
—Albert Einstein

INTRODUCTION

The promise of the EHR is the opportunity that computerization offers for improving processes of care and the performance of our organizations. The ultimate goal of the billions of dollars and untold person-hours dedicated to health information systems implementation is improvement of effectiveness in quality of care and in reduced costs of care. Achievement of these goals is not attained by IT implementation alone. Fundamental changes in work processes are an essential ingredient. As Brown, et al. suggest: "The purchase of advanced IT without a commitment to work process redesign can be a wasted investment by the institution. The total cost to the institution may be even greater than the direct cost of the IT system itself."[1]

In this chapter, we'll discuss the many ways Davies Award winners designed and implemented process improvements in their hospitals and physician offices. Factors related to the ROI, or value added, that Davies Award-winning providers experienced will be discussed in Chapter 9. In Chapter 4, we briefly discussed the way work processes must be addressed in systems planning and design. Here we build upon Chapter 4 and pick up the discussion of the ongoing demands of work process change during initial planning, design, acquisition, implementation and post-implementation.

Why Do We Need to Do This?

If there is one lesson that the Davies Award winners share, it's that workflows should be assessed even before the information system is selected, designed and implemented.

Consideration of process begins with the readiness assessment discussed in Chapter 3. Change in processes starts at the beginning of commitment to systems implementation and continues even after the system is up and running. Without process change, the organization will simply be superimposing technology on processes that are laden with inefficiencies and prone to human error.

In some instances, current processes have been retained in the move to the EHR but not without some level of assessment of whether they would work and/or could be improved in the new electronic environment. Goals of reduced costs, improved competitiveness and better patient care will not be realized without addressing the way in which functions are carried out. As Richard Lang, editor of *The Journal of Healthcare Information Management* and CIO at Doylestown Hospital in Pennsylvania, said in a recent issue: Healthcare "IT has made much progress....But without a fundamental change in the way we work and process information, we will continue to spend billions of dollars on technological advancements just to do the same inefficient things, only faster."[2]

MacClaren puts it another way: "The need to simplify and eliminate wasteful activities in hospital processes is a prerequisite to implementing an EHR system that will produce positive outcomes on patient care quality. The implementation of instantly accessible patient records is merely a piece of the infrastructure necessary for excellent healthcare processes."[3]

Brown, et al., add: "The reality is that the processes of patient care in healthcare systems do not flow smoothly. Few, if any, departments in a hospital are linked and services are often delivered in 'batch and queue' fashion. The result is a patchwork of handoffs that generate unnecessary costs and variability. An EHR system that incorporates these broken processes will fail to deliver the promise of improved operational efficiencies and patient care. The solution to this dilemma is the implementation of process improvement programs in advance of implementing EHR."[1]

2009 Davies Organizational Award-winner MultiCare in Tacoma, WA, committed at the start of their EHR implementation not to simply build the system around current processes. Their approach to future state workflow design was one that focused on "eliminating waste and exploiting system capabilities to their greatest advantage." (see the full quote in next paragraph).

Their purpose was captured in a quote from Bill Gates, chairman of Microsoft: "The first rule of any technology used in a business is that automation applied to an efficient operation will magnify the efficiency. The second is that automation applied to an inefficient operation will magnify the inefficiency." The organizational challenge is that we, or some of us, may assume our processes are efficient, only to find a surprise when we transition them to the new system.

WHERE TO START

Step 1: Tie Process Change to Organizational Strategy and EHR Vision

You've read this in earlier chapters, but it can't be overemphasized. The point at which an organization gets the idea that a new systems implementation is in their near future occurs when someone, or several people, realize that their vision for the organization, for improvement or for better workflow can only occur with the implementation of IT in both the business and clinical functions.

MultiCare, for example, was explicit about its goals. There was a commitment to "avoid designing and building a system that would simply mimic our existing processes.

The approach to future state workflow design was one that focused on eliminating waste and exploiting system functionalities to our greatest advantage. This was made possible through the collaboration between clinical and operational subject matter experts, system build analysts, physicians, and our vendor partners."

When embarking on their EHR journey, 2005 Davies Organizational Award winner Citizens Memorial Healthcare (CMH), in Bolivar, MO, identified specific processes they wanted to target in their implementation and kept their vision in the foreground. As they addressed their processes, they tied each back to their organizational strategies. They were guided by a vision of what the ideal state would be in achieving their goals and then focused directly on specific activities and functionalities. Table 6-1 shows how they targeted specific processes to achieve their project vision and goals. It is their framework for process improvement and implementation decisions:

Table 6-1: Citizens Memorial Healthcare Process Improvement Targets. (From Citizens Memorial Healthcare, used with permission.)

Goal/Strategy	Vision	Processes Targeted
Enhance access to care and improve continuity of care.	Enable a patient to enter anywhere into the continuum of care and have a personal identity maintained across that continuum.	ADMISSIONS/REGISTRATION & SCHEDULING: Patients will be asked to supply information only once. Patients will be able to schedule appointments from any CMH location.
Provide physician connectivity.	Physicians will have access to all of a patient's medical information within the healthcare continuum.	MEDICAL RECORDS: Providers will have access to easy-to-use, reliable, timely, accurate, and complete information available from any location. Information will be stored digitally in a retrievable format. Paper documents will be phased out.
Gain operational efficiency.	Providers will be able to document efficiently and safely.	CARE DOCUMENTATION & CHARGING: documentation will be captured at the point of care. Charges will be captured automatically as providers document in the system.
Support facility & services expansion.	Enable the continuum to become technologically advanced and poised to grow to meet demand and offer new services.	COORDINATION OF CARE: Implementation will be done from an organization-wide perspective, with recognition that CMH serves the same patients across care settings.
Push quality/performance improvement.	Providers will be supported by clinical decision support that will prevent medical errors.	CARE DELIVERY: CMH will employ the new system tools to enhance patient care, improve delivery and safety of care and support decisions with access to knowledge bases.

2003 Davies Organizational Award-winner Cincinnati Children's Hospital Medical Center took a similar approach in tying system objectives to organizational strategies and defining specific functionalities that would achieve their objectives.

Step 2: Analyze the Workflow

Having started with vision and tying IT strategy to organizational strategy, the "roll up the sleeves" work begins with the analysis of workflow. In the physician's practice, this step in the process may move quickly; in the hospital environment, with its complexities and scope, more time will be spent on workflow analysis. Let's look at how some of the Davies Award-winning organizations approached this part of the process:

Allina Hospitals & Clinics, Minneapolis: A 2007 Davies Organizational Award-winner, Allina reported that the reason for process change with the EHR was that existing processes were too inconsistent and convoluted to have an electronic system "dropped on top" of them.

"Almost every clinical and revenue cycle process was impacted by the implementation…The integration between inpatient and ambulatory, as well as between clinical and revenue cycle, forced Allina to look at all processes and to redesign those processes. The integration highlighted the interdependencies of the sheer number of applications that were designed and implemented together—i.e., surgery, pharmacy, ED, registration, billing, scheduling, CPOE, clinical documentation, HIM, documentation management."

MultiCare: MultiCare was intentional about not just layering technology over existing process, but instead used the implementation of MultiCare Connect as a catalyst to transform the way patient care is delivered. "There really was no process that did not undergo at least some minor modification."

For example, they re-designed their entire medication reconciliation process. Prior to the implementation, some of the major issues with the medication reconciliation process were that it was not standardized, roles and responsibilities were unclear, and there was incomplete or conflicting understanding of process requirements. As a result, organizational compliance with medication reconciliation suffered. The new functionality was approached in a step-by-step process that was easily embedded into the provider and nurse workflow navigators.

Center for Behavioral Health, Bloomington, IN: 2006 Davies Organizational Award winner Center for Behavioral Health found that, "while the technology of implementing an EHR may be difficult, the challenge of analyzing workflow was even more daunting." They had to understand how information flowed across the organization, formally and informally. To achieve this, they mapped all the work processes of the organization. When those work processes varied between departments, they standardized them. For example, they had many types of treatment plans in use by different departments. "All were driven by a well-intentioned but erroneous perception of clinical uniqueness. But multiple treatment plans would not work once an organization-wide EHR was established, so they were standardized into one."

Cincinnati Children's Hospital Medical Center (CCHMC): This 2003 Davies Organizational Award-winner found that: "As is common with the introduction of electronic systems, bad practices or broken processes are uncovered. The goal of the thorough workflow analysis during implementation planning is to minimize the occurrence of surprises once the system has been implemented. Despite CCHMC's efforts at methodical analysis of processes, several imperfect systems were discovered after implementation."

Village Health Partners (formerly Family Medical Specialists of Texas), Plano: Village Health Partners, a 2007 Davies Ambulatory Care Award winner, speaks of how their implementation "drove us to do an analysis of workflows." The organization studied clinical and business workflows, not only in the departments that would be directly impacted by the system implementation, but in all departments that interrelate to the directly impacted departments.

They found that the workflow for labs offered "another huge efficiency gain." They now order labs electronically in the EHR. For common things such as annual exams and diabetic visits, their nurses follow the re-designed clinical protocol. The results come back electronically unsigned into the patient chart and on the ordering doctor's desktop the same night. The results are then sent by the physician via secure e-mail or secure voicemail to the patients.

Palm Beach Obstetrics & Gynecology PA, Lake Worth, FL: For this 2008 Davies Ambulatory Care Award winner, almost every workflow was transformed by the implementation of the EHR. For example, every clinical phone call is documented as a message in the patient's chart, and any decisions made and recommendations given are also written into the chart. Each medical assistant has a task list that organizes their duties and reduces the chance of forgetting something important.

Cardiology of Tulsa, Oklahoma: This 2006 Davies Ambulatory Care Award winner reports that: "Installation of the system required that workflow throughout the organization be evaluated. The exercise allowed practice leadership to overhaul and eliminate all areas of systemic inefficiency."

Piedmont Physicians Group (PPG 775), Atlanta: This 2006 Davies Ambulatory Care Award winner also took an approach of using the EHR implementation: "As an opportunity for process improvement." From the very beginning of their process, they determined that their EHR would not be implemented around existing processes. Instead, the practice identified optimal processes for the flow of information and the delivery of care and built the EHR around those processes. They then hired an industrial engineering consulting group to complete a series of time motion studies related to workflow throughout the office.

These studies identified key areas for improvement, and the in-house work group used the results to develop future state workflows. Coincidentally, the practice was undertaking a major physical renovation concurrently with EHR design, so the design and layout of the practice were completed with the EHR-enabled workflows in mind. "This process allowed the practice to identify key benefits and expectations for the EHR and to develop appropriate future-state workflows, knowing the physical layout of the practice would support them. The results of this process were also used to identify ideal locations for computers, printers, scanners, and other assets."

The case of Allina Hospitals & Clinics allows a deeper look into the approach they took to workflow re-design.

Case 6-1

A STUDY IN WORKFLOW REDESIGN AT ALLINA HOSPITALS & CLINICS

Allina Hospitals & Clinics started their EHR implementation by redesigning workflows and then building and installing the software to support these new workflows. Early on, the steering committee knew that to succeed most, if not all, workflow processes would need to be examined and redesigned. Existing processes were too inconsistent and convoluted to have an electronic system "dropped on top of them" as referred to earlier.

Project management assigned a team leader to each of the seven different operational areas involved, as well as a team led by IS and a training team led by the chief learning officer (CLO). In deciding team leaders, project managers selected individuals who had clinical experience, process redesign and performance improvement experience, and who had the trust of the operations staff. This team would be responsible for the detailed planning and preparation for the implementation.

To prepare for what was to be the most challenging part of the entire project, team leaders and key physician leaders participated in a training class on the capabilities of the new software.

With this understanding, team leaders began to redesign workflows throughout the three hospitals. For three months, they led more than 150 end-users through a complete analysis of the patients and information flow throughout their areas and the organization. This analysis touched every workflow and revealed redundancies, workarounds, and hand-offs that significantly slowed the flow of patients and information and created numerous opportunities for error.

With this insight into current processes, the team leaders then worked intensively with end-users to redesign the flow of information and create integrated workflows. The result was 500 integrated high-level workflows that provide for consistency in managing clinical information across the organization. These 500 eventually developed into 2,000 detailed workflows.

The high-level workflows laid the foundation for the simultaneous development of:

- Deeper, more detailed department and unit workflows (see next section).
- Policies and procedures to support the new workflows.
- Training materials.
- System planning and build.
- Communications for change management.

As teams proceeded with the redesign of deeper workflows, they simultaneously gathered all paper documentation tools and order sets. Working with clinicians, the teams also analyzed and classified the data elements that were collected and reviewed. This enabled a complete redesign of the clinical information gathering by units. They then worked with IS to build the documentation in the Epic system, so that users would enter data into the system only once. From there, it could be shared, retrieved and reused by any clinician in the care and outcomes management of the patient across the continuum of care. A sample flowsheet is shown in Figure 6-1.

For the 68 office practice sites, the ambulatory team developed a basic set of workflows to serve as a model for all sites. The standardized workflows ensured that each office performed critical workflows in the same efficient manner, while allowing for the unique set of physicians, specialties, personnel mix and physical characteristics at each location and practice.

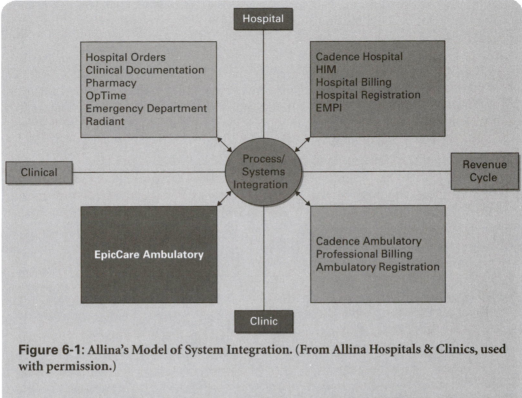

Figure 6-1: Allina's Model of System Integration. (From Allina Hospitals & Clinics, used with permission.)

Organization-wide registration conventions ensured that equivalent information was collected and entered into the system in the identical way from largest site to smallest outlying office. This helped to establish basic routines from co-pay collection and payment posting to scheduling patients or taking phone messages from patients. Skeleton processes were formulated to standardize clinical workflow, while leaving ample room for individualized patient care.

WORKFLOW IMPROVEMENT MEANS CHANGE!

There is a big "catch" that is an inherent part of workflow and process improvement: CHANGE. Once processes are re-designed, then the humans implementing those processes must adapt to the new; they must change the way they do things. This is where implementation can get really difficult.

Our resistance to change can unhinge even the best intentioned and well-funded EHR implementation. Change is not limited to the tangible workflows of the hospital or the physician's office; it must inherently be enveloped in a culture that embraces change. As you read in Chapters 2 and 5, top leaders must be champions of change. They are responsible for sustaining morale and for creating a culture that embraces change. The process of systems implementation can have the transformative impact that comes with embracing change. This transformation is the point at which improvements in quality and financial performance will find the opportunity to reveal themselves.

Davies Award winners have found effective ways of addressing change and engaging providers and staff in designing and adopting changes in their day-to-day procedures and their decision-making processes.

Village Health Partners (formerly Family Medical Specialists of Texas) described how "the culture change in our office has been dramatic. Our staff is now keenly aware of the importance of workflow and process improvement. Our monthly meetings focus on this and how we can more efficiently care for our patients. This has allowed our staff to move from being scared of change to embracing change." That change will not be limited to one area of the hospital or medical practice. It will be found throughout the entire organization or at least in all areas that are touched in any way by the EHR.

MultiCare created a series of events called "Workflow Walkthroughs & Tunnel Tours" to introduce their employees to the new technology, and at the same time, check out the impact on workflows and point out ways in which those workflows could be further improved, as depicted in Figure 6-2.

Figure 6-2: Example of MultiCare Training Their Staff. (From MultiCare, used with permission.)

THE VENUE FOR PROCESS CHANGE

In changing processes, IT is an enabling technology. It offers the opportunity for improvements that support clinical services, business services and overall communication. "Considerable evidence describes how IT can be used to enable the fundamental redesign of work processes that produce exceptional levels of operating efficiency and strategic advantage."[1]

Process Change in the Clinical Setting

It is in the clinical setting that the major change happens with the implementation of the EHR. With that implementation, information is available and flows more directly and efficiently among clinicians from the way it flowed pre-implementation. Collected in the electronic medium, rather than on paper, patient and clinical information can be made readily available to the clinician at the point of care and to multiple clinicians and staff simultaneously. This supports timely, evidence-based diagnosis and treatment regardless of where the patient or the clinician is located. The case of Alpenglow Medical provides a clear picture of information flow in the practice setting.

Case 6-2

WORKFLOW IN THE PAPERLESS PHYSICIAN PRACTICE

The EHR is fully implemented at 2006 Davies Ambulatory Care Award-winner Alpenglow Medical, PLLC. All intended users (physicians, MA, office manager and receptionist) are using the EHR to accomplish their work. Every scheduled appointment includes nursing pre-work listed on the master schedule, as well as a box in the upper right hand corner for signaling readiness; that is, when the patient enters through the front door, whoever is at the front desk puts an 'X' in the box, which is the visual cue that the patient is ready for rooming. Physicians and MAs always have the schedule open on their computer, even if they are working within an individual medical record or are seeking other electronic information. The medical assistant enters vitals, updates the current medication list and enters the chief complaint and any secondary complaints into the EHR system.

A typical office visit begins with Dr. Griffin and the patient entering the exam room together and accessing the electronic system. The opening screen shows a picture of the patient, all demographic and insurance information, current lab and x-ray reports, prompts from the disease-specific concept, and current problem and medication lists. The interview is conducted with the patient and Dr. Griffin viewing the screen while the doctor enters relevant notes. Medication reconciliation is a routine part of every visit.

Following the examination, the patient and Dr. Griffin return to the computer to enter further information as needed. Dr. Griffin verbalizes all entries into the system while typing to ensure accuracy, to allow for corrections or additional patient input and to serve as an educational intervention. He places a high priority on fully answering patient questions and schedules appointments with that goal. After the concurrent visit documentation is completed, he and the patient leave the examination room together and go to the front desk, where prescriptions, tests and referral orders and billing information are printing. The front office staff has access to the follow-up recommendations section of the clinical encounter and schedules the next appointment before the patient leaves, whenever possible. At the conclusion of the visit, all documentation is completed, with no pending data entry.

When a plan is generated from within an examination room that indicates need for scheduling or arranging, such as for laboratory or consult intervention, a popup appears on the front desk computer and the receptionist or office manager begins calling to arrange these appointments, printing any required instructions and/or physical directions and indicated patient education materials. Prescriptions automatically print to the computer behind the front desk and are added to the paper information given to the patient. Following lab tests, the medical assistant manages an electronic tickler system that sends alerting messages to check for lab results.

The receptionist and office manager are responsible for scheduling patients, either based on phone call requests, or when present in the clinic, typically after a physician appointment. Patients are scheduled according to type (acute, chronic care needs, lab follow-up, physical exam, etc.) and are put into the schedule with color-coding. Standard appointment time allocations are based on Dr. Griffin's estimation of the time required, plus a buffer of several minutes to ensure adherence to the no-waiting policy. If an unusual number of patients request same-day appointments, office protocols guide the staff in placing additional visits into the schedule, or they are individually cleared by discussion with Dr. Griffin.

The physicians at Alpenglow routinely use UpToDate, an evidence-based clinical decision support tool, to access clinical information at the point of care. In addition, Alpenglow recently incorporated First Data Bank, National Drug Data File Plus into their EHR system, which allows providers to access drug screening information as they prescribe.

More Process Change in the Clinical Setting

The practice of Village Health Partners (formerly Family Medical Specialists of Texas) significantly changed workflow related to prescriptions refills. Learning from benchmark data that this process can take more than a day and cost several dollars for each refill, Village Health Partners gained the ability to electronically send all prescriptions directly to the pharmacy. Whether the request comes in by phone, fax, e-mail or while the patient is in the office, it is forwarded to the physician who reviews it and sends it on electronically to the local pharmacy or pharmacy benefits manager (PBM).

This process takes seconds. Patients' refills are completed within the hour of their request because the physician can quickly dispose of them when he/she is in-between patient visits. Additionally, the physician can quickly review the chart and identify and respond to other patient needs. This improves both quality of care and practice revenue.

Yet, with all of this efficiency, the physician takes about as much time on refills as was required in the paper world; the difference is that no one else has to be part of the workflow. The limited number of "pass offs" significantly limits errors. Village Health Partners reports that this workflow saves at least 50 calls per doctor per day, and refilling a prescription now costs pennies.

In the health system environment, the EHR supports the workflow of care delivery in many ways. At Allina, order entry enables the flow of information from the provider to every other discipline. In some cases, printed requisitions alert an ancillary department of an order; in other cases, the order populates a system list (a type of work queue), which the ancillary department will reference and manage. Results from tests and procedures are available at the order level, making it efficient to access a result related to the order. External results may be interfaced with the EHR or scanned and made accessible through the order. In the new system, providers and other clinicians are alerted to new results through their patient census lists.

Patient transfers are also improved with the EHR implementation. At Allina, patient flow is enhanced through EHR tools. The immediate access to information by all clinicians enables nursing units to better prepare for transfers. Outpatient orders populate work queues for schedulers, prompting them to schedule patients. Scheduled patients then appear on work queues to be pre-registered by the registration department. Handoffs between departments are streamlined, taking less time than previous methods of communication and providing greater accuracy.

The sophisticated integration of applications (Figure 6-1) has led to greater dependency between functions and the need to understand the impact of one department's work on all other departments. The development of integrated workflows to understand handoffs and interdependencies was accomplished through a matrixed approach of the various applications involved in the care and revenue processes, as well as the ambulatory and hospital settings.

Workflow and Patient Charts

Providers who have implemented the EHR widely report that the effect on updating, maintaining, finding, pulling and re-filing patient paper charts is dramatically impacted, and the process is made infinitely more efficient. The electronic chart is immediately available to the clinician without having to be found, pulled, updated and placed at the exam room door or on the physician's desk, only to be re-filed after the patient visit and physician notes are completed. Most Davies Award-winning practices report that lost, misplaced or queued charts awaiting input are a thing of the past.

In the EHR environment, charts are updated simultaneously during patient visits. Billing occurs immediately, improving cash flow—sometimes dramatically. Lab and other diagnostic tests are automatically incorporated into the record when those tests are completed, assuming that the diagnostic devices are interfaced with the EHR. Alpenglow Medical, for example, achieved 100 percent concurrent, real-time documentation."

In the words of Village Health Partners: "Pulling charts, finding charts, and waiting on charts is no longer a reality. The ability for everyone to be in the same chart at the same time and the chart always being available, especially remotely, has greatly enhanced our efficiency."

Cardiology of Tulsa found that "the practice realized significant benefits through process improvements—not necessarily because physicians worked faster but because the installation of the system required that workflow throughout the organization be evaluated."

Valdez Family Clinic now captures "complete medical information in real time, at the point of care." Not only has this added to the efficiency of the practice, the EHR has also eliminated the endemic problem of lost charts in the workflow of so many physician practices. When the chart is "lost," the patient visit is hampered, and the ability of the clinician to make quality clinical decisions is impeded; staff time is wasted in searching for the chart; patient satisfaction diminishes; and billing may be delayed.

In the words of the Valdez Family Clinic: "Missing (paper) charts are almost never lost; rather, only one person knows where they are at any given time." The effect on the doctor is the same.

For example, in early 2006, "…while the clinic was still paper-based, auditors from the state visited Valdez Family Clinic to monitor childhood vaccination records. The clinic was asked to pull 300 charts for the examiners' review. In the meantime, some of these patients came in for treatment, and those responsible for pulling their charts had no idea where they were. Even if the charts had been easily located, finding a specific chart amid the examiners' work would have caused unacceptable delays." The EHR made the process smooth.

The Oklahoma Arthritis Center anticipated that the EHR program would increase efficiency and provide better time management in their daily operations. Rather than spending hours a day searching for charts, they would be easily accessible via the computer. Staff would be able to get patients into the exam rooms to see their provider faster by inputting all their problems and medications into the system, as opposed to handwriting everything in a paper chart. Interfaces allow other systems to send information directly to the provider without additional manual entry.

Palm Beach Obstetrics & Gynecology PA found that the EHR reduced employee movement since they are not continually looking for charts. As an added bonus: "the complete elimination of charts and written notes made our nurses' station, checkout area, and doctor's offices look clean and professional."

At Citizens Memorial Healthcare, patients' charts were, until a few years ago, physically housed in the medical records departments of their facilities in several counties. Those charts were moved in stacks from the care areas to the physicians' desks, to coding, to billing, then to racks and racks of file folders.

Now access is available to multiple providers and staff concurrently. Figure 6-3 illustrates access to one of the most "popular" charts in this sample period. During this

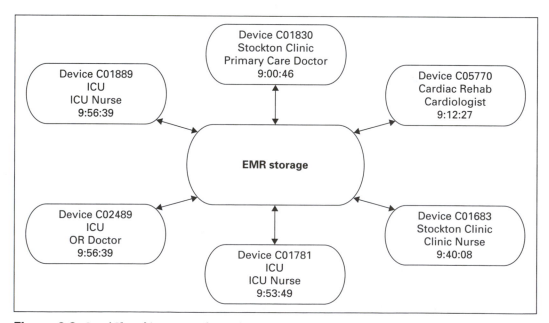

Figure 6-3: One 'Chart' in Many Places. (From Citizens Memorial Healthcare, used with permission.)

hour, the medical record for Patient 8099 was accessed by six healthcare professionals in six locations. The devices, or computers, used illustrate the accessibility of the EHR. The record was viewed in OR, ICU, the cardiologist's office at the hospital, and in the primary care physician's clinic, 25 miles away.

Patients' conditions can change quickly, the clinician needs to be alerted; but what happens when the clinician is not in front of the computer screen?

Generations+/Northern Manhattan Health Network found a workflow solution to a situation in which time is often of the essence. They found that "the best way to alert clinicians to changes in a patient's condition and to workload activity is to use a large number of electronic bulletin boards in the various departments. These boards display department-wide indicators and alert staff through changing colors and objects to conditions that require their attention. Now clinicians do not have to be signed on in the ED to see lab results, or the radiology tech does not need to be logged on to know that a STAT CSR was just ordered in ICU. These constantly updating monitors bring real-time alerts to clinicians all the time."

Business Efficiency

Business processes are also changed with the implementation of the EHR. In both the practice and the hospital setting, coding is made more accurate, revenue flow is enhanced, FTE time devoted to billing is reduced, efficiency is improved and compliance is increased.

At Village Health Partners, the physicians had always done their own coding prior to implementation of the EHR. With the EHR, the doctors continue to do their own coding, but with electronic order sets for common diagnoses the process is quicker and more accurate. In fact, before a patient leaves the office, coding is completed, insurance benefits are reviewed, and the patient pays his or her portion of the bill. As Village Health Partners put it: "This has had tremendous financial ramifications" and note that, for example, a data entry person is no longer needed. On the other hand, "collections at the time of service increased significantly."

At Cardiology of Tulsa, after implementation, the handling of patient phone calls was significantly improved. Before the implementation, the process required staff to log all calls and their purpose, pull the chart, deliver it to the clinical staff, retrieve the completed chart, log it back in and then return it to the file—a 15-minute process when the chart was in the file at the beginning of the process. After implementation, the process of handling phone calls was reduced to five minutes, and the three employees who had been handling phone calls were re-assigned.

MultiCare in Tacoma, WA, found that a significant new process in the revenue cycle resulted in the reduction of claims denials. Work queue functionality was built upon rules designed to catch issues with claims before they were sent to the payor and to support pre-authorization processes. This process change alone resulted in a $5 million reduction in payment denials.

Communication

Oklahoma Arthritis Center describes the importance and impact of workflow change related to the flow of communication: "Through the implementation process, communication between the different departments of the practice became more streamlined with in-office messaging. Additionally, the various departments are now able to work simultaneously within a patient's chart without having to wait for the chart to be found.

"For example, if a patient calls requesting a prior authorization as well as medical records, the billing team no longer has to wait for the medical records team to return the chart before working on the prior authorization. Both teams can begin to process the patient's request at once, thus creating a more efficient work environment and superior customer service. The physical environment has also become more organized as charts, and the necessary storage associated with them, have disappeared. Without the constant distraction of 'chart-hunting,' staff and patients now enjoy a more tranquil environment throughout the clinic and have more time to spend with patients."

Palm Beach Obstetrics noted that almost every workflow was transformed by implementation of the EHR. Communications that once occurred via telephone or through face-to-face contact, are efficiently handled and documented with internal e-mail. Palm Beach reports having fewer interruptions and distractions. Every clinical phone call is documented as a message in the patient's chart, and any decisions made and recommendations given are also written in the chart. Each Medical Assistant has a task list that organizes their duties and reduces the chance of forgetting something important. Patient charts are better organized since documents can be placed in customized folders, making them easier to find and track over time.

Village Health Partners automated confirmation and recall systems for patients, consultants and anyone else needing patients' medical information. They have a patient portal on their Web site that allows patients to request prescription refills, make appointments, request a referral, change demographics or ask a billing question. Patient utilization of these features helps the practice to lower phone volume and batch non-urgent tasks with asynchronous communication. Approximately 10 percent of patient appointments are now made online. For a nominal fee, patients can e-mail their physician to view a portion of their chart online. Prescriptions are refilled in seconds and can be electronically sent at the point of care, so they will be ready when the patient picks them up. This alone saves the practice about 60 phone calls a day.

Case 6-3

COMMUNICATIONS AND WORKFLOW AT GENERATIONS+

Generations+/Northern Manhattan Health Network found that "nurses love the electronic health record and take great pride in our medication administration time and accuracy—after implementation, their administration time was cut in half. Nurse-nurse and nurse-doctor handoffs are now simplified and accurate. True multidisciplinary engagement with the patient has become easy, not only for the doctors and nurses but for social work, dietary, etc."

When an online order placed for a late tray results in a quick response, the patient and nurse are both happy. Streamlining their workflow, reducing redundancy, and providing tools to monitor patients have increased nursing satisfaction.

Specific workflow initiatives included:

Improvements in Alerts

A program of integrated medication management, including the online administration of medications, has been implemented at all hospitals. The system has dose and allergy checking and warns of drug interactions. Reminders and review queues are in place. Patient-tracking tools such as bed boards and ED white boards are used.

In addressing the issue of alerts to patient condition, we recognized that clinicians cannot stay chained to a computer waiting for things to happen. Computers are great at alerting users to many different care issues, but those alerts only happen if the clinician is signed on. At Generations+, we believe that the best way to alert clinicians to changes in patient condition and workload activity is to use a large number of electronic bulletin boards in the various departments. These boards display department-wide indicators and alert staff through changing colors and objects to conditions that require their attention. With these in place, clinicians do not have to be signed on in the ED to see lab results or the radiology tech does not need to be logged on to know that a STAT CXR was just ordered in CCU. These constantly updating monitors bring real-time alerts to clinicians at all times. Electronic information resources are available through separate query.

Elimination of Redundant Processes

A complete elimination of redundant patient queries, e.g., allergies and histories, has been achieved. The referral process has also eliminated redundancy through the nursing admission assessment notes; patients meeting criteria for referral to social work, dietician, physical therapy, etc., trigger an immediate referral. Regulatory requirements are stringent and strictly monitored—high-risk patients must been seen within twenty 24 hours, and our compliance is above 90 percent. Duplicate phone calls, paper forms and scheduling no longer exist.

Improved Work Processes

The EHR system has served as a vehicle to automate these departments and facilitate interdepartmental communications and processes. In the OR, booking requests are electronically generated. These requests route to the preadmission area for health and financial clearances and to the booking area for scheduling. Managed care information, including the patient's health maintenance status, is available. Guest relations document patient satisfaction surveys in a secured procedure in the EHR.

The ED workflow, including triage, patient tracking, order entry, rounding and documentation has been automated, shaving valuable time off ED triage. This change has only slightly decreased the mean length of stay (LOS) but has significantly reduced the standard deviation. In the clinic cycle, availability of the online chart has reduced waiting time in the clinic, and overall, the system has enabled us to improve communication with patients. For abnormal test notification, letters to patients are automatically and immediately generated. Discharge instructions are also generated automatically.

Because we can trend results, patients can actually see these results—doctors can point right to the screen to show trends, graphs and progress. Seeing their results helps patients engage in their own health maintenance. They can also go home with growth charts, trended results for the lab, immunization records, etc.—all printed out instantly. We anticipate a further expansion of patient communication through an e-health initiative that was recently approved. Part of the patient demographic will include e-mail address and cell phone numbers as point of contact.

PROBLEMS MAY ARISE

One of the "natty" elements of workflow improvement is the detail that must be assessed and addressed. Some Davies Award winners reported elements in which they found that attention to the little things mattered a great deal—and offered opportunity for business improvement at little cost and with opportunity to learn from problems.

As in any change process, problems will arise. Humans may be resistant, and in the very complex world of healthcare delivery, some process issues may not surface until a problem presents itself.

For example, Valdez Family Clinic "experienced the range of problems inherent in a paper-based office. Take lab results as a case in point. As the practice grew and the pace of work increased, the pre-implementation environment was one in which labs occasionally fell through the cracks. In some cases, the results would not come back, or the patients themselves would not comply by avoiding the test, or results would be misfiled, never to be seen by Dr. Valdez. From a patient care and a liability perspective, that was unacceptable. Simply having the right labs in the right chart results in better patient care."

Cincinnati Children's Hospital Medical Center acknowledged that "as is common with the introduction of electronic systems, bad practices or broken processes are often uncovered. The goal of the thorough workflow analysis during implementation planning is to minimize the occurrence of surprises once the system has been implemented. Despite CCHMC's efforts at methodical analysis of processes, several imperfect systems were discovered after implementation. The design teams and Patient Care and Access Process Initiatives (PCAPI) took the lead in investigating these practices and worked toward their resolution. These are depicted in Table 6-2.

Table 6-2: Cincinnati Children's Hospital Medical Center—Summary of Process and Practice Problems Identified after ICIS Implementation. (From Cincinnati Children's Hospital Medical Center, used with permission.)

Broken Process/Imperfect Practice	Process Improvement Solutions
Delayed placement of patient registration into the system. Delays in getting the patient account set up in the clinical system resulted in delays in order placement and the ability to document care.	The admitting and registration process underwent a complete performance improvement initiative to anticipate the arrival of scheduled admissions and place them in a temporary unit until the actual patient arrival. This allowed preliminary orders to be placed on the patient before their arrival.
Placement of the order "Home meds per routine". In the manual world, some clinicians would write the above.	The resolution of this issue is not an information system fix, but it uncovered the practice.
Unanticipated Consequences	**Process Improvement Solution**
Verbal orders entered under the incorrect physician. Although the ICIS has led to a significant decrease in the number of verbal orders, there have been cases where the nurse attributed the order to the wrong physician.	In the isolated cases when verbal orders are accepted, the nurse is asked to confirm if the correct physician was selected from the list of physician names.

(Continued)

Table 6-2: (Continued)

Unanticipated Consequences	Process Improvement Solution
Excessive COE clinical alerts. Too many alerts were being generated by normal practice, especially in intensive care units where multiple sedation agents, vasoactive medicines, antibiotics or other potential conflicts are common usage. Too many alerts led to desensitization to warning alerts.	Rather than simply remove all generic and therapeutic duplicate checks, alerts were evaluated for helpfulness and those that were deemed a nuisance were removed from the system. The allergy checking and dose range checking both remain. Certain absolute maximum doses have been added for very high-risk drugs.
Unanticipated Expiration of Medications. The CCHMC policy for limiting treatment duration of certain drugs was engineered into the system in the form of default expirations. The ordering party may accept the default in haste. The physician would find out after the fact that the medication was no longer being administered due to expiration of the order.	Several system features were built into the system to alert clinicians to orders approaching expiration. These orders are indicated on the active order display; the last dose of a medication is labeled as such by the pharmacy; and the nurse administering the medication gets an alert as the last dose of the medication is charted on the Medication/IV Charting.

CONCLUSION

Changes in processes and workflow are at the heart of a successful implementation. Overlaying technology on old processes that are not examined in light of the technology leads to not only lost opportunity to gain the benefits of the implementation but may actually result in increased inefficiency. The cases and vignettes discussed in this chapter highlight not only the importance of workflow re-design but also practical approaches that are useful. Process improvement does not have to be overwhelmingly complicated, though in some cases it inevitably is as many departments and disparate providers are connected. In the latter case, professional process engineers may need to be engaged. In the less complex situation, staff may just gather around a conference table with all their process points prepared on sticky notes or charts. As one practice described, once the staff gathered and looked at all the points that each staff person used to complete their part of a process, it became clear where steps could be eliminated and efficiency gained through the intervening technology. There is opportunity in an EHR implementation as demonstrated by each of the Davies Award winners described in this chapter.

References

1. Brown GD, Stone TT, Patrick TB. *Strategic Management of Information Systems in Healthcare.* Chicago, IL: Health Administration Press; 2005;6.

2. Lang RD, ed. Editor's Report: The evolution of the primary caregiver. *J Healthc Inf Manag.* 2009;23(1):3.

3. MacClaren B. Electronic Health Records Destined to a Rocky Start without Healthcare Process Improvement. *NOVACES.* Available at: www.novaces.com. Accessed August 15, 2009.

CHAPTER 7

How We Got Our Physicians to Adopt the System

Alice Loveys, MD, FAAP, FHIMSS

"Attitude is a little thing that makes a big difference."

—Winston Churchill

INTRODUCTION

Physician engagement is key to the successful implementation of technology. At an organizational level, legions of failed technology implementations have been left in the wake of purchase decisions made by administrators or information systems departments with a paucity of end-user involvement.

In fact, without such involvement, an entity is unlikely to realize the full potential of a system, with resulting diminished return on investment and risks morale issues.

In the small office, a single unengaged partner can derail the entire effort. Several Davies Award applicants relayed stories of practices dissolving or partners quitting because of tension during an implementation. When these departures or dissolutions are examined, one finds that a lack of physician consensus or even of seeking all partners' opinions toward alignment was the critical fracture point.

In contrast, a well-done implementation can actually result in physician retention and recruitment. Of the many elements of a successful implementation, the ones that get physicians to fully use the system are the very ones, when extended systemwide, that assure an optimal implementation. This chapter will examine those elements across a variety of ambulatory settings—from the solo physician to organizations with multiple hospitals and remote clinic settings.

THE SOLO PRACTICE

Several solo physician practices have received the Davies Award. While it may seem an empty exercise to include the solo office in a discussion of physician engagement, an extrapolation in solo decision-making and psychology exists that "scales up." Solo physicians migrate to that practice setting for a variety of reasons, and chief among them is the ability to set the course for the practice. They have flexibility in decision-making and can rapidly adjust when a decision does not work out as planned. They assure their own training and oversee the staffs' training, and the resulting competency is readily apparent.

Communication within the office is straightforward. The solo doctor also is the chief executive officer and chief financial officer; he or she bears the ultimate risk but also garners the reward of his/her decisions. The solo doctor then, must be convinced of the positive impact that implementing an EHR will have on the quality of patient care, practice life and the financial bottom line.

For solo-office Davies Award winners, once they started the process of implementation, there was no going back; their personal commitment assured success. These themes of having convincing evidence to go electronic, involved decision-making consistent with the culture of the organization, adequate training, clear communication, as well as the theme of flexibility and responsiveness during implementation are evident in larger, successful practices and provider organizations as well.

SEVEN KEY REQUIREMENTS FOR SUCCESSFUL PHYSICIAN ADOPTION

Whatever the size of the Davies Award winners, strong physician leadership and involvement set the tone. The first area critical in physician involvement is creating the vision statement and strategic plan. The vision for going electronic has to be in keeping with the values of the physician. Davies Award winners have consistently found that the commitment and enthusiasm of physician leaders created an atmosphere that drew in the staff.

Likewise, if one of the partners did not consistently attend staff meetings or support time needed for training, the staff lost confidence in the effort. Organizational leaders—from CEOs to board members—actively sought physicians to participate in every phase and to support the effort. Organizations kept the mission to go electronic at the forefront using a variety of communication and marketing tools. They gave projects clinical credibility by making sure someone with clinical experience was a liaison between administration and information system departments.

Requirement 1: Physician Involvement in Creating the Vision

The first area critical to physician involvement is creating the entity's vision statement and strategic plan. The need to go electronic is then aligned with that plan. Consistently, Davies Award winners describe the vision as having strong clinical themes of improving the quality and safety of care. In these cases, physicians were eager to engage with a plan consistent with their values. Marketing campaigns and recruitment brought people together to realize those goals. Physician and clinical leaders created a clear outline of the goals and their responsibilities in meeting them and helped craft project charters or strategic plans. Change could not be force fed; it had to come in response to building strengths and improving on quality. Effective change only came with consensus on these goals.

Requirement 2: Communications

Communication is critical, and for the Davies Award winners, a variety of communication methods kept physicians involved. Leaders reviewed the electronic vision status at meetings, held at least monthly within the office or at organizational medical staff meetings. CEOs gave presentations at board meetings as well and were clear in their support of the projects. Practice or organizational newsletters also emphasized the message, and posters advertised the mission around the organization or office.

Requirement 3: Training

Training is another key ingredient to active physician involvement. Among Davies Award winners, continued physician acceptance of systems depended on adequate training and on going support. Many doctors first needed training in computers in general before working with their EHR.

Keeping in mind the adage one practice had of "never embarrass a doctor in the exam room" in every case, organizations and physician practices created training environments in which physicians could train and master the skills they needed to navigate the system.

Requirement 4: Financial Security

Financial security was an important element as well. On the organizational level, this was communicated by administrative leaders allocating monies and personnel to the efforts. The organizations were willing to make the investment in order to achieve their quality and safety goals. They had capital campaigns to back up their vision. But smaller ambulatory settings however had to be convinced of their ROI. One practice was not only convinced of the ROI, they saw it as a financial necessity to go electronic; they feared going bankrupt if they didn't invest in technology and gain efficiencies.

Requirement 5: Enhanced Physician/Patient Relationship

Physicians—regardless of the size of their practice or organization—value a personal relationship with their patients. They respond to physical settings that allowed them to maintain eye contact with the patient. Some organizations offer scribes to enter data during visits, so the physician can focus solely on the patient. Doctors also want to provide personalized care. They would comply with standards of care and uniformity of delivery if they were involved in creating them and had a sense they could customize the care.

Requirement 6: Improved Work-Life Balance

In this era of work-life balance, Davies Award winners also valued the way in which going electronic allowed them to achieve this balance. The ROI in improving the quality of practice life was not as easy to define, but many physicians reported an improved sense of satisfaction in the care they delivered, while being able to leave the office on time. We'll take a look at a few of the Davies Award winners from different size organizations to see how they engaged their physicians.

Requirement 7: Reward of Goal Achievement

Whatever the size of the entity, implementation champions made a clear case for using technology to improve the quality of patient care or practice life. Those goals had to be clearly displayed with the result that physicians responded to the public display of their performance in reaching those goals. This may have been taking advantage of a characteristic common to many doctors, a competitive spirit with high personal standards for achievement.

CASE EXAMPLES

Adoption in the Solo Practice

For the solo office setting, there is no shared risk and reward. An examination of the solo physician's decision-making process to go electronic, how he or she successfully implemented a system and the rewards garnered reveals essential elements on which one must focus when engaging physicians in larger settings.

Solo physicians are by default leaders of their teams. At San Antonio, TX-based Valdez Family Clinic (2007 Davies Ambulatory Care Award), the physician leader was able to make the leap only after a partner left, and Alicia V. Valdez, MD, was on her own to keep the practice afloat.

Jeffrey L. Harris, MD, of 2005 Davies Ambulatory Care Award winner Wayne Obstetrics and Gynecology, Jesup, GA, took on the ultimate responsibility for the success of the project, as did Jeffrey D. Cooper MD, FAAP, of 2003 Davies Ambulatory Care Award winner Cooper Pediatrics, Duluth, GA. Each felt empowered to lead change. These physicians also had a vision for their practice and believed in the potential of the EHR to realize it.

The solo physician also is intimately engaged and has an understanding of every aspect of the practice and how each comes together to meet practice goals. In the small-office setting, there is a sense of family; so physicians must have a way to communicate their vision to the rest of the office and nurture the culture of change.

Dr. Valdez said, "We are not only a small business, but we are a small family business. Open communication, collaboration and mutual support are encouraged."

She recognized the need to engage her entire staff in the process. During vendor selection, she asked a member representing each role in the office to evaluate systems based on just his or her perspective. When they came together to select several vendors and evaluate systems, the team was unanimous in their decision as to which vendor product to purchase. Dr. Harris worked closely with his office managers on selection, training and implementation. Dr. Cooper worked with his office manager for installation, training schedules and maintenance, and his nurse for ongoing education and training.

These successful practices all enjoyed success in meeting quality, financial and personal goals. Cooper Pediatrics realized improved quality review scores and improved patient care with immunization rates at 99 percent for all the two-year olds in the practice, and a 102 percent increase in profits, all while decreasing the amount of time spent in the office.

Valdez Family Clinic went from a 4.5-day work week to a four-day work week and realized a 325 percent ROI. Wayne Obstetrics and Gynecology improved the quality of documentation and patient services, which resulted in greater patient retention. Because of these improvements, their malpractice carrier removed a rider on their malpractice policy allowing them to do vaginal birth after cesarean (VBAC) deliveries.

So, as the solo physicians teach us, engaged physicians have a sense of leadership, an understanding of every aspect of a practice; an investment in the decision-making process; an understanding of the risks and rewards; a sensitivity to engaging the entire staff in moving toward the goal; and knowing how to leverage the EHR to meet those goals.

In the end, they reaped the benefits of a successful implementation with improved patient care, improved working environment and hours, and a financial award. Let's see how organizations of increasing size build upon these characteristics to engage their physicians and what complexities are added as the number of physicians increases.

Adoption in the Small Practice

Physician offices of two to four doctors generally operate as true partnerships. Though one physician might be the "leader," consensus is essential for success. The doctors generally have a shared vision of patient care, practice atmosphere and finances.

2007 Davies Ambulatory Care Award winner Village Health Partners (formerly Family Medical Specialists of Texas) Plano, TX, operates without an office manager. It is run by the physicians, so each is aware of the various facets of the practice. During EHR implementation, they were unified in attitude and managing staff expectations and never had any "strong points of contention."

Likewise, partners of Pittsford, NY, Pediatrics @ the Basin, 2004 Davies Ambulatory Care Award winner, enjoyed a lock-step attitude toward EHR implementation. Their decision-making process is one of brainstorming. Either partner can make a suggestion with the caveat that nothing is too outrageous to consider. They brainstorm until there is a solution that feels right to both of them.

Not all offices had outcomes with as smooth a consensus. For example, 2008 Davies Ambulatory Care Award winner Palm Beach Obstetrics & Gynecology PA, Lake Worth, FL, had periods during which the physicians were not as equally engaged. The doctors felt they had the most to learn while continuing to focus on patient care and productivity. Palm Beach Obstetrics overcame this problem by providing super-user support and by instituting short daily huddles and longer weekly meetings.

The original partners of Augusta, GA-based Evans Medical Group, 2003 Davies Ambulatory Care Award winner, had a great implementation, but things became rocky when one physician left for personal reasons and two new doctors joined the practice. The remaining original partner was accustomed to being able to make decisions and implement them with his original partner's full support. Therefore, he did not seek out permission to make changes with his new partners. The friction this caused ultimately resulted in one partner leaving the practice. However, the original partner learned to adjust and seek his remaining partner's consensus before moving forward. He also led by example. As the number of physicians expanded, he would try something new, then perfect it before presenting it to the other physicians in his practice. These tried-and-true solutions were then more easily accepted by the other doctors.

Almost all of the offices adopted an expectation of decreased productivity during the first few weeks of implementation so as not to overwhelm the doctors. However, Birmingham, AL-based Sports Medicine & Orthopedic Specialists, 2005 Davies Ambulatory Care Award winner, were a notable exception with almost disastrous results.

Physicians worked overtime during those first few weeks to continue to see patients and master the process of documenting in the new system, a plan that was so difficult that at one point their physician leader thought a "mutiny" was imminent. Only through a group consensus to push forward did they survive day to day during the first few months of implementation. Among other lessons, they learned to provide training to new doctors and the people supporting them prior to bringing them into the practice.

So for the small two- to four-physician office, consensus is key, along with added support for those physicians who are engaged, but not necessarily leading. Communication becomes more formal with weekly meetings and daily huddles recognized as leading to success. Physicians also responded to formal feedback.

Adoption in the Medium-Sized Practice

Davies Award-winning practices of five to eight physicians, such as Atlanta-based Piedmont Physicians Group (2006 Davies Ambulatory Care Award), built upon these techniques. Their physician leaders led by example. They had super-users in place when the entire staff went to go-live. New doctors joining the practice were trained by their peers, with the competitive nature among physicians helping to foster their mastering of the system. PPG placed physician users in one of three categories:

Fundamental users. This is the minimum standard for all users, with all basic functions, including use of documentation templates, coding wizards and basic ordering. PPG estimates that the average annual savings for a fundamental physician user is $14,500.

Average users. Most physicians have become proficient in the fundamental uses of the EHR and have learned to use more advanced functions to increase clinical productivity, decision support and professional and patient satisfaction.

Power users. Several physicians have fully embraced the EHR and are using it extensively for quality and revenue improvement, and management of the entire patient population. Examples of power use include the use of voice recognition for transcription, the use of flowsheets and protocols and the use of MAs to collect and manage data.

At Piedmont, physician compensation is based in part on meeting clinical quality standards, which are set annually. The practice also utilizes the Press-Ganey patient satisfaction measurement survey for feedback and have achieved above-average ratings.

Georgia-based Roswell Pediatric Center (2003 Davies Ambulatory Care Award) achieved 100-percent physician buy-in through the center's annual strategic planning retreat at which they identified their practice's strengths and weaknesses. As a result, they targeted the following areas for improvement: universal access to the chart, quality of documentation, intra-office communication, workflow and forms and referrals processing. An EHR was considered essential to meet these goals.

During the planning phase of their implementation, they spent the first week developing a "project charter" and discussed specific details about the practice and implementation of the EHR. Expectations were also defined at the beginning, and their inclusion at this point and throughout the process was an important factor in leading to a successful implementation that met all of their objectives.

Outlined in the charter in detail were the scope of the project, the various phases and the timelines. The result was a 51-page project charter that fully outlined their objectives and responsibilities, as well as their vendor's responsibilities. The project charter served as the guiding force of the entire process and is considered a huge part of their success because it put all of them on the same page. They knew what was coming, what their roles were and what to expect from the overall process. They even knew the risks involved and how to avoid those risks. The project charter was a key reason they went live on their targeted go-live date. The project charter defined roles and created an understanding between all project stakeholders about each of their roles and responsibilities. All physicians signed the charter, thereby commiting to attend all scheduled meetings regarding the EHR. Participation was not optional.

Two larger practices made going electronic a campaign effort. Beaumont-based Southeast Texas Medical Associates (2005 Davies Ambulatory Care Award) named their effort Project Fahrenheit 451.

"We published a booklet entitled *More Than a Transcription Service: Revolutionizing the Practice of Medicine with Computerized Patient Records.* We gave copies to our providers, our patients and our payors… to anyone who would listen. We talked implementation, we dreamed implementation and we implemented. It was with 'sheer dogged endurance' that we accomplished the task. Decisions were made early that implementation of the EHR and construction of templates would be by consensus, rather than being individualized. This allowed for standardization of care, standardization of documentation and comparison of care and comparison of documentation. This is probably the most important decision we made and is one that directly impacted our success."

At Nashville, TN-based Old Harding Pediatric Associates (2004 Davies Ambulatory Care Award) the decision to move forward with an EHR came in three phases that began with the launch of a campaign called Compassionate Care 2000.

"'Compassionate' meant providing quality service focused on kindness, understanding and accessibility. 'Care' meant being committed to excellent pediatric medical care, education, prevention and providing a nurturing workplace; and '2000' signified that our future was focused on technology, quality assurance, research and dedication to education for future physicians."

The second phase was the development of a strategic plan for which they formed a strategic planning committee, with representatives from every aspect of the office, including patients. Goals and a clear vision were identified, along with areas of improvement: facilities, personnel, communication, technology and external influences.

The annual director's retreat was the third phase of the decision-making process. The physicians reviewed the Strategic Planning Committee report, and subsequently the directors set the EHR goal for one year.

"Ultimately, our overwhelming success with implementation is credited to physician buy-in of the product. All physicians had some level of apprehension about such a monumental change of practice style, but they could also see the benefits that connecting with the electronic world would have on the care we could provide for children. Our Implementation Team's dedication to the project was the other main cause of success. Even when filled with doubt and nervousness, the team members displayed eagerness to all of the staff. This team served as a constant 'safe place' to which staff could voice concerns and frustrations and receive encouragement and accurate answers to questions."

Adoption in the Large Physician Practice

As practice size increases, communication, buy-in, training and feedback become increasingly more important. Large practices, such as Cardiology Consultants of Philadelphia (2008 Davies Ambulatory Care Award) needed special techniques to ensure physicians were engaged and part of the decision-making process and invested in the overall workings of the practice. They engaged 79 doctors in their implementation in 21 locations. Inclusive decision-making, unique communication tools, an effective feedback mechanism and excellent training all figured in Cardiology Consultants' success.

Decision-making was inclusive on several levels. Each location had a representative on the Cardiology Consultants Board who voted on the decision to adopt an EHR. Cardiology Consultants had an EHR committee with clinical representation, which made key decisions regarding workflow changes, chart transitions, training timing and the like.

To communicate the details of these team meetings and resultant decisions and timelines, Cardiology Consultants utilized an intranet. All staff could log on at anytime to view timelines and key policy decisions.

Go-lives at the various locations were scheduled at intervals of four to six weeks. A single trainer was assigned to each physician and remained on site during one to two weeks after go-live.

"Experienced" users from locations that had gone live also came into implementing offices to share their experiences and add support. EHR committee meetings were opened to all those in the early go-live stages, giving a platform for feedback. Details of the concerns staff expressed and team solutions also appeared on the intranet. Cardiology Consultants also had a unique EHR support team that rotated through the sites to assure workflow adherence, assess quality controls and concerns, as well as train new employees. Yet, they did not take standardization to an extreme such that it usurped the physicians' needs to give a personal touch in communications to referring physicians. Cardiology Consultants allowed customization for each physician's preference for how his or her letters read.

In sharing a lesson learned, Cardiology Consultants believes they made one decision that had far-reaching impact on morale and workload. The decision allowed some doctors to delay their implementations. These resistant physicians represented one end of the spectrum of perceived utility and value of an EHR. Allowing them to delay their implementations resulted in confusion on a unified goal and in duplicative workflows.

The resistance was eventually overcome with attention to training and technology improvements.

In contrast, Oklahoma-based Cardiology of Tulsa (2006 Davies Ambulatory Care Award) took the opposite approach. They began implementation with their most resistant users. Cardiology of Tulsa put an emphasis on training one physician at a time, so as not to overwhelm their 18-physician, four-office location practice. Physician proficiency was not left to chance with Cardiology of Tulsa. They also had an iterative analysis of the success of their implementation strategy, which allowed them to rapidly improve their process.

The phased implementation plan relied upon a calendar of go-live dates, with the first physician beginning to utilize the EHR on January 17, 2001. Implementation was rolled out among the various practice sites, so that no single location had every physician going live in quick succession.

The final physician began using the EHR on September 2, 2001. Cardiology of Tulsa initiated the process by installing high-speed Internet access in all physicians' homes, so they would be able to review patient records after hours and when on call. Each was then required to take a four-hour classroom session with a trainer, who provided thorough hands-on exercises in all aspects of the EHR. At the end of classroom work, the physicians were given an open book proficiency test with case studies. Only those who passed the exam proceeded to the next stage of training. They then spent a half-day learning the flow of the EHR and observing how it affected the dynamics between physician and patient in the exam room setting. Immediately before the go-live date, the physician super-user spent a half-day in each physician's office as well, to ensure they were comfortable with the technology before signing off on their go-live plan.

To prepare each office for physicians' transition to the system, Cardiology of Tulsa installed eight computers in the practice's boardroom for one month and scheduled all-day classes for staff members to attend. Training was customized for various departments. Subsequently, super-users were identified and given additional training. They then worked with clinical staff in a training room, where two-hour sessions were scheduled to review specific functions and to role play anticipated clinical scenarios. They were also tested and had to demonstrate proficiency before their physician's go-live date. The Saturday before the first go-live, clinical staff came into the office from 9 a.m. to noon to conduct a run-through and troubleshoot potential problems.

During the session, super-users simulated an abbreviated day's schedule, including patient check in and checkout, exams and related workflow processes. Teams of clinical staff at each practice site were assigned two physicians whom they would support during implementation. No team was allowed to bring its second physician online, however, until all teams throughout the practice had their first physician using the application comfortably. This allowed the practice as a whole to make the transition to EHR more gradually and to address stresses on the organization as they arose.

In addition, all affected personnel—from the receptionist to the business office—were debriefed at the end of each physician's adoption of the EHR to discover what worked well and what did not. This allowed Cardiology of Tulsa to adjust its strategy as it went along, making subsequent implementations easier. In fact, it took the first physicians about a month to fully utilize the EHR's functionality, while the last users were brought online in less than a week. Further, Cardiology of Tulsa began working with some of the most challenging physicians first—specifically, those who were skeptical about the EHR.

Besides being able to learn more about the flaws in its implementation approach early in the process, practice leadership believed that initial success with those most resistant to change would encourage subsequent adopters. Key to the success of the training, scanning/abstracting and implementation efforts were motivational strategies the practice implemented.

For instance, go-live t-shirts were distributed to staff members in each office as their physicians began using the EHR. Project CHEARTBURN playing off the cardiology related term "heartburn" and providing a not so subtle reference to the fact that the explorer Cortez burned his ships so his crew could not mutiny and return to the Old World kept the drudgery related to the elimination of paper records bearable. Scanning and abstracting staffers were given targets and prizes for reaching their goals within specified time frames. For example, the practice held after-hours "tropical" parties complete with margarita machines and the chance to throw water balloons at the administrator.

Adoption in the Physician Practice—In Summary

Whatever the size of the practice, physician engagement is dependent on tying EHR implementation into physician core values and their vision for the practice. Upfront retreats and the development of charters can define these within their setting. Physicians respond to clear goals, open communication and feedback. Physicians must feel competent on a system, and they don't want to sacrifice productivity while becoming so. An emphasis on training and support is crucial to move forward. Holding small and frequent meetings at the outset to address concerns and support allows physicians to master the system without feeling overwhelmed.

PHYSICIAN ADOPTION IN THE HOSPITAL AND HEALTH SYSTEM

Davies Organizational Award winners broaden the scope of stakeholders. Given the sheer numbers of people, locations and complexity of information technology projects, Davies Organizational Award winners used "all out" campaigns in the adoption of EHRs. Their campaign names included: Patient First Initiatives Program, One Patient, One Record and Project Infocare, to name a few.

Davies Organizational Award winners also tended to use structured methodologies for project management and change management, such as Lean Six Sigma, Franklin Covey Leadership or Adaptive Design. Physicians in these settings may only comprise a fraction of the total clinical and support staff. They may not be the organization's leaders, but instead are part of a hierarchy in which they report to CEOs, CIOs or a board of directors. Governance structures may be quite complex.

Organizational Award winners, however, recognized that implementation is impossible without physician engagement and demonstrated a variety of ways to bring them on board in keeping with the same principles used in small provider settings. As part of their campaigns, Organizational Award winners wove going-electronic into every level of the organization—from board meetings to daily rounds. Communication efforts were multi-faceted. Training for all organizational units was extensive, required and tested. Going electronic was written into bylaws and system policies. Each organization also had or developed ways to immediately log and resolve any issues.

In the case of Bangor-based Eastern Maine Medical Center (EMMC), going electronic was part of their campaign, Patient First Initiatives (PFI) program, a tri-fold approach to delivering high-quality patient care by transforming care delivery, adopting a patient-focused culture and implementing a technology plan that supports, but does not drive, the care delivery process. EHR implementation was a project within this initiative. EMMC won the Davies Organizational Award in 2008.

EMMC's 400 physicians work with more than 3,000 clinical and support staff. The physicians who were engaged in the project were private, community-based, regional and hospital employed. The planning process for the implementation of an EHR at EMMC was guided by the goals of PFI. The project vision, as depicted in Figure 7-1, is founded on the Eastern Maine Healthcare System (EMHS) Together Project vision, which states: "All EMHS providers will be able to treat a patient using one shared electronic record system,

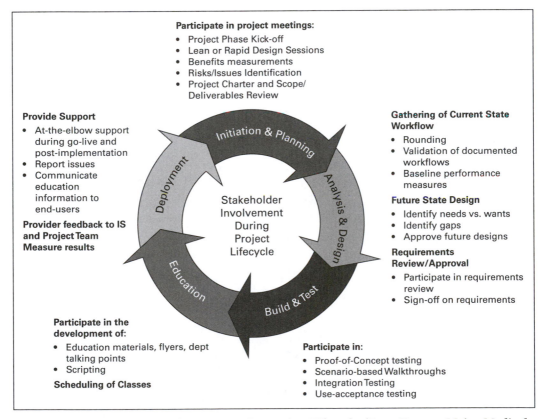

Figure 7-1: Stakeholder Involvement During Project Lifecycle. (From Eastern Maine Medical Center, used with permission.)

no matter where in EMHS the patient seeks care." The project team employed several methods to engage physicians in planning the EHR.

Because the EHR implementation spanned a number of years, effective communication of the EHR strategy was key to EMMC's successful EHR implementation. The project team's communication strategy was to provide consistent and timely information to all project stakeholders and keep them informed and engaged throughout the life of the project. For each major EHR implementation, the project team used the same communications path: awareness, understanding, acceptance, alignment and commitment.

The project team used both internal and general communications planning methods, depending on the need and scope of the project. Examples of these methods are listed as follows:

General communication plans. Media releases, company newsletter—such as the *Eagle Newsletter*—in addition to the EMHS and EMMC Web sites.

Internal communication plans. Promotion/awareness at department meetings, and other forums—such as presentations at operations council, medical staff meetings, employee update meetings, service and section meetings, memos, notices in provider lounges, PowerNews (*CMIO Newsletter*), and *CURRENTS* (EMMC staff newsletter), which features articles on CPOE and other EHR implementation status. EMMC's executive leadership team provided strong support of these initiatives throughout the organization."

Acknowledging the need for end-user participation during the design and test phases of the project and the challenges of their busy schedules, EMMC compensated all clinical participants, including private physicians, for their time. Change management teams assured physicians were included in process design, which drove the written policies on which they signed off. Physicians were able to give ongoing feedback in several ways—through multi-disciplinary committees on issues such as hardware selection, new and/or modifications to clinical applications, decision support, standardization of care, change in downtime and care processes and use of technology. They also could use the EMMC CPOE intranet for providing feedback and checking on the status of reported issues. Through the EMMC CPOE intranet, clinical staff could send their questions and/or feedback. A team of clinical coordinators from the Office of the CMIO, Information Systems staff and clinical educators review the feedback to identify and resolve any technical, process or training issues. This Web site also provided complete transparency to all end-users on the status of reported issues.

Risk management is key in projects of this scope. To avoid resistance among physicians, EMMC required use of the system as part of the bylaws. Training and competency testing were not optional. All clinical staff were required to attend training and demonstrate EHR competency. The overall strategy and approach to training was to require training prior to attaining access to the system and as part of any system upgrade. Information Service Process and Education continued to issue quarterly updates to introduce new system features, thereby minimizing classroom training. Multiple ways of distributing education materials included: tri-fold information guides, Web-based tutorials and tip cards for providers.

EMHS identified several successful training strategies, as well as training challenges:
- Sent letters outlining expectations to all attendees prior to the class.
- Engaged/worked with department heads to ensure all staff members were scheduled for the class. Non-attendance was reported to department heads or provider office practice manager for follow-up and/or rescheduling.

- Utilized dedicated training environment for all education.
- Maintained dedicated IS education staff, with majority having clinical experience.
- Utilized super-users to provide assistance with large classes.
- Held one-on-one classes for targeted users.
- Developed Web-based tools on various clinical processes that were accessible via the Internet and the EMMC intranet.
  Challenges to training:
- Rescheduling classes was an issue when there were large numbers of students.
- Group training was not as effective for some providers. Individualized training would have been more effective for those providers.
- Long training classes proved to be too much for some providers. IS Education may consider splitting up the topics and combining them with hands-on training

Like smaller organizations, EMMC recognized the need for "at the elbow" support for physicians during the first few weeks of go-live, and super-users were on the units at all times. The change management teams reinforced physician education by rounding with the team. Physicians then had immediate support and answers to their questions on the EHR and a place to give feedback on concerns.

"All EMMC clinicians use the EHR as the main source of clinical information. CPOE was implemented for all in-patients on November 12, 2007, and the compliance rate has been exceptional. Three weeks after the start of go-live, all inpatient units were on CPOE. As of December 31, 2007, approximately 96 percent of all EMMC providers had started using CPOE, entering about 93 percent of all orders electronically."

Physicians and other caregiver satisfaction is measured through formal surveys, quick polls, user feedback sessions, electronic feedback forms, medical staff meetings, super-user meetings and user groups that define enhancements to existing systems. Based on an August 2007 pre-CPOE survey, approximately 91 percent of providers use EHR regularly to view patient information. Thirty days after the CPOE initial launch implementation, approximately 93 percent of providers indicated that their CPOE experience was much better than expected, or at least time-neutral.

EMMC is relatively small compared with the 2007 Davies Organizational Award winner, Allina Hospitals & Clinics, Minneapolis, with more than 23,000 employees, 11 hospitals, 65 clinics and 5,000 physicians. In 2002, Allina committed to a campaign with the vision of One Patient, One Record. This vision was the work of two teams commissioned by senior leadership, a clinical care team and a revenue-cycle team. Physicians were part of the executive leadership team from the start. This singular vision drove the selection and implementation of their current system. More than 750 people participated in developing requests for proposals and vendor evaluations. The process of inclusion for this campaign was the most extensive employed by Allina to date and was very well received.

Critical to success, given the scale of their governance structure, was the formation of a Physician Engagement Team (PAT), created to foster stronger physician engagement of their EHR. Part of PAT, were Site Physician Champions, appointed by the clinic physician lead or hospital Vice President of Medical Affairs. They championed the physician from go-live to system compliance.

As an example of the role they played, during development, all order sets were e-mailed to the physician champions prior to the monthly PAT meeting where they were endorsed.

Upon endorsement, physician champions were asked to communicate new and changed orders set(s) to their colleagues.

The physicians were part of user groups providing two-way communication between sites and Allina leadership. They detailed:

- Prioritization of system enhancements, build, redesign and support-related project work.
- Evaluate, recommend and approve Allina-wide system design configuration.
- Prioritization of system enhancements, build, redesign and support-related project work.
- Idea sharing and best practice identification.
- Championed the EHR within the organization.
- Promoted adoption and proper use of the system.
- Participated in Allina-wide initiatives, such as system upgrades.

Allina, like other Organizational Award winners, used specific methodologies to enhance processes and improve implementation. And similar to small office settings, they had super-users who were the first to train on the system and then participate in workflow redesign.

Allina used a change management methodology called Adaptive Design.

"Adaptive Design uses principles from the Lean production model and puts the responsibility for understanding what the work should be and how the tools will support that work in the hands of the super-users."

Again, end-user accountability fostered success. Training was not optional, and each user had to complete training and pass an assessment. Accountability was a two-way street. At the end of each site implementation, Allina sought feedback on user satisfaction with resolution of issues. Support services had to achieve a score of at least 18 out of 20 on user ratings. As implementations were rolled out, Allina continued in this iterative analysis of the "good, the bad and the ugly." Leadership then responded to feedback they received. Perhaps one of their best examples was coming up with a solution to poor adoption by physicians of CPOE.

"A new ad hoc team, called the adoption team, was formed from staff already working on the implementation. The main areas of focus for the team were revising physician training, updating order sets, improving surgical services tools, improving flowsheets and resolving ergonomic and hardware issues. The team was in place for six months, and changes in workflow and in the system were made to address the issues. During this time, a mandate for adoption of CPOE was initiated by Allina leadership. The major outcomes of this work were the successful adoption of CPOE by the physicians and the successful adoption of documentation by the nurses."

Allina also responded to the evident need for post-implementation training and support by hiring a permanent physician support team to provide "at the elbow support" for physicians both during and after implementation. Currently, use of the EHR is required for all caregivers.

"Policies are in place to promote adoption and consistency of care, including policies to address noncompliant users. Site leadership is accountable for enforcing these policies." Site leadership generally offered more training or workflow tips for users who were noncompliant.

Allina enjoyed 100 percent adoption, and in 2006, 75 percent of physicians were entering directly into the EHR with templates and approximately 25 percent had their dictated notes transcribed into the EHR.

The 2005 Organizational Award winner Citizens Memorial Healthcare's (CMH), Bolivar, MO, implementation campaign was called Infocare. It was employee-driven with full administrative support. Of those 1,500 employees or admitting staff, approximately 100 were physicians. Of those 100 physicians, 71 were from privately held offices and 28 were employed. As part of their communication and engagement plan, CMH used the Franklin Covey Leadership model (see Table 7-1) with a facilitator trained in the model.

Table 7-1: Four Roles Planning Highlights (Franklin Covey Leadership model).

Information Systems Implementation Planning 4 Roles Planning Highlights	
Pathfinding These key stakeholders were identified: • patients & community, • physician & other caregivers, • system end users & employees, and • administrative decision-makers & Boards of Directors. The Project Infocare vision statement was enthusiastically developed and embraced.	*Aligning* Understanding the importance of aligning to achieve the vision, the team agreed to use these techniques and practices in the implementation: • understand and become experts on the system before training, • train in the basics of computer operations so end users won't feel intimidated by the new technology, • begin with current users and gain support, • phase in functions and applications in order to ensure sufficient resources for support during training, implementation and post-live, • build a foundation upon which an EMR can be developed, • seek process improvements in each step to enhance workflow for end users, • identify problem people and make a positive effort to engage them in the process, and • market the project to end users throughout the continuum of care.
Modeling The role of the ISSC was determined to be to • allocate resources, • remove obstacles, • establish parameters, • serve as cheerleaders, • implement system to maximize functionality, and • serve as communication liaisons.	*Empowering* The planning team identified the need to form Implementation Teams for the many applications to be implemented. Key qualities to seek in Implementation Team Leaders were decided on and included: knowledge of department or function, trusted/respected, works well with other departments, interest/enthusiasm, communicator/listener, organized/can meet deadlines, and motivated. An Implementation Kick-Off event was planned to include the CMH CEO with all team members. A meeting was scheduled to introduce the project and responsibilities to the chosen Implementation Team Leaders. A chart was developed to show the organizational relationships of the Implementation Teams, IS Staff and Administration.

Physician engagement highlights include multiple avenues for communication, feedback, training and ongoing support. Unique to Davies Organizational Award winners was a cross departmental approach. This assured that users understood how processes affected CMH as a whole. They also were cognizant of the physicians' need to deliver personal care.

CASE 7-1 HOW CITIZENS MEMORIAL HEALTHCARE ACHIEVED PHYSICIAN ADOPTION—IN THEIR OWN WORDS

The CMH strategy for managing the change for physicians was to be very open and provide ongoing, proactive communication about the project. The team and project manager did not "duck" problems, but rather solicited issues.

Once issues were identified, they were logged, prioritized and resolved; follow-up was done with the suggesting physician. The team intentionally provided many avenues for feedback, so that no matter what style of communication a physician preferred, each had an opportunity to make his or her issues known. Avenues included one-on-one interaction, paper forms for submitting issues, open forums, presentations at medical staff meetings, special forums on specific issues and a constant presence of support staff in the Physician Resource Room during rounds.

CMH's CEO was kept apprised of the progress and issues surrounding the project and was supportive both in his approach with physicians and in his willingness to provide the resources necessary to complete the implementation of CPOE.

CMH found that physicians went through stages as they gave up paper processes—denial, then anger, followed by depression, bargaining and finally acceptance.

During some of these phases, particularly when you consider the position from which physicians bargain, it was tempting to "give in" and abandon or modify the objectives of the project. Instead, CMH weathered each phase for each physician and used every possible opportunity to gain more insight into how to make the system better. One of the most successful strategies in the implementation of CPOE was to "make it personal." CMH did this by creating physician-specific order sets and favorites, which were presented to them during training.

CMH did not develop these sets and favorites by asking physicians to fill out a form or spend time thinking about their practice patterns, but rather by developing reports to identify the most common orders written by a physician (and entered by ward secretaries) over the six months prior to the implementation. The team then created those as favorites, so that physicians were provided with one-click ordering ability for most of their orders from day one.

TRAINING FOR PHYSICIANS

After attempting training of physicians using a physician-to-physician model and a classroom model, CMH achieved success using one-on-one training in short sessions provided by a CPOE team member. Training was conducted in 30-minute sessions whenever and wherever physicians requested. Follow-up was done during rounds at the hospital. Team members staffed the Physician Resource Room (a room with computers for physician use only on the medical/surgical floor) full-time during the implementation to answer questions and immediately make system changes upon request. Key to the success of physician training was the use of qualified staff members who had both clinical and communication skills.

Newsletters. During the implementation, a newsletter, *Project Infocare*, published at least once per month, outlined the milestones achieved, as well as upcoming phases. A separate newsletter, the *MEDITECH Minute*, was developed for the medical staff to focus on issues specific to physicians. The *MEDITECH Minute* continues to be published and distributed at medical staff meetings.

Project Infocare forums. Also, during the implementation, an informal forum arose within the hospital to address cross-application implementation issues, such as terminology and functionality. With an integrated system, a high level of communication is required to assure that maximum benefit is achieved. The forum was held over lunch on a weekly basis. IS specialists attended and team members were encouraged to attend. Each attendee was asked to report on how the implementation was proceeding and what questions, concerns or issues had arisen. This cross-application discussion served an important role in solving problems and assuring that the system implementation was successful.

Physician order management team. The physician order management team was open to any and all physicians. The team met regularly during the implementation of CPOE. Physicians were encouraged to attend regular meetings to discuss issues and make decisions.

Board communication. A one-page monthly report was prepared and presented to the board of directors. In addition, the CIO attended board meetings and presented live demonstrations of software as the implementation progressed. This effort ensured that board member questions and concerns were addressed throughout the implementation and helped secure their continued support for Project Infocare.

Ongoing support for users is provided in numerous ways, including a Help Desk, IS specialists, and super-users. An IS help desk is available Monday through Friday, 7 a.m. to 5 p.m. Two support people are on call for all other hours to respond to hardware, network and software support issues. CMH is fortunate to have 39 super-users and they have accepted the additional responsibility of being the primary liaison between IS and the end-users in their areas. Super-users train end-users, assist in developing training materials, and test new functionality. Super-users sign an agreement that they will serve this role and are paid a stipend for the additional responsibility. As described earlier, in order to assist physicians and solicit suggestions for system improvement an IS specialist or super-user is usually present in the physician resource room, where most physicians enter orders and daily notes during morning rounds.

CMH used Project Infocare forums to gain feedback from end-users. These forums provided an opportunity for end-users or team members to discuss any concerns regarding the project. For physicians, regular meetings of the physician order management team were held and the IS staff members present in the physician resource room obtained immediate feedback from physicians as they were in the process of using the system. Solicitation of feedback and issues tracking continues to be used as the final phases of the EHR are implemented.

CMH shared important lessons learned during their implementation:

- While they initially began with classroom training for physicians, they found one-on-one training in 30-minute sessions whenever and wherever physicians wanted was more effective.
- Instead of ending physician support upon go-live, they recognized a need for continued support and made a physician resource room available during morning rounds.
- Instead of training hundreds of end-users for each change in functionality and upgrade, they implemented HealthStream online training system.
- Instead of casual follow-up on physician issues, they developed a documented process for soliciting, logging, tracking and following up on physician issues.
- Teams that focused too narrowly on their single application during configuration and testing created a lack of respect for the "I" word (integration) and the impact of each part on the whole. So they began Project Infocare forums for discussion of cross application issues and testing and parallel runs that cross applications and care settings for all.

CONCLUSION

No matter the size of office or organization, several themes emerged for physician engagement. Having this engagement depends on strong inclusive leadership with clear support for achieving goals consistent with physician and practice or organization values and vision. Support came in the forms of financial and personnel commitments and adequate training. Support also came with clear expectations for physician participation.

End-user accountability is essential. Frequent communications via meetings, newsletters and marketing materials provided encouragement and incentives for continued involvement and alignment. Success came with usable systems that conformed with workflow and allowed for personalized care.

Whatever the setting, physician engagement and satisfaction with an implementation depended on personalized workflow analysis with training before, during, and after implementation. One on one, or "at the elbow" training was the most effective for physicians. They also benefited from two-way communication that allowed them to express their concerns. Organizations of every size needed a game plan to rapidly record, respond to and resolve these concerns. Transparency in this process is essential. Physicians were enthusiastic supporters as they began to realize they were reaching quality goals, a financial return, improvement in the ease of providing care and an improved work-life balance.

CHAPTER 8

Staff Acceptance of Electronic Health Records

Nancy R. Babbitt, FACMPE

"What is past is past. Today we start anew, and what we do today will make our life for tomorrow."

—*William Thomson Hanzsche*

INTRODUCTION

According to 2007 Davies Ambulatory Care Award winner Village Health Partners (formerly Family Medical Specialists of Texas), Plano, "Transitioning to an EHR is an art." The involvement of staff in the change to electronic records also is an art, of a particularly crucial type. They have the power to make or break this all-important project. If they fear their jobs may be cut, they can find ways to make it not work. Preparing, reassuring and involving staff are crucial steps to being successful.

As you read this chapter, you will find that themes emerge, such as the importance of staff involvement and participation in the decision-making process, of soliciting and honoring their feedback, of training and then training again, of providing lots of support at go-live and of recognizing achievement. Each story of EHR implementation has a different context, but each offers insight into what worked and helped to position these hospitals, health systems and physicians' practices to become Davies Award winners. First we offer some tips for staff engagement—tips that emerge from themes consistently found in the various stories of EHR implementation. Then we tell the staff stories—many in their own words.

Tips for Staff Engagement in the EHR

Staff engagement, hopefully enthusiastic engagement, in the implementation of the EHR is essential to success, as mentioned. So let's start with some helpful hints learned from those who have walked this path. When launching your EHR project, during the stressful implementation and then later, with continuing the ongoing process improvement, you'll want to:

Involve. Begin involving and discussing the technology well in advance of beginning your search. Use this opportunity to engage staff in solution brainstorming and to reassure them, they will not lose their jobs.

Communicate. Keep the lines of communication open. Host meetings at the onset of the project, during the project and on an ongoing basis. Take notes, follow up on questions, encourage involvement. Make them feel they are part of the process. Let them help to re-engineer their own positions to improve the patient flow process for better patient care, safety and efficiency. Carry this over after the initial implementation to continue to use technology for continuous process improvement.

Train. Invest in your most valuable asset—your people. Budget time and money for training and support that is structured, uninterrupted and tailored to the individual and collective needs. Begin training as soon as you can. Consider including education and training as part of your strategic plan to let your staff know how important they and their training are to this project and to ongoing success. Be sure to plan for education and training on an ongoing basis for new hires and upgrades. Take advantage of the vendors' "user groups" for ongoing training and networking.

Support. Provide plenty of vendor/computer support and/or use internal super-users to assist staff. Having this backup and support will give your staff the confidence needed to make this project a success and keep it a success.

Motivate. Celebrate your successes. Nothing motivates staff to rise to a challenge like recognition for a job well done.

Engage. Make if fun! This helps with the stress level and creates a team environment— we are all in this together! Recognize that: The best EHR in the world accomplishes nothing if staff refuses to use it! Recognize them for their (and your) achievement.

THE MEDICAL PRACTICE—ACCOUNTS OF STAFF ACCEPTANCE

Samuel Goldstein, MD, is an orthopedic surgeon at 2005 Davies Ambulatory Care Award-winning Sports Medicine & Orthopedic Specialists in Birmingham, AL. This four-physician, 15-staff practice handles 20,000 ambulatory visits a year.

Dr. Goldstein describes his clinical staff as highly educated and skilled. A major consideration of their decision to go to an EHR was the ability to better utilize their clinical personnel and physician time. In their paper system, the clinical assistant would perform the history and physical and present the findings to the physician. On many occasions, however, the physician would be ready for the presentation, but the assistant would be in with another patient.

Today, the physician can review the findings in the EHR when he or she is ready, making the entire office more efficient.

Dr. Goldstein informed his staff at the start that all would be held accountable for the success of the EHR implementation. Two physicians and an RN were in charge of the clinical implementation and patient flow organization, while the business manager and billing clerk were responsible for the clerical aspect of the transition. The formal training session was a two-day event held on a Friday and Saturday. The office was closed to allow staff to concentrate without interruptions of a typical workday.

Staff and physicians learned the basic functionality of the system and then divided into groups for more intense training in specific areas. Using fictitious patients, they spent the next two weeks practicing with the system and encouraging each other. Despite recommendations to do otherwise, the practice did not cut back on the patient schedule during go-live. After weeks of planning and hard work, they were excited and a little anxious, but could not wait for their go-live day.

On go-live day, two trainers were on site. One trainer was positioned up front with front office staff and one was positioned with clinical staff. Staff quickly discovered that what used to take three to four minutes to document on paper per visit, now took 15 minutes to complete as data entry in the EHR. And every patient was now a new patient to the EHR.

After the first day, however, policy changed so that, temporarily, only one quarter of the visits were entered into the EHR; after the physicians regrouped with staff to evaluate their progress and plan, they decided to limit the schedule for the following two weeks.

In fact, the following two weeks were full of challenges. They had wireless network problems, messaging workflow issues and continued to work long hours. By Wednesday of the second week, mutiny was imminent. At noon they closed the office for an emergency lunch meeting. The options were given to the staff: forge on with their goal to enter all patient visits in the EHR, use the system partially or abandon the project.

The decision was unanimous: "Let's just go all the way with this and get the bad days over with."

Due to dedicated and hardworking staff, within six weeks the practice was back to its normal patient volume and all staff were leaving on time. While the practice uses a trainer from the vendor to train new physicians, their staff trains new staff members. Dr. Goldstein believes the success of EHR at Sports Medicine & Orthopedic Specialists is entirely due to total physician commitment and a dedicated office staff.

Alicia V. Valdez, MD, with Valdez Family Clinic (discussed shortly) noted that "in the clash between culture and technology, culture wins." This is seen in the way staff acceptance of an EHR and the resulting change in culture are critical to a successful implementation and ongoing process improvement after the initial implementation.

Most of the EHR implementation focus is on the dollars and cents of technology, and it is easy to overlook how technology can affect patient outcomes and the daily lives of the frontline staff. However, the change that staff must endure during implementation is critical to recognize since they have the power to make or break this all-important project. It is therefore essential to realize the need to improve the fundamentals of staff engagement and education. Many times when you ask why an implementation has failed or the staff refuses to use it, staff responds by saying: nobody asked us!

I have been the administrator for a large pediatric practice in Atlanta for the past 22 years. In our practice, Roswell Pediatric Center, a 2003 Ambulatory Davies Award winner, we started discussing EHR with our staff more than a year before taking the plunge. At staff meetings when problems and solutions were discussed, we began considering how an electronic solution could be used. Asking your staff to keep a list of issues they have and getting them to think about how an EHR might solve those issues is very powerful. It will gain their buy-in into the process, thereby helping them better tolerate the extra work and major changes involved in implementing an EHR. A successful implementation is achieved from re-engineering workflow to provide better care and more efficiency. Take advantage of the staff's knowledge. They do the job every day and probably have some great ideas how technology might improve their area.

We started by involving staff in implementation committees. We had billing office representatives on the interface committee to the practice management system. We had clinical staff on the customization committee and a few brave staff volunteers on the hardware committee. This made the staff comfortable in that they had input on the areas that would affect their job responsibilities and patient care workflow. Getting them vested in the project and making it fun and exciting were keys to our success. They also became our super-users and trainers as we moved forward.

We set up our training area in a classroom of our main location for one week. Everyone had two hours of formal training the week prior to go-live. This was a quiet area with no interruptions, compared with our normal pediatric office full of kids. For those who needed extra training or one-on-one help, we met again on the Saturday morning before our go-live week. We helped them and then practiced common office scenarios to build their comfort level. For the first two to three days of our go-live week, we had trainers from our vendor present in all areas of the office to help whoever needed it. This provided a great deal of reassurance to our staff during the very stressful go-live time.

During the training, we observed some staff members who still seemed hesitant, many of whom were our phone triage staff. We take approximately 300 triage calls a day, giving parents advice on what they can do at home or if they need to bring their child in for a visit. Many of these triage staff had no experience with computers, never even having used a mouse, Windows, Word or e-mail. So the thought of the EHR had them anxious. I asked several of our billing staff members to learn how to chart the triage calls in the EHR. The billing staff was very familiar and comfortable with computers, as they were already using computers in accomplishing most of their work. They quickly learned the EHR charting and sat next to the triage staff during go-live, assisting as needed. We also developed some "cheat sheet" type documents that explained how they would chart their information in the EHR. To chart a call would take about 10 clicks in addition to typing in information if it was not already formatted in a template. Both the additional training and the billing staff support gave the triage staff the confidence they needed at go-live. After entering the first 100 or more calls, it became very routine and comfortable for them to accomplish this task very quickly.

Many theories exist on the best way to roll out an EHR. As was discussed in some detail in Chapter 3, the Big Bang approach is one in which you move to a complete electronic chart from your go-live date forward. This has its benefits, but puts lots of stress on everyone. The more successful implementations using this approach limit their schedules or procedures to allow for a learning curve and to take off some of the stress. However, this can have a significant impact on revenue at a time when expenses are increased with implementation costs. Another approach is the phased implementation; that is, bringing up one module or area at a time. A successful strategy to get buy-in from physicians and clinical staff in this approach is to bring up electronic prescribing first. This is a great tool to help practitioners manage medications, interactions, refills, etc., very efficiently. It gets them used to viewing clinical information on a screen and allows them access to additional information, such as insurance company formularies.

In our practice we had always assumed that at go-live it would be mandatory for everyone to use the EHR for every visit from that point forward. My vendor counseled me on the stress we would be putting on our staff and encouraged a different "phased in" approach.

When we "went live" in November 2001, it was impossible to limit our schedule during the busy winter season because of sick children needing to be seen. So we started our go-live day only entering every third visit into the EHR. We still had all of the paper charts pulled and ready to go, so if at any time staff fell behind or felt as though they were going to lose it—they could easily return to using the paper chart to get caught up. We found right away we could chart our sick visits faster in the computer than on paper. Check-ups, however, took a little longer just because of the more complicated workflow.

Our vendor's project manager kept track of our progress, and at the end of each half-day, would share what percentage of each provider's visits was being charted in the EHR. This was great in spurring some internal competition to be the first to reach 100 percent. By the end of the second day, all of our providers reached 100 percent and we've never looked back! By the time we went live, the staff was ready, excited, and of course a little nervous. We accomplished our implementation in eight weeks—on time and within budget. Our practice and staff used humor and the desire to provide better patient care as an impetus to accomplish our goal. (See Figure 8-1).

Figure 8-1: From Left to Right: Dr. Catherine Bowman, Dr. Howard Silverman and Dr. Evan Landis of Roswell Pediatric Center. (From Roswell Pediatric Center, used with permission.)

Setting a tone of humor, but also determination, with the staff helped to support all of us for that day in November 2001, when Roswell Pediatric Center went live with their EHR.

Our next account is about a solo practitioner, Alicia V. Valdez, MD, with 2007 Davies Ambulatory Care Award-winning Valdez Family Clinic, which serves an economically disadvantaged and medically underserved community in San Antonio, TX. With a staff of six, open communication, collaboration and mutual support are encouraged and also help to make this family practice a working family business.

Three specific goals they intended to accomplish with their EHR implementation were to decrease overtime costs, see the same number of patients in four-day week, rather than a 4.5-day week, and to move billing in-house without adding staff.

Dr. Valdez involved her entire staff in the selection process. She took them to a trade show where several vendors were exhibiting. She asked them to evaluate the systems from the perspective of their individual roles, not on whether they thought she would like it or not. They returned from the show with their list of what would be in their "ideal" EHR. They then ranked their top three vendors and brought them in for a demo for all the staff to see. Their selection process resulted in a unanimous vote.

They used the same collaborative methodology for their implementation phase. They divided the work among staff based on their role in the practice.

"Each staff member shared a vision of the benefit: that once in place, the EHR would make everyone's job easier." They worked hard to get the patient charts scanned and ready for the first visit. They had a few bumps in the road, mainly with billing and claim submission, but the staff worked through the problems with their vendor to resolution. The practice met all of their success criteria, with the exception of one specific claim transmission goal, within four weeks of their go-live date. That final goal was met within 90 days.

Attitude made the difference for this practice and their EHR acceptance. They made a group commitment to the transition. The staff involvement in the selection and the fact that a specific EHR was not imposed on the staff contributed greatly to their success, which reaffirms Dr. Valdez's belief that people support their own decision. Once they had committed individually and as a team, there was no turning back. Moving a practice from paper to an EHR is a huge challenge. This practice has proven the way to be successful is by engaging and involving staff.

Oklahoma-based Cardiology of Tulsa (2006 Davies Ambulatory Care Award) is an 18-physician, eight mid-level provider practice, which saw more than 57,000 patients in 2005. Although, they did not expressly state at the onset of their EHR project that staff benefits from increased efficiency would have such a positive impact, they recognize it now. They have decreased stress, improved the work environment and eliminated work backlogs and the need for overtime. The staff appreciates getting their work done efficiently, while providing better care and quicker responses. This has increased morale.

One of the staff's responsibilities was to coordinate the interfaces between the EHR vendor and their device manufacturers. For example, when a patient is brought to the exam room area, he or she is first taken to a special chair that has built-in blood pressure and other vital signs equipment. The data collected at this station are entered directly into the patient's chart as the result of the interface the staff has created. There are many other interfaces and interactions the staff is responsible for, depending on the job tasks. For example, the health information system (HIS) staff has maintained primary responsibility for the EHR system.

Most of the template designs and workflow architecture were accomplished by the staff. The Saturday before go-live, the staff gathered to run through fictional scenarios. They simulated an abbreviated one-day schedule and practiced working out the kinks. The practice rolled out their system two physicians at a time, training the staff along with them.

Keys to the success of their training, scanning/abstracting and implementation efforts were motivational strategies to keep it fun. They gave out "Go-Live" T-shirts to all employees as their physicians began using the EHR. And they were given targets and prizes for reaching their goals within specified time frames, including after-hours tropical parties complete with margarita machines and the chance to throw water balloons at the administrator.

"A change of this magnitude is very stressful; it is worth the time, effort and money to infuse the process with motivational and fun activities, such as parties to celebrate goals met, casual days for training and contests and prizes to keep spirits up."

Cardiology of Tulsa allowed their staff to capitalize on the successes along the way, which helped maintain enthusiasm and lead to a successful EHR implementation.

In Lake Worth, FL, Palm Beach Obstetrics & Gynecology (2008 Davies Ambulatory Care Award) proudly discusses their EHR implementation. This practice has six providers and 19 staff members. "In two locations and having four hospitals means your practice has to be on top of things, not only in the office, but especially when births are occurring. Most of the staff quickly adapted to the new system and programs; however, there were a few employees who were clearly uncomfortable with the new environment, mainly due to their lack of basic computer skills."

Their vendor asked them to identify six super-users who would, as the process evolved, become the support resource for the rest of the practice. They split implementation responsibilities into the following team areas: administration, scanning/medical information, check-in/out, clinical nursing, billing/collections, EHR vendor's roles and responsibilities, and initial and ongoing IT support.

They chose a phased implementation and allowed employees to attend classes based on their job responsibilities. They also had access to online training and opportunities to learn with a decreased patient load. For the week prior to their go-live, they stopped seeing most patients in the offices and just attended deliveries at the hospitals. This way staff could attain training and concentrate on their classes and still assist the few patients who needed to be seen.

When employees were having trouble, the trainers would spend more time with them as they returned for each phase of the implementation. The level of stress increased during the second phase of the implementation, as they started entering more of the clinical information into the patients charts, and all new patients had to start with an electronic chart. Further ramping up the stress level were the decreased revenues from the shortened schedule during training. Within a few months, however, the staff was more comfortable with the new system and program. Their office now ranks in the top 2 percent of practices successfully implementing their vendor's program. Morale is at an all-time high as the practice now serves as a reference and demonstration site for the vendor.

The managing physician partner for the group, who was the inspiration for the EHR, notes that "one of the important areas of value that the EHR has brought to the practice is the reduced office noise and foot traffic level. The staff no longer has charts and paper over all their work spaces, nor do they have to chase charts, test results, messages, etc. all day. Their work areas are neat, pleasant spaces in which to work, where they have access, tools and equipment to efficiently do their job."

Challenges they encountered included staff reaching a plateau of expertise and not wanting to move beyond that level; the time needed for new hires to master all the intricacies of their processes; and circumventing the practice of fitting staff into tasks that are a poor fit by looking for tasks that suit the staff member's valuable qualities. They found that weekly meetings helped to keep everyone informed about issues, problems and progress. This helped with acceptance of the EHR and in finding resolutions to issues and problems.

The practice sends several staff members to the vendor's annual users' conference. It is a great opportunity to meet practices from around the country that share the same problems and frustrations and train on the same software, allowing time to discuss how to improve acceptance and usage of their EHR. Staff attends formal classes and has the chance to network. They improve their skills, return with new ideas and their enthusiasm is renewed. The practice finds this type of networking invaluable in the training of staff, improving processes and getting the most out of their EHR.

Village Health Partners opened in 2001, and implemented their EHR in 2003. From the very beginning of their process toward implementing the EHR, the physicians spent a lot of time managing staff expectations and addressing their fear of change. As the leaders of the practice, they knew that it was important that they remain uniformly positive throughout the process. They had the good fortune to have one LVN on staff who had previously worked with an EHR, and she did "a lot of behind the scenes grassroots evangelism to help demystify the EHR to the staff."

All staff were included in all workflow discussions from the beginning, and their input was found to be extremely valuable time and time again, as well as improving buy-in to the EHR.

Their application makes a very telling statement about how this benefited the staff: "They were able to see for themselves how 'inefficient and sometimes dangerous' the existing processes were. They also saw how the EHR would 'offer vast improvements in accomplishing their daily tasks and providing better customer service.'"

HOSPITAL AND HEALTH SYSTEMS—STORIES OF SUCCESS (AND CHALLENGES)

Now we move into the accounts by Davies Organizational Award winners. The challenges of a large hospital or integrated delivery system can be similar to ambulatory practices but usually on a much larger scale.

2007 Davies Organizational Award winner Allina Hospital & Clinics in Minneapolis is a non-profit system with 23,000 employees, 5,000 physicians and 2,500 volunteers dedicated to meeting the needs of their communities. With a desire to standardize work processes across the organization and use best practices when possible, they proceeded with an implementation, which included a sophisticated level of delegation to committees, departments and individuals. They developed system-wide work groups, advisory groups and user groups to support ongoing two-way communication between the vendor and the sites. Among their many continuing duties are prioritizing projects and enhancements, idea sharing and best practice identification, promoting adoption and proper use of the system, and helping with upgrades.

They learned from their first go-live site and carried that knowledge over to all subsequent site training programs and included centralized training sites, schedules, a learning management system and patient-rich training environments. By having centralized training, they could set requirements by role and by name. This enabled scheduling six to eight months in advance to plan and accommodate large, diverse staff populations. The learning management system helped class offerings to be part of a real-time enrollment tracking process and provided a platform to securely deliver eLearning modules. Managers could easily enroll their staff and know their status at any time. The system delivers scores and triggers security access or remediation for the user.

Allina developed a customer satisfaction survey to obtain feedback from staff. Eighty-two percent rated the EHR as good, very good or excellent. Continuing to solicit feedback from the staff through workgroups, advisory groups and user groups is crucial to their continued success. Some unanticipated effects of the EHR implementation were the high level of emotions involved that sometimes carried over to other areas and the opportunity for individual growth of staff members. Many stepped up, using the implementation to grow significantly and positively as leaders in the organization and among their peers. "Allina's 'One Patient One Record' vision was to enable a seamless care experience across the organization for patients, their families, and Allina's caregivers."

As stated by an Allina nurse and super-user: "It's been very helpful to have one source of patient information. I also work at the clinic and often use the chart review to triage patient calls. It's very helpful to look back at clinic records to see what a patient's prescriptions and diagnoses are when they come to the emergency department. It helps the doctors and nurses provide better care and triage properly."

New York-based Generations+/Northern Manhattan Health Network won the Davies Organizational Award in 2006. This large, integrated delivery system includes three hospitals, 38 neighborhood family health centers, child health centers and school-based clinics. The total number of employees in the healthcare network is more than 7,200.

The leadership believed involving key staff contributed to the success of their project. "A participatory decision-making process was encouraged in the pursuit of an EHR." The system had an information system committee that oversaw the project. They also included the CIO and IT directors by having them participate in clinical leadership meetings, including medical board and nursing committees. This kept everyone informed and kept the project moving.

To reduce risks of failure, hospital-savvy clinicians were commandeered to be active members of the team and also keep their fingers on the network's pulse. Tasks included a thorough assessment of each facility's workflow, database design and training, comprehensive testing, and transition planning. The user support was structured to ensure patient safety.

As a result of staff training, education and support, their EHR implementation was successful. They used a multifaceted approach, starting with an assessment of each individual's computer skills. Both individual classroom training and online training were provided. The training was organized based on the clinical role and function. At the conclusion of each class, the participant completed a self-assessment test and left with an easy to use "cheat sheet."

The EHR has reduced human error in patient care at Generations+. Both their caregivers and patients feel more satisfied and safer because of it. "The positive effect of the EHR on patient safety has motivated our caregivers to be creative and engaged in developing new and better uses for IT—and for raising the bar for patient safety."

2005 Davies Organizational Award winner Citizens Memorial Healthcare (CMH) opened its doors in 1982 with 53 beds and 90 employees. Today it employs more than

1,500 staff, 25 of whom were part of the original 90. This fully integrated healthcare delivery system in Bolivar, MO, invited the board and medical staff to participate in all product demonstrations. To achieve total buy-in, they were given a demo by the preferred vendor and a consensus of support was obtained. Part of application notes, "The selection process at CMH was employee-driven."

A key committee in the successful project was the IS steering committee, which had broad representation from across the organization, including members from clinical, non-clinical and financial areas of the system, as well as representation from across the continuum of care—hospital, long-term care, home care and physician offices. Their responsibilities included recruiting team members, leading discussions, scheduling and organizing demonstrations, analyzing responses, site visits, ROI analysis and final recommendations to the board and the CEO. They were the overall driving force behind planning and implementation, providing continuing guidance, long-term planning and budgeting.

By involving their staff from the beginning and using them in all aspects of the planning and implementation, CMH has been very successful and improved patient care for all in the community.

Finally, we must include the account of staff engagement in the most recent health system winner of the 2009 Davies Organizational Award: MultiCare. In the early stages of their project, they "ran an internal marketing campaign called Reasons to Get Excited about MultiCare Connect. The campaign featured clinicians and users from all areas of the three hospitals aimed at engaging all employees and educating them about the upcoming implementation."

They also made sure to engage staff in the change management and adoption process. With the full support of leadership, staff was involved in the design of new workflows and received abundant education on system functionality. They stayed involved in workflow change and validation through formal validation sessions, called Workflow Walkthrough demonstrations, and through their Tunnel Tour workflow display events.

Education was particularly focused on students, nurses and ancillary clinicians who were required to pass a competency test to receive their user-names, passwords and full functionality passes. "Broad participation by nursing and ancillary clinical staff was obtained by providing sufficient agency staff to relieve them from clinical duties and allow them to focus on their classes." Through this process, the health system found that it was most helpful to provide a full-day, rather than a part-day, course because staff had too much difficulty trying to attend classes during work breaks.

CONCLUSION

These Davies Award winners' stories have brought to light the common traits of staff acceptance of technology. Selecting, purchasing and integrating EHR software is a challenge in itself, but getting staff invested in learning and using the technology is quite another. If the introduction to the new system is not strategic or well-planned, the backlash can be significant and costly. Focusing on staff buy-in is critical to the successful implementation and usage of EHRs.

CHAPTER 9

Value and Outcomes: What the System Has Meant to Our Practice and Our Patients

David Collins, MHA, CPHQ, CPHIMS, FHIMSS, and Alice Loveys, MD, FAAP, FHIMSS

"Price is what you pay. Value is what you get."

—Warren Buffett

INTRODUCTION

The promise of the EHR is to improve quality and efficiency in healthcare delivery and therefore, improve outcomes, all while reducing costs in the system. However, the implementation of an EHR to achieve these goals requires a significant organizational investment in effort, time and monies. Davies Award winners proved to be exceptional in realizing an ROI on their implementations, while deriving significant value and improved patient outcomes.

Several forces are behind an organization's drive to implement an EHR, both internal and external. As was outlined in Chapter 6, internal forces for EHR implementation are, in part, driven by widespread campaigns to improve patient safety, quality of care and practice life, while controlling costs or enhancing revenues.

External forces are at play as well. The media has heightened awareness of the all-too-frequent adverse events and tragedies that occur within the complexities of healthcare delivery, as well as its escalating costs. Purchasers of healthcare, such as the federal government and employers, have looked for various ways to achieve value in healthcare, wanting to purchase care that is both safe and of high quality at a reasonable cost. Value for them is the price they pay to derive desired, achievable outcomes. As they look for greater value, they apply external forces to organizations for accountability in the form of accreditation or seek to share costs savings with organizations in the form of pay-for-performance incentive programs. Healthcare purchasers are behind a multitude of national quality programs designed to put stop-gaps and check and balance points in place. These programs have set a new norm for monitoring and tracking healthcare-related data and the payout of incentives.

One example is The Joint Commission core measure set. Physicians in paper-based offices are unable to meet all internal and external forces, as the dollar amount, time and effort to do so are substantial, and the rewards in many of the incentive programs, such as Physician's Quality Reporting Initiative, have been too low. That is changing.

What Is Value?

The Davies Award evaluates four primary categories in EHR implementation: management, technology, functionality and value derived from an EHR system. While all categories are important, the greatest interest (and emphasis) by each of the Davies Award Committees is the demonstration of value the organization has been able to achieve from leveraging health IT. Successful organizations infuse health IT as a tool they use throughout the organization's culture. They derive value through the process of setting, monitoring and achieving system-wide business, operational and clinical objectives. In doing so, data are not merely collected and submitted for purposes of filling in a checkbox but are trended, analyzed and converted into usable information to effect real clinical change.

The end result may be a positive impact on quality outcomes and improved patient safety. In this data critical environment, if the EHR itself is not being utilized to effectively alter behavior, then resources will still be misaligned and physicians will not derive the true power of digital medicine. Running queries against available data in an EHR, with an integrating reporting application and process measures, provides a "beginning level" of performance level comparisons among providers can be provided. Automating the capture and reporting of data and analyzing these data to create information to effect changes in provider behavior, based upon outcome measures, is where the real power of medical informatics impacts the practice of medicine.

The Davies Award continues to evolve each year along with industry expectations, facilitated by technologic advances and the proven track records of past winners. They have proven what can be accomplished by the effective utilization of health IT as a tool, as part of their programs and processes, resulting in substantial changes in derived value.

The 2009 Davies Organizational Award application criteria for "Value" provided the following expectations:

> Documenting the actual value of the EHR system serves several important purposes. The investments in system components and implementation are huge. Consequently many organizations set very explicit expectations for the implemented system in terms of its impact on overall quality improvement. Important areas to consider include patient safety, effective care delivery, patient care efficiency, clinician efficiency, regulatory compliance, user satisfaction, access to care, equity in care.
>
> ROI and other strategic objectives. The ability to understand and articulate actual progress is important to justify the investment to those who funded it and to obtain funding and approval for pushing ahead. It takes years to achieve the maximum benefit from such an investment. The Value section should highlight the initial benefits derived, the metrics and methodology that have been chosen to evaluate these benefits and the plans for future measurement of improvements and ROI.
>
> For those managing the project, a clear understanding regarding the results actually achieved can be extremely useful as a checkpoint to verify the success of implementation (both during pilot implementations and full-scale roll-outs), to guide expectations for further rollout within the organization and to indicate opportunities for increasing value through enhancements to capabilities and fine-tuning the implementation strategy.

Implementing an EHR is a community effort, requiring extra work and energy from virtually every employee of the organization. Publicizing and celebrating EHR achievements validates the accomplishments of individuals and the community as a whole.

The EHR projects that have had the greatest influence on the health care industry have communicated their experience with achieving value from their EHR projects by providing detailed analyses of both the resources expended and the returns gained from their project.

- Additional areas to be considered in this evaluation include:
- Improvement in important patient safety metrics.
- Enhanced effectiveness of care delivery.
- Reduced admission or re-admission rates.
- Reduce infection rates.
- Greater efficiencies in patient care or with clinicians.
- Improved compliance with "standard protocols."
- Improved documentation compliance.
- Improved compliance with regulatory agencies.
- Enhanced customer satisfaction.
- Improved access to the care within the organization.
- Improvements in equitable care delivery.
- Important additional gains may include streamlining information access and reducing time spent searching for missing information, improving continuity of care across providers and settings, improving timeliness and reliability in communicating test results to patients and/or improving the effectiveness of teams by facilitating communication and organized work flow.

As described in these criteria, applicants are challenged to demonstrate the success of their programs by demonstrating integrated, system-wide use by providers to improve the delivery of care. Value is not only captured in the traditional hard dollars and cents of ROI but also within the soft and stretch benefits of the care provided through the EHR, as described in the Davies Award application criteria in the bulleted list previously shown, with specific examples in Table 9-1 and Table 9-2.

Table 9-1: Understanding Hard and Soft ROI, Davies Organizational Award Recipients.

| *Benefits Realization— "Hard & Soft ROI"* | MultiCare ('09)—4 hospitals | • Total cost of ownership over a 10-year period (go live 6/1/07) $126 million (implementation hardware, implementation software, implementation operating expenditures, implementation, personnel, facilities, ongoing capital expenditure, and ongoing operating expenditures) ($58.4 million for implementation expenses and $67.4 in ongoing expenses).
• ROI: Improved staff efficiency, reduction in practice variation, improved reimbursement, improved "patient responsibility" cash collection, improved billing cycle process, adverse drug reaction avoidance, and hospital-acquired condition avoidance. Initial net benefit $42.6M. ROI projections show 2012 break-even. |

(Continued)

Table 9-1: (Continued)

Quality Improvement— "Hard ROI"	Eastern Maine Medical Center ('08)—411 Beds	• 50% decrease in use of blood products resulting in a cost savings of $1.2 million. • For the CMS Physician Quality Reporting Initiative (PQRI) Reporting, EMMC reports data on diabetics (HgbAlc, BP and cholesterol meeting targets), coronary artery disease patients on aspirin and fall risk assessment as ascertained from the EHR -approx $28,000 annually.
Patient Safety— "Soft ROI"	Allina Hospitals & Clinics ('07)— 11 hospitals	Improved nursing documentation—examples include: • 28% improvement in nutrition screening. • 26% improvement in documentation of response to pain intervention. • 17% improvement in discharge screening. • 3% improvement in weight documented within 24 hours.
Patient Safety— "Soft ROI"	Generations+/ Northern Manhattan Health Network ('06)—3 hospitals	• 40% reduction in medication errors in the first 12 months after CPOE implementation was reported. Errors due to illegible orders were virtually eliminated. Errors due to incomplete orders were reduced by 70%. • Online medication administration resulted in a 66% reduction in administration errors by Nursing, with a 94% satisfaction rating by Nursing. • Reduction in medication administration by almost 50%, improving nurse productivity.
Patient Flow— "Hard ROI"	Citizens Memorial ('05)—74 beds	• 23% increase in net patient revenues after the EMR implementation, with positive patient volume influence.
Reducing and Reallocating Resources— "Hard ROI"	NorthShore University HealthSystem ('04)—200+/facility	• Savings—Increased volume with its EMR equivalent to eliminating 65 full-time employees throughout the corporation ($4M); eliminating forms, a scheduling system, and dictation ($1.94M).
Billing Improvements— "Hard ROI"	Maimonides Medical Center ('02)—705 beds	• '96 profits $761,000, '01 profits $6.1M post-implementation; 25% revenue increase from EMR, 9.4 % ROI annually. • 4.84-year payback on its $43.8 million investment.
Patient Safety— "Soft ROI"	Maimonides Medical Center ('02)—705 beds	• 58% decrease in medication orders, 55% decrease in medication discrepancies. • Decision support feature—"High alert medications," confusing look-alike and sound-alike drug names, patients with similar names. • Identified 164,250 alerts, resulting in 82,125 prescription changes.
Process Improvement— "Soft ROI"	University of Illinois Chicago Medical Center ('01)—450 beds	• 75% reduction in chart pull requests, expected to increase. • 12 paper forms eliminated. • 100% availability patient records (previously 40%).
Regulatory Compliance— "Soft ROI"	Ohio State University Health System ('01)— 849 beds	• Full compliance institutional do-not-resuscitate orders and restraint orders. • Allows daily reports to Ohio State Pharmacy Board, controlled substances compliance.

Preventing Errors, Achieving Value—Clinical Decision Support

Clinical decision support (CDS) can provide real-time positive influence on clinical decision-making and affiliated outcomes and differentiates merely implementing and using a system, from truly utilizing the system to its greatest potential and thereby deriving value. As Davies Award winners demonstrate over and over again, CDS is a powerful tool in improving overall organization performance and in achieving clinical quality improvements at the point of care.

Goals of CDS. The starting point in implementing CDS is to establish performance goals. These guide decisions about data analysis, evaluation of results, report sharing, and process change. The goals of CDS include the ability to[1]:

- Detect potential safety and quality problems and help prevent them.
- Detect inappropriate utilization of services, medications and supplies.
- Foster the greater use of evidence-based medicine principles and guidelines.
- Organize, optimize and help operationalize the details of a plan of care.
- Help gather and present data needed to execute this plan.
- Ensure that the best clinical knowledge and recommendations are utilized to improve health management decisions by clinicians and patients.

Table 9-2: Understanding Hard and Soft ROI, Davies Ambulatory Care Award Recipients.

Condition	Possible Efficiency Gain		Ambulatory Care Davies Recipients—Actual Examples
Increase physician productivity— *"Soft Benefit"*	IF physicians have extra capacity & get "faster" with EMR	0%–15% revenue gain	**Virginia Women's Center ('09)—25 MDs, 5 sites, 5,629 avg pt encounters/provider/yr** • Volume of patient throughput was increased. Pre EHR, average number of annual patient visits/provider 5,314. Post implementation, 11% increase to 5,629. • Average number of annual relative value units (RVUs)/provider jumped over 13% with EHR. • Average profits per shareholder physician stayed level during implementation, and 19% increase in the year post implementation.
Reduce transcription— *"Hard benefit"*	IF dictating AND willing to change	$5k–$15k/yr costs cut	**Cardiology Consultants of Philadelphia ('08)— 79 MDs, 21 sites, 2,710 visits/year/physician** • 88% reduction in transcription costs, pre-implementation cost of $800,000, post-EHR reduced to <$100,000.
Capture lost charges— *"Hard Benefit"*	IF charges are now being lost	1%–5% revenue gain	**Valdez Family Clinic ('07)—1 MD, 1 site, 9,600 visits/yr** • Increased the accuracy of coding—Pre-EHR: 948 patient visits, $91,904 was billed Post-EHR (by 3-months): 772 visits, $94,175 was billed. • Move billing in-house without adding to staff–Svgs: $31k/yr—the avg of yrly cost 3rd-party billing company; Offset the cost of software.

(Continued)

Table 9-2: (Continued)

Condition	Possible Efficiency Gain		Ambulatory Care Davies Recipients—Actual Examples
Staff efficiency— *"Soft Benefit"*	IF overtime being paid, or IF staff ratio can be reduced	0%–15% cost reduction	**Alpenglow Medical, PLLC ('06)—1 MD, 1 site, 10,000 visits/yr** • Post-EHR, only 1 MA needed for 2 clinicians (annual cost savings of $30,000). • Post-EHR no need for medical records staff or transcription (annual cost savings of $20,000). • Post-EHR ability to see more patients per time spent in the office with increased profitability (1 extra level 3 return per day adds $10,000/yr in profit.
Increase physician productivity— *"Soft benefit"*	IF physicians have extra capacity & get "faster" with EMR	0%–15% revenue gain	**Wayne Obstetrics and Gynecology ('05)—1 MD, 1 site, ~6,000 visits/yr** • Work hours devoted to documenting patient encounters decreased by 4 hours/week. • Number of patients clinicians able to see increased 225%.
Increase preventive & management services— *"Hard Benefit"*	IF new services are profitable AND capacity exists	5% revenue gain	**Southeast Texas Medical Associates ('05)—24 MDs, 3 sites, 200,000+ visits/yr** • Improvements in E&M service coding increased average billable charges for office visits 4.23%, adding more than $150,000 in billable charges.
Staff efficiency— *"Soft Benefit"*	IF overtime being paid, or IF staff ratio can be reduced	0%–15%cost reduction	**Southeast Texas Medical Associates ('05)—24 MDs, 3 sites, 200,000+ visits/yr** • Number of administrative staff required to handle patient charts decreased by 76.7% (from $2.65 per visit down to $0.62. • Annual savings of more than $120,000 in administrative costs.
Reduced chart pulls— *"Soft Benefit"*	IF practice charged for pulls	$5/pull or $6k/yr/MD	**Sports Medicine & Orthopedic Specialists ('05)—4 MDs, 1 site, 20,000 visits/yr** • Spends $1,000 per month on the EMR, post-implementation, compared with the $6,000 per month the practice used to spend pulling paper charts. • The systems freed up an estimated $75,000 in staff time.
Reduce claims denials and delays— *"Hard Benefit"*	IF denials or delays are common	15–30 day A/R speedup	**Riverpoint Pediatrics ('04)—1 MD, 1 site, 6,800 visits/yr** • Increased collection rates from 52% to 88% in 4 years. • Eliminated claims denied due to coding errors. • Insurance-payment turnaround time fell from between 30 and 60 days, to approximately 15 days.

Condition	Possible Efficiency Gain		Ambulatory Care Davies Recipients—Actual Examples
Reduce transcription— *"Hard Benefit"*	IF dictating AND willing to change	$5k–$15k/yr costs cut	**North Fulton Family Medicine ('04)—7 MDs, 2 sites, 51,000 visits/yr** • Elimination of transcription, recouped costs since implementation total ~$775,000. • Transcription processing time/day reduced from 705 mins to zero.
Reduce costs of chart storage and archiving— *"Soft Benefit"*	IF office goes paperless and chart room eliminated	$1k/yr per physician	**Pediatrics @ the Basin ('04)—2 MDs (1FTE), 1 site, 4200 visits/yr** • As a result of paper charts no longer being pulled in the office, $4 per chart request saved, totaling approximately $16,800 per year. • Not having to conduct written data entry saved another $1,400/yr while eliminating transcriptions added $10,000 to the bottom line. • $5,000 annually by eliminating storage costs.
Capture lost charges— *"Hard Benefit"*	IF charges are now being lost	1%–5% revenue gain	**Roswell Pediatrics ('03)—9 MDs, 3 sites, 82,000 visits/yr** • Before go-live, 18.3% of procedures performed escaped documentation, therefore not billable. • 1-year post implementation, billing for procedures (e.g. venipuncture), increased from 353 to 8,324, the number of handling fees jumped from 968 to 1,734 and medical management charges jumped from one to 34.

Examples of the use of CDS. Two examples of the use of CDS include medication management and radiological testing,[2] which include suggesting brand-to-generic substitutions for medications, for alternative, more cost-effective therapies, or for more formulary compliant drug options. As well, selecting complex dosages (renal failure or geriatrics) and supporting drug-level monitoring are additional advantages of CDS. Support at the point of ordering can guide physicians toward the most appropriate and cost-effective, radiological tests. Alerts and reminders are certainly an important component of CDS, but are often misunderstood. Because they are so visible to the provider, they are often viewed as the only functionality of CDS. In fact, CDS is far more powerful. Its functionalities include:

• Alerts and reminders.
• Clinical guidelines.
• Order sets.
• Patient data reports, dashboards.
• Documentation templates.

- Diagnostic support.
- Reference information delivered.
- Other tools to support decisions within clinical workflow.

Appropriate use of CDS can be a pivotal point in deriving system value. For example:

2002 Davies Organizational Award winner Maimonides Medical Center, Brooklyn, NY, identified 164,250 alerts, resulting in 82,125 prescription changes. As a result, problem medication orders dropped 58 percent, and medication discrepancies by 55 percent. They addressed "high-alert medications," confusing look-a-like and sound-alike drug names, as well as patients with similar names.

2008 Davies Organizational Award winner Eastern Maine Medical Center (EMMC), Bangor, in contrast was challenged with alert fatigue and providers overriding alerts without reading them. This action is counterintuitive to the intent of the alerts. To minimize this risk, EMMC opted to start slowly with the minimum number of alerts to the providers, yet allowed all alerts to the pharmacists to provide for check-and-balance. As a result, there was a reduction in drug-drug alerts to providers, which significantly decreased the "noise" and negative impact on provider ordering, while maintaining patient safety, driving 17,498 alerts per month down to 2,401 per month. This required a customization of the alerts to a minimum number to providers.

Case 9-1

EASTERN MAINE MEDICAL CENTER—OPTIMIZING ALERT FIRING, REDUCING ALERT FATIGUE

Rules-based alerts fire to providers based on specific patient care situations. The alerts warn providers of conditions and recommend actions to take, such as ordering certain medications. The following are specific examples of alert use:

- When opening a patient's chart, the provider is alerted to medications that require renewal within 48 hours.
- When closing the patient's chart, the provider is reminded of orders that have been "planned" but are not yet initiated. This is a reminder to providers that they may have forgotten to do part of the process needed to implement a plan of care.
- The provider is alerted if the diet has been changed to NPO and there is existing insulin therapy that needs to be reviewed.
- Notifications are sent to a shared clinical pharmacist mailbox letting them know of combinations of results and orders that could result in bradycardia, so that dosing can be reviewed and the provider consulted if needed. Other conditions monitored are renal toxic drug orders, low potassium level results in the presence of medications that can result in potassium depletion, lab results indicative of life-threatening hematological events.
- Since pharmacists no longer receive a written order, an alert fires to them when they review an order, drawing their attention to special instructions that may have been entered by the provider.
- Alerts are used to assure that the code status of a patient is entered when the patient is admitted. The information is then easily viewed within the EHR.

A key benefit to EMMC: The system resulted in an overall medication incident decrease of 27 percent over three years (2004 to 2007).

Alerts and reminders are only one type of CDS. The true power of CDS comes from a combination of tools that must be applied to positively impact patient care, including:

- Clinical guidelines.
- Order sets.
- Patient data reports, dashboards.
- Documentation templates.
- Diagnostic support.
- Reference information.

2007 Davies Organizational Award winner Allina Hospitals & Clinics, Minneapolis, implemented a system of clinical guidelines by creating a process to reduce drug utilization. Allina's ability to generate a system list of specific IV medications, which can be changed to PO medications, without contacting a provider, resulted in the following benefits:

- PO medications are a less costly route of therapy.
- The incidence of infection from IV use is also decreased.
- Average length of stay is reduced.
- Pharmacy and nursing time to prepare and administer medication is reduced.

Illinois-based NorthShore University HealthSystem (formerly Evanston Northwestern Healthcare) (2004 Davies Organizational Award) experienced unanticipated issues with the pain medication Dilaudid (hydromorphone hydrochloride) for certain patients. With the ability to reconfigure its EHR quickly, a change in recommended dosing was streamlined. Evanston changed all order sets and 22 preference lists in just three hours and notified every clinician of the change through the EHR system.

Now when a physician orders Dilaudid, the EHR raises an alert to evaluate the patient for previous experience and selects the dosing accordingly. Nursing documentation in the system ensures that nurses conduct the correct assessments at the correct time. Prior to the EHR, this type of change to processes and affiliated order sets would have been very time-consuming and cumbersome, compromising patient safety. With paper processes, pre-printed orders would have needed to have been changed, along with checking individual physician prescriptive habits on a patient-by-patient basis, with the pharmacist directly calling the physician for consultation and change, and providing nurses with multiple in-services.

Cardiology Consultants of Philadelphia (2008 Davies Ambulatory Care Award) has leveraged patient data reports and dashboards to derive value from its EHR system. Prior to implementing its EHR, its offices relied on the patients to return for repeat INR blood tests.

With 7,267 patients in the practice who are currently prescribed warfarin (Coumadin), (incidentally, an unknowable count prior to its EHR), this was an inefficient process and placed the burden of compliance solely upon the patient. With the EHR in place, this second largest cardiology practice in the country customized its encounter form for warfarin management to include weekly reports to identify patients overdue for their warfarin level check. Patients overdue as much as six to 12 months can now be identified, and nurses contact these patients, facilitating compliance with anticoagulation monitoring and optimizing value in the patient care experience.

A second telling example of Cardiology Consultants' ability to leverage patient data reports and dashboards is in regards to the device recall of Medtronic's Fidelis defibrillator lead. Upon learning of this recall, the practice queried the EHR database, which helped it to identify all patients implanted with this lead within just ten minutes after recall notification.

More than 100 patients were identified beyond those in the records of the device manufacturer. Leveraging the mail-merge form-letter functionality within the EHR, all patients were notified within hours (not weeks, as would have been the case pre-EHR). Incidentally, the device manufacturer modified their local processes for collecting implanted lead data.

Documentation templates provide a means of leveraging CDS for greater efficiencies. Maimonides Medical Center developed a process to involve its physicians and nurses in the development and use of its templates. At the time of their Davies Award submission, Maimonides reported that all clinicians using their Ambulatory Care CPR system began from a master screen that serves as a launching screen to the various pathways tailored for each category of user. This master screen pulled information that was entered from various templates (e.g., the chronic conditions master list, chronic conditions addressed today, chief complaints, and alerts for special patient needs—deaf, blind, interpreter required.). From the master screen, physicians accessed any template specific to gathering medical data during the patient visit. These templates were developed by physicians working with the project team to fit their workflow and method of data gathering.

Nursing staff also accessed their templates from the master screen and participated in developing templates structured to their needs. Nurses determined which orders were to be acted on at the time of the visit, using data presence fields (e.g., medications or treatments to be administered). From the development and active use of these documentation templates, Maimonides reported improved regulatory compliance for the current problem list from 67 percent to 97 percent; allergy documentation from 88 percent to 100 percent; and the quality of pain assessment documentation improved to 95 percent.

The regional Picture Archiving and Communications System (PACS) at EMMC, provides for improved diagnostic support within clinical decision making. This system enables access by fifteen organizations to images and concurrent review by multiple providers in separate locations across the region. This continuity of patient information facilitates the ability of radiologists and other specialists to access studies for timely online comparison from the same PACS system, allowing broad and rapid access to images and improving clinical effectiveness and patient outcomes.

Reference information provides system value as it allows providers access to information such as drug references at the point of care. At NorthShore, desktop access is possible via the Intranet to Micromedex, OVID, ENH Formulary, ENH Drug Use Guidelines, ENH Policy & Procedures, IV Administration Guidelines, and several other secondary and tertiary medical references.

We have been discussing the clinical value that is achievable through implementation of the EHR and its CDS functionality. Let's turn attention to the business value that our two most recent Davies Award winners achieved (clinical improvement measures are included as they also drive improved business performance).

The most recent winner of the Davies Organizational Award, MultiCare, Tacoma, WA, reports having become more flexible and nimble as a result of their EHR implementation.

Case 9-2

CITIZENS MEMORIAL HEALTHCARE

2005 Davies Organizational Award winner Citizens Memorial Healthcare (CMH) has leveraged the organization's investment in health IT through grant funding. In addition to the initial $6 million that CMH invested between 2001 and 2004, CMH has been awarded more than $4 million in grant funding.

The grants have been awarded by federal government agencies and private foundations. Grant funding has supported the expansion of the CMH EHR system, quality measure extraction and reporting, and telehealth applications.

The findings of those grant evaluations have been another way for CMH to demonstrate the value of health IT.

One grant, from the Agency for Healthcare Research and Quality, funded the expansion of the CMH EHR into 15 physician practices. The practices include primary rural health clinics and specialty clinics.

CMH found, as predicted, an initial period of reduced productivity and net income for a period that varied from a few weeks to a few months in each clinic. But after that period the clinics showed a significant increase in net income, compared with the pre-EHR period, as depicted in Figure 9-1.

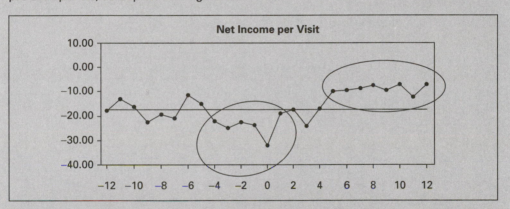

Figure 9-1: Net Income Per Visit. (From Citizens Memorial Healthcare, used with permission.)

Another grant, from the Healthcare Resources and Services Administration, Office for the Advancement of Telehealth, funded a study using in-home telemonitoring for patients with chronic conditions. Of particular interest were home care patients with the highest likelihood to be re-admitted to the hospital or to require emergent care.

CMH implemented 40 in-home telemonitoring units and provided those units to 516 patients during the three-year study. The findings showed that although patients received fewer in-person visits during each episode of care (because they were being monitored daily using telemonitoring), their outcomes were improved; in particular, their need to be re-admitted to the hospital or to require urgent care or an emergency department visit.

Overall, the rate of re-admissions for home care patients at CMH is less than 18 percent, compared with a national rate of 29 percent. The rate of emergent visits at CMH is also less than 18 percent, compared with a national rate of 22 percent, as depicted in Figure 9-2 and Figure 9-3.

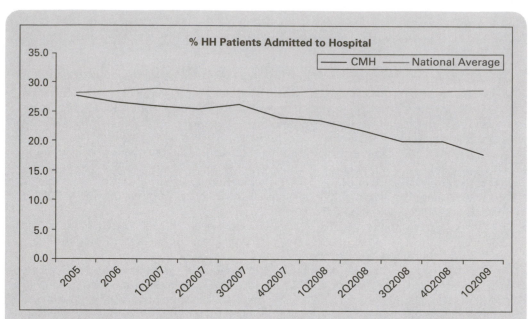

Figure 9-2: Percent of CMH Patients Admitted to Hospital Compared with National Average. (From Citizens Memorial Healthcare, used with permission.)

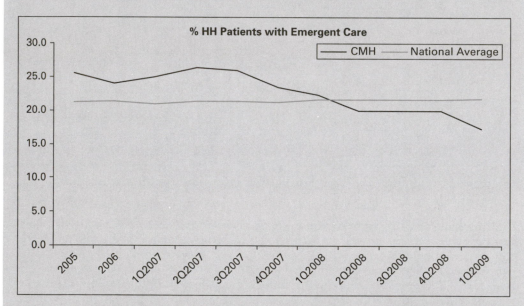

Figure 9-3: Percent of CMH Patients with Emergent Care Compared With National Average. (From Citizens Memorial Healthcare, used with permission.)

They report an array of improvements in patient safety, which had been established as the number one goal of their implementation. The following are a few specific measures of performance improvement:

- 13 percent decrease in the use of unsafe abbreviations.
- 13 percent decrease in Adverse Drug Reactions within the first 2.5 months of implementing CPOE.
- Estimated 108 lives saved among diabetic patients.
- Mean laboratory turnaround time reduced by 30 percent at all three hospitals.
- Median imaging order turnaround time reduced by an average of 50 percent at all three hospitals.

In their financial performance, MultiCare reported achievements of:

- $12 million in net benefit as a result of improved Patient Responsibility collections.
- More than $1 million in avoidable write-offs.
- $20 million in improved cash collections.

In its commitment to achieving expected benefits from its EHR implementation (called MultiCare Connect), MultiCare developed a Benefits Realization Program, and in its own words, under that program "determined that its total 10-year cost of ownership was near $126 million ($58.4 million for implementation and $67.4 in ongoing expense). The ROI projections were determined based on targeted process improvements, as well as efficiencies created simply by automating processes. This analysis included the determination of whether the returns were expected over a multi-year period or as a one-time benefit. The major ROI categories included: improved staff efficiency, reduction in practice variation, improved reimbursement, improved 'patient responsibility' cash collections, improved billing cycle process, adverse drug reaction avoidance, and hospital-acquired condition avoidance.

MultiCare has measured an initial net benefit in excess of $42.6 million since June 2007. Given continued commitment to optimize MultiCare Connect, ROI projections indicate break even in 2012."

MultiCare also reported other ways in which they achieved performance improvement in both clinical quality and business functions—more than we can relay to you here. They are certainly a harbinger of ongoing benefit that EHR implementations have in store.

Having taken a brief look at how MultiCare achieved benefit, it's appropriate to also review the report of value from the most recent Davies Ambulatory Care Award winner: Virginia Women's Center. In their own words, at the beginning they:

> … Braced for a 10 percent to 15 percent decrease in productivity as a consequence of implementation. The value proposition turned out to tell a story of fantastic ROI for us. Most notable is the marked profitability growth post-implementation. Average profits per shareholder physician stayed level during implementation, and the year post-implementation resulted in a 19 percent increase!
>
> The expected immediate $300,000 elimination of transcription costs proved to be true. However the anticipated reduction in FTEs did not occur. In fact, the staff to provider ratio rose from 4.01 to 4.41 during the implementation and fell to 4.33 the year post-implementation. (Their) business model has always

included a higher than average staffing complement to allow productivity and patient services that result in higher than average revenue production.... Workflow efficiencies and enhanced revenue cycle management contributed to favorable profitability. The volume of patient throughput was increased. Pre-EHR, the average number of annual patient visits per provider was 5,314. Post-implementation, it rose 11 percent to 5,629. The average number of annual RVUs per provider jumped to more than 13 percent, with the EHR. On the cost side of the financial report, operating costs, as a percentage of revenue, decreased from 61 percent to 59 percent.

In addition, clinical and patient care value propositions show improvement with the EHR system ... Internal quality assurance reports allow monthly reporting of adherence to universal best practices, such as ante-partum compliance with genetic test offering, cystic fibrosis, and nuchal translucency screening for chromosomal abnormalities. As well, time-sensitive treatments in pregnancy, such as Rhogam administration, are monitored.

In each of the cases presented in this chapter, the organizational leadership set out at the beginning of their EHR quest to define and measure the results they expected from their implementation. With those goals in mind, each has successfully achieved the very measurable results at the core of the plan that drove them forward.

CONCLUSION

It's clear from the Davies Award winners that value from the implementation of an EHR can and does result in value returned to the organization and to the patient. Safer practices and reduced errors are universally reported, and, to the surprise of many, financial returns are achieved over time. While the initial investment is challenging, it is essential that all medical providers move to an electronic system that provides not only improved business functions but also critically needed and improved clinical functions. When designed and implemented correctly, they do provide value!

References

1. Osheroff JA, editor. *Improving Medication Use and Outcomes with Clinical Decision Support: A Step-by-Step Guide.* Chicago: HIMSS; 2009.

2. Osheroff JA, Pifer EA, Teich JM, et al. *Improving Outcomes with Clinical Decision Support: An Implementers' Guide.* Chicago: HIMSS; 2005.

Chapter 10

The Ultimate Goal: Performance Improvement

Louis H. Diamond, MB ChB, FACP, FCP (SA), FHIMSS

"To raise new questions, new possibilities, to regard old problems from a new angle, requires creative imagination and marks real advance in science."

—Albert Einstein

INTRODUCTION

Improving the quality of care, given the knowledge of the current gaps in quality, is arguably the most important task facing healthcare professionals, and in fact, all stakeholders.[1] We must, out of necessity, expand the focus from quality improvement to performance improvement, the latter encompassing not only a quality perspective but also the costs of care delivery and, by extrapolation, efficiency considerations. To place this in perspective, the nation is facing a triple threat when it comes to healthcare delivery and maintaining the health of the population: covering the uninsured, bridging the quality gap and controlling costs. It is the latter two on which this chapter is focused.

The discussion will deal with the following: data types; the quality national measurement enterprise; the point-of-care decision, often referred to as clinical decision support (CDS); controlling costs and achieving efficiency; quality and performance improvement; and implications of ARRA.[2] The discussion will provide an outline of these activities and their components, with emphasis on measurement and the health IT needed to support these activities.

DATA TYPES

Data from various sources are needed to support measurement and decision-making at the point of care, and then at the ultimate goal of performance improvement, focusing on improving processes of care and achieving desired patient outcomes. A description and definition of the various data elements needed should start with the data that are easily available, usually termed administrative data, or otherwise described as claims data. This data set is designed and used for payment of services, and now increasingly to support performance measurement. While distinct from clinical data, to be described later, administrative data do have clinical data elements embedded, such as ICD-9 and CPT codes—the former describes diagnosis and the latter describes services provided by physicians and other healthcare professionals. Some data elements that fall under the definition of administrative data include patient name, address, gender and other demographic data, as well as insurance status.

The term clinical data is used to describe information about the patient (history and physical examination), what is done to the patient (diagnostic test results and treatment provided), and what has happened to the patient (outcomes). So, there is some blurring of definition between administrative and clinical data. All of these categories can be further disaggregated, e.g., patient management into medications, education, procedures and surgery, physiotherapy; laboratory tests further disaggregated into chemistry, hematology, anatomic pathology and serology.

As clinical data are used, either alone or to enrich administrative data, the support and robustness of performance measures are enhanced. Such data are similarly needed to support decision-making at the point of care (Figure 10-1). As can be seen from this diagram, as we move from left to right, and access clinical data, the linkage between process and outcomes strengthens, and levels of accountability can be enhanced, as the robustness of the clinical performance measure is increased. An example of a measure set focused on diabetes can be seen in the box.

The work at the National Quality Forum (NQF), focused on Automating Quality Measurement with the Quality Data Set (QDS), is described by Dan Rosenthal.

Meaningful healthcare quality measurement depends on collecting and reporting precise performance data. EHR systems should facilitate the seamless collection of these data, but most EHR systems are insufficient to support quality measurement, as it is envisioned to assist broad health reform efforts.

National comparison of performance requires that all quality indicators measure the same concepts equally. Most health information standards were created to send information from one computer system to another, focusing on the "envelope" for the information

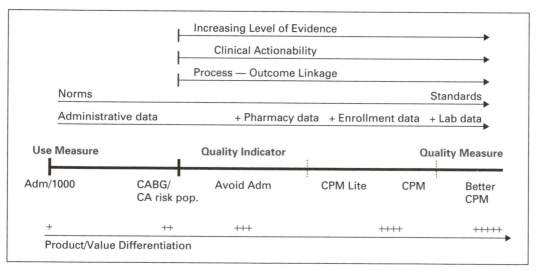

Figure 10-1: **Sample Spectrum of Use/Quality Measures.**

more than the content, but it is the standard information that is required for measurement. The lack of a set of precisely defined, universally adopted clinical definitions—i.e., the information—remains a major obstacle to measuring and comparing quality.

Thus, with support from the Agency for Healthcare Research and Quality (AHRQ), the NQF in 2007 assembled an expert panel, the NQF Health Information Technology Expert Panel (HITEP),[3] to accelerate standardization. In a report published the following year, HITEP spelled out a set of common data types across a prioritized set of measures to identify standards for how this information could be expressed. To build on that effort, and to assist the healthcare field in its efforts to meet health IT and quality goals in recent legislation, HITEP reconvened in 2009 to define a draft quality data set (QDS) that could be used nationwide to support automated quality measurement.

The QDS is a set of data elements that can be used as the basis for developing harmonized and machine-computable quality measures—a dictionary of standardized electronic clinical terms for the purpose of automated quality measurement. The QDS, as conceived by NQF HITEP, does not populate that dictionary directly. Rather, it is a framework or classification system by which measure developers can offer and refine QDS terms.

The QDS Framework (Figure 10-2) contains two levels of information:

Standard elements. Standard elements consist of a single clinical concept and the atomic unit of information, identified by a data element name (e.g., diabetes); a code set, or taxonomy (e.g., ICD-9-CM); and a code list comprising one or more enumerated values (e.g., 250.0, 250.1). Standard data elements should be reused and aligned among measures and measure developers.

Quality data elements. The quality data element is composed of a standard element, as defined, and a quality data type. The quality data type is the context in which each standard element is used in a clinical care process. Quality data elements reuse the standard elements and should be reused by other measures and by clinical guideline and CDS developers. Examples include, in the case of diabetes:

- Active diagnosis of diabetes.
- Family history of diabetes.
- Diabetes medication dispensed.
- Diabetes medication administered.

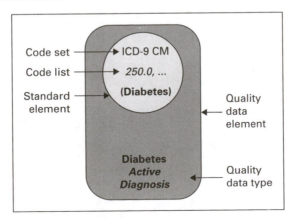

Figure 10-2: QDS Framework. (From NQF, used with permission.)

To determine how best to gather data as a seamless part of care delivery, facilitate improved quality measurement and reporting, and drive improved care outcomes, NQF's HITEP also sought to establish a framework for "data flow"—a way to express how data move within the clinical workflow so that a measure developer can easily identify the authoritative source for each element of information in the measure. While the QDS describes the pieces of information needed for quality measurement, additional data flow information connects the QDS to the right source, recorder, setting, and health record field. The data flow elements provide a concise and direct means to describe what is currently included in lengthy measure abstraction guides.

As conceived by HITEP, data flow contains four elements (Figure 10-3):

1. Source. The source is the originator of the quality data element. The source may be an individual or a device.
2. Recorder. The recorder is the individual or device that enters the data element into a health record field.
3. Setting. The setting is the physical location at which the data element is captured.
4. Health Record Field. The health record field is the location within an electronic record where the data should be found.

The QDS framework is intended to represent clinical and administrative information required to calculate quality measures. These elements will be used to construct, with measure-related logic, numerators and denominators. The QDS aims to provide direction to measure developers, EHR vendors, and other stakeholders on how to define quality terminology without ambiguity.

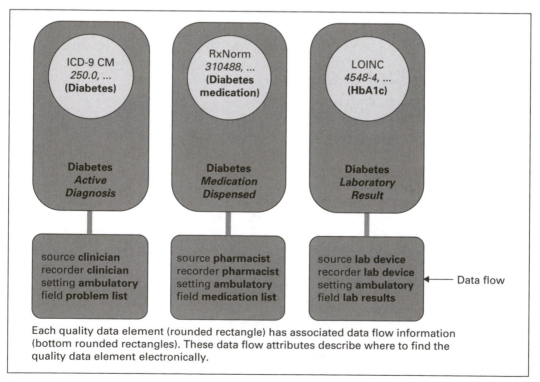

ICD-9 CM
250.0, ...
(Diabetes)

RxNorm
310488, ...
(Diabetes medication)

LOINC
4548-4, ...
(HbA1c)

Diabetes
Active Diagnosis

Diabetes
Medication Dispensed

Diabetes
Laboratory Result

source **clinician**
recorder **clinician**
setting **ambulatory**
field **problem list**

source **pharmacist**
recorder **pharmacist**
setting **ambulatory**
field **medication list**

source **lab device**
recorder **lab device**
setting **ambulatory**
field **lab results**

← Data flow

Each quality data element (rounded rectangle) has associated data flow information (bottom rounded rectangles). These data flow attributes describe where to find the quality data element electronically.

Figure 10-3: Data Flow Model. (From NQF, used with permission.)

As measures are created and continually updated, the QDS will need to reflect these changes. HITEP recommended maintenance of the QDS content at regular intervals. Because of the importance of the QDS as a framework from which EHR developers can extract data for performance measurement, adherence to the QDS likely will become a requirement for NQF endorsement.

Once the QDS is widely accepted and adopted, other health IT standard groups can begin to make the necessary connections to electronic clinical information—so that a standards group can easily find an acceptable, agreed-upon interoperability standard describing a term such as "patient information." Simultaneously, health IT vendors can connect their systems to those health IT standards, so that an EHR vendor can define where to find those terms (e.g., "patient information") in its system. Measure developers would not have to map to every single EHR system; rather, the QDS would map to common standards. The goal is for quality content and clinical information to meet in the middle, using those common health IT standards (Figure 10-4).

To support the adoption of the QDS framework, NQF also sponsored the development of an electronic measure standard in the international standards organization, Health Level 7 (HL7). The eMeasure representation of the Healthcare Quality Measure Format (HQMF) was successfully balloted as a draft standard for trial use (DSTU) as of November 3, 2009.

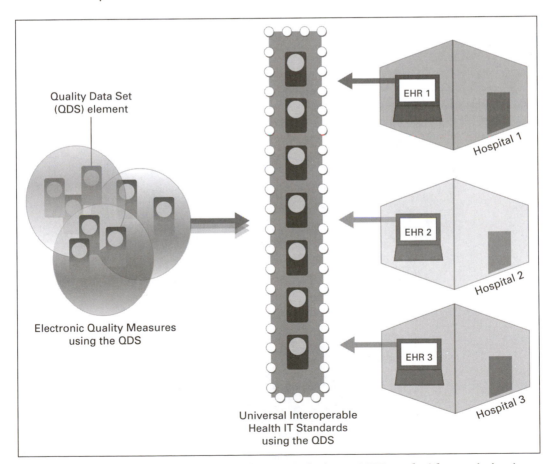

Figure 10-4: Quality Measures Meeting the Hospitals. (From NQF, used with permission.)

The structure is based on the QDS framework, connecting (or binding) the code list and the concept (the standard element) and the quality data type (context of use). An authoring tool will be developed to enable creation of the eMeasure directly by measure developers. Each of the HITEP quality data types was also mapped to the clinical document architecture (CDA) as part of the Healthcare Information Technology Standards Panel (HITSP) data dictionary (component C154), to enable the EHR and the quality measure developers to more directly meet in the middle as outlined earlier. Each of these efforts will be tested during the early 2010 initiatives to retool a large number of existing NQF-endorsed measures for use in EHR systems. NQF will also be expanding on these efforts with activities in health IT standards for CDS and care coordination.

THE QUALITY NATIONAL MEASUREMENT ENTERPRISE

Quality measurement is an essential building block, as we focus on the ultimate goal: quality and performance improvement. The national quality measurement enterprise is still evolving, but slowly, standardization and harmonization are occurring.

The starting point as we try to understand this national enterprise and the data needed to support quality performance measurement is a definition of the quality of care. A reasonable definition is: the degree to which healthcare is expected to increase the likelihood of desired health outcomes for patients and populations, consistent with current professional knowledge.[1]

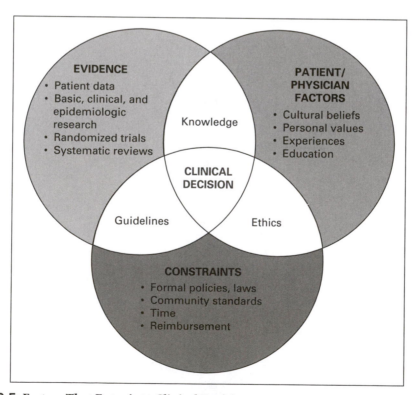

Figure 10-5: Factors That Enter into Clinical Decisions.

One of the keys to this definition is the focus on individual patients and patient populations, an important shift in our thinking and a desired outcome "based on current knowledge." All these issues influence the kinds of data needed to support measurement. The reference to "based on current professional knowledge" leads to the recognition that the basis for quality measurement is a commitment to evidence-based medicine, the application of the best available evidence, while taking into account other considerations in decision-making, such as patient preference and the clinical judgment of the physicians and the other members of the healthcare professional team. As can be seen in Figure 10-5, a robust set of data elements are going to be required to support quality measurements.

These principles, with a commitment to evidence-based medicine (EBM), are applicable to the care of the individual patient, and now, with the use of EBM as a building block for quality measurement, through the development of EBM-derived performance measures, they can also be made applicable to populations.

The national quality measurement enterprise starts with the development of the evidence, through the conduct of clinical trials, to the synthesis of the evidence, using structured methodologies, to the development of clinical practice guidelines (CPG)[4], which are "systematically developed statements, to assist the decision-making of healthcare professionals and patients."

Figure 10-6 describes the relationship between the conduct of research, with the generation of the evidence, with connections to the development and application of measurement tools; in turn connected and related to point of care decision support tools. Feedback of information, in associations with other needed components to achieve change

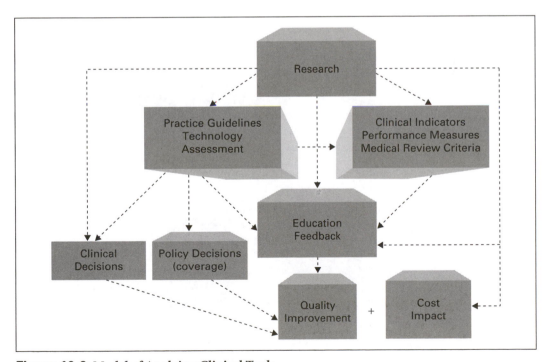

Figure 10-6: Model of Applying Clinical Tools.

and improvement, closes one loop. The second loop, not shown in the figure, is feedback to the research enterprise to inform future research.

All these aspects of the enterprise have an impact on the kind of data that will be needed and the kind of healthcare information infrastructure that will be required.

In brief, the final common pathway is the conversion of CPGs or, based on the highest level of evidence, convert to both quality measures and clinical decision support tools, the former applied to populations and the latter applied to individual patients.

The organizations engaged in these measurement activities are described in Figure 10-7 and Figure 10-8.

Figure 10-7 describes, in a simplified fashion, the national quality enterprise, while Figure 10-8 describes the evolving health IT "enterprise," the latter evolving rapidly since the enactment of ARRA.

In regards to the former, measure developers are at the core, with these functions still diffused among multiple groups, including but not limited to the Joint Commission, National Committee for Quality Assurance (NCQA), Physician Consortium for Performance Improvement (PCPI), academic medical centers and others in the private sector.

There is now a common final pathway for endorsement of quality measures for the purposes of public report, namely the National Quality Forum (NQF). The processes utilized for developing measures, and the use of the evidence from which quality measures are derived are well described by the PCPI.[5] The process for NQF endorsement, the National Consensus Process, and the criteria for measure endorsement are described on the NQF Web site.[6]

All these processes and selection criteria are increasingly needed to take into account the data elements needed to support, and the health IT standards needed to cost effectively collect, transmit and aggregate the data, to support public reporting and use healthcare

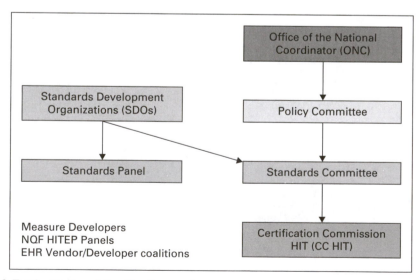

Figure 10-7: The National Quality Enterprise.

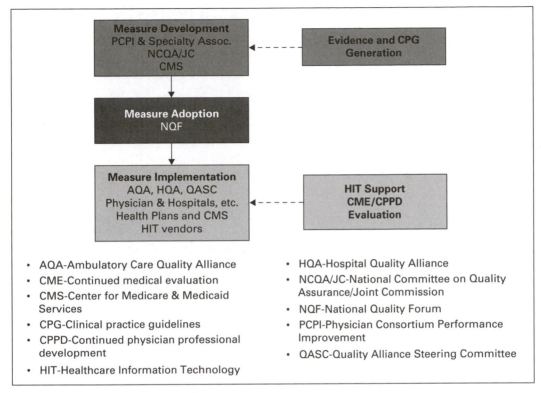

Figure 10-8: Evolution of Health IT.

professionals to achieve improvement. Implementation is currently being orchestrated by multiple organizations of loose coalitions, alliances, such the Hospital Quality Alliance (HQA), Ambulatory Care Quality Alliance (AQA), etc. (see Figure 10-8).

In addition to what was described earlier, we now have a rapidly evolving set of activities focused on the health IT aspects of measurement and improvement, including the Policy Committee of the Office of the National Coordinator, various IT standards panels, to set standards and product and application certification originations, such as CCHIT. This entire "enterprise" focused on measure development, endorsement, and implementation is focused on quality measurement for the purposes of public reporting, with the ultimate and perhaps unproven goal of generating improvement activities and patient choice, a subject that can not be explored at this time (Figure 10-8).

As alluded to earlier, the challenge is to facilitate electronic data collection, transmission, aggregation and reporting. Moving toward a system of data input and collection once, as an integral component of work flow, with the use of the data for multiple purposes, will require standardization of data elements, and the use of health IT standards to collect, transmit and store data. We could not function efficiently even in today's manual data collection environment without some standardization and the ability to utilize diagonalizable data elements. The projects being undertaken by NQF as described next. are taking giant steps toward the creation of a health information infrastructure needed to support healthcare delivery, measurement, and improvement.

CLINICAL DECISION SUPPORT

Clinical decision support (CDS) is the "front end" and necessary component of an infrastructure needed to improve performance, the other being performance measurement, of both quality and financial dimensions. Given the existence of an evolving infrastructure of standardized content, data definitions and health IT standards in support of EBM-derived quality measures, it seems logical to build the CDS infrastructure off those building blocks.

We will have to deal with the related nature of the two dimensions, while recognizing the important differences. CDS deals with individual patients and confidentially with the patient's encounter with the system and members of the healthcare professional team who interact with the patient. Measurement, on the other hand, deals with patient populations, at various levels of aggregation, e.g., the practice level, the hospital level, and other levels of aggregation, like geographic areas.

Tami Mark writes: "Increasingly, the information generated as part of healthcare services is becoming digitized and transmitted electronically. The healthcare community has recognized the value of capitalizing on these data to push forward the need for more and speedier comparative effectiveness information. Furthermore, providers, researchers, federal and state agencies, and others are working to further enhance the developing healthcare data infrastructure to improve its value in developing a more efficient and effective health care system."

Figure 10-9 describes some of the transactions and interactions that routinely occur in the course of clinical care that are being widely digitized.

Medical care claims that payment routinely occurs through electronic submission of claims, and the same is true for prescription drug claims. Large, third-party payors, such as insurance companies, Medicaid and Medicare, have enrollment records that can be used to link medical and prescription drug claims, so that an individuals' healthcare utilization can be tracked over time. This information is increasingly being augmented with other data, such as results from laboratory tests. Additionally, many traditional health maintenance organizations such as Kaiser have developed EHRs.

The development of this data infrastructure is primarily being driven by the demand for more efficient healthcare processes, such as claims payment and information storage and retrieval. The usefulness of this developing data infrastructure for comparative

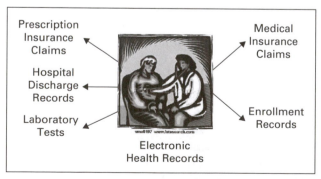

Figure 10-9: Healthcare Information That is Becoming Routinely Digital.

effectiveness research will depend in large part on the types of questions being asked. Fundamentally, for the data to be useful for comparative effectiveness, it must capture the interventions being evaluated and the outcome measures needed to measure effectiveness, as well as control variables necessary to adjust for differences in the populations being compared.

Many comparative effectiveness questions are being addressed with the electronic data that already exist. Other questions will require that additional data collection efforts or databases be merged together.

A well-known example of merged data is the SEER Medicare database, which has linked Medicare claims data with cancer registry information. Other examples include the merger of hospital discharge abstracts with birth and death registries. In the area of pharmaco-vigilance, prescription claims are being used to detect signals of adverse events, but paper medical charts are then checked on a subset of signals to verify their validity. The usefulness of the emerging electronic data infrastructure will also depend on the extent to which data are formulated, using common data elements and a common vocabulary.

For some variables routinely collected, a common standard exists, such as the International Classification of Diseases (ICD) for diagnoses and some procedures, the Current Procedure Terminology Codes (CPT) for procedures, and the Logical Observation Identifiers Names and Codes (LOINC®) for laboratory tests. For other data types, standards and common vocabulary are still emerging, such as for EHRs and prescription drug codes. Developing common data elements, classification systems, and vocabulary will be a critical task in developing a robust data infrastructure that can support comparative effectiveness research.

The ability of the emerging data infrastructure to support comparative effectiveness will also depend on the quality of the data being input. If a physician decides to omit a substance abuse diagnosis in concern for a patient's privacy, then the usefulness of claims data for understanding patterns of substance abuse treatment becomes more limited. Additional efforts are needed to understand the strengths and limitations of the data that are entered electronically. These efforts may include validating electronic data against medical chart information and surveying providers about their documentation practices.

Electronic healthcare data are evolving at a rapid rate and will increasingly be able to support an array of inquires into comparative effectiveness.

There is no "national enterprise" dealing with CDS. The activities described earlier at the NQF Forum, and the development of the QDS, do begin a process of harmonizing performance measurement at the back end and CDS at the front end from a data definition and health IT standards' perspective. Data and health IT standards in support of CDS and performance measures will have to be integrated into work flow.

This means, in part, collection as a component of practice. They will also have to be integrated in formats amenable to one time data collection in an electronic form and then transmitted and aggregated electronically. A related issue is that the content and EBM from which data are derived should be similar. Given that quality measures which are utilized for public reporting are endorsed by QNF, a question could be raised as to why not a similar "endorsement process" for CDS, raising issues of the public domain status of such content. An additional issue that must be addressed is the need for pricing and related financial information that is required, at the point of care, by both healthcare professionals and patients, to maximally inform diagnostic and therapeutic decision-making. All these issues, as they are resolved, will have an impact on the data and the health IT infrastructure needed to support both measurement and improvement.

COST OF CARE AND EFFICIENCY METRICS

Measuring and improving performance, across any level of aggregation and accountability, implies that we will be able to assess multiple dimensions of performance. Currently, as described earlier, a national enterprise to develop and endorse, i.e., standardize and harmonize measures, is focused on the quality dimensions and is still developing and evolving. Not so explicitly for financial metrics. We do have in existence a claims-based system developed to support payment for services. This system is functioning electronically at many levels, with many elements being standardized. There is, however, lack of standardization to further the claims-based payment systems. Harmonization across the various sectors is needed to achieve this.

So building off this system that was developed for payment purposes is the potential to create a system of measuring and making transparent various financial metrics. One aspect of these efforts is to create a framework for measuring and reporting on meaningful financial metrics and, by extrapolation, efficiency metrics. Work on this aspect has commenced at the NQF (described next). The kind of metrics needed are fee schedules, unit price and total costs, the latter over time.

The financial content, or some of the content and metrics, will need to be available publicly,[7] through public reporting programs, while similar information will have to be made available at the actual time of decision-making by the patient and members of the healthcare professional team members, physicians and others.

Many of these metrics will require assessment based on an episode of care construct. NQF reports on this subject lay out a framework for the utilization of episodes of care.[8]

A description of this episode-based framework is described in Figure 10-10. This construct charters the life cycle of a disease, following the phases from staying healthy, recovering from acute diseases, dealing with chronic disease, and disability and end-of-life care. Each phase will require different metrics to measure and improve quality and control costs. A central tenant is the diversity of the data elements needed to support measurement, POC DSS and improvement and the need for access to data over time and across settings.

In brief, this episode contract does require the collection of data over time and across settings. Episodes are of care, not illness, and are usually initiated in an encounter with the healthcare delivery system, and end at some designated time, e.g., for chronic diseases, at the end of a year. Data are aggregated during the entire episode to reflect all the services, medications, and tests delivered to that patient based on the disease/condition driving the episode. The episode is then case mix adjusted to capture the severity of the primary disease/condition driving the episode and the data to capture the number and severity of the patient's co-morbid conditions. All these considerations, in structuring the episode, drive the need for standardized data and health IT standards and are similar in principle to those needs in support of both PMs and POC DS.

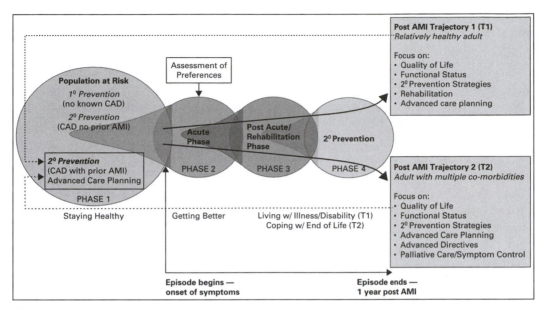

Figure 10-10: Episode-Based Framework. (From NQF, used with permission.)

QUALITY AND PERFORMANCE IMPROVEMENT

Performance measurement and point of care decision support systems are a necessary but insufficient requirement to accomplish performance improvement (PI) at any level within the healthcare delivery system. PI can and must be tackled at many levels within the entire system from the point of delivery, e.g., the hospital or physician office, to health plan or other level such as geographic level. We also need to take into account that the delivery system per se has the capacity to impact only perhaps 25 percent of improvement in patient outcomes and the maintenance of health.[9] The remaining impacts are driven by the environment, genetics, and personal behavior. These latter considerations have data and information needs but are beyond the scope of this chapter and will not be discussed.

A number of ingredients required to conduct PI include the execution of leadership and their affirmative commitment to provide the resources and oversight locally, feedback of relevant performance information and creating a culture of improvement and patient safety to mention but a few. All these dimensions can and should be supported by data and information. Specific information and software tools in support of PI also include tools that facilitate flow, run, control and Pareto charts, histograms, as well as scatter and cause-and-effect diagrams.

A particularly new and innovative dimension, in support of PI, is the conduct of and integration of continuing professional development into PI initiatives. For physicians, CME, now termed performance improvement based CME (PICME), is an example of such programs. These interventions use the Internet and deploy adult learning tools and asynchronous learning. Performance Improvement CME provides healthcare professionals with the framework to assess their current practice based on performance measures, connect to interventions for improvement and re-measure on an ongoing basis. One of these platforms is provided by CeCity.[10]

In 2005, the American Medical Association (AMA), American Academy of Family Physicians (AAFP), and the American Osteopathic Association (AOA) developed the criteria to award CME credit for physicians participating in practice-based PI initiatives. These organizations can approve twenty credits for completion of a PI cycle. This process includes three stages. Physicians may receive five credits for completion of each stage, with a bonus of five credits for completing all three stages. The system is data driven, with the educational intervention focused on the gaps in care, documented either at an individual or professional team level.

A vision for the future is depicted in Figure 10-11, a data- and information-driven system, as is now being referred to as a "Learning System,"[11] an integrated approach to genergation of evidence, development of clinical tools, such as CPGs, CPMs and CDS, with an overlay of PICME (and CE for all healthcare profesionals). Not displayed are the other evidenced-based comments of the interventions required to achieve improvement.

CONCLUSION

Given recent developments, especially with the meaningful use provisions of ARRA, future efforts to solicit best practice reports and case studies will have to increasingly focus on these evolving programs.

This new focus will have to emphasize PM and reporting, use of point of care decision support tools, engagement of patients and health information exchange, all deployed from a standards-based health IT infrastructure.

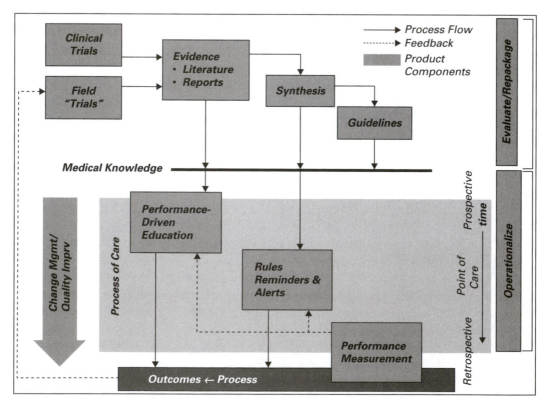

Figure 10-11: Convergence Model.

This focus has not been evident in prior efforts to describe experience with deploying health IT in support of these activities. A format for reporting for these efforts, case studies, and reports is becoming standardized by the adoption and use of the SQUIRE tool, a tool helpful in organizing thoughts and standardizing the component of these reports.[12,13]

The SQUIRE reporting tool specifically provides for specific descriptions, such as the nature of the performance problem being addressed, the intended improvement desired, an articulation of the planned intervention and the specific interventions achieved. A modification of SQUIRE to focus attention on the health IT components necessary to support meaningful use should be explored.

References

1. Institute of Medicine. *Crossing the Quality Chasm: A New Health System for the 21st Century.* Washington, DC: National Academy Press; 2001.

2. American Recovery and Reinvestment Act of 2009. Available at: http://frwebgate.access.gpo. gov/cgi-bin/getdoc.cgi?dbname=111_cong_bills&docid=f:h1pp.txt.pdf. Accessed February 20, 2010.

3. National Quality Forum. *Measure Evaluation Criteria.* August 2008. Available at: http:// qualityforum.org/uploadedFiles/Quality_Forum/Measuring_Performance/Consensus_ Development_Process%E2%80%99s_Principle/EvalCriteria2008-08-28Final.pdf?n=4701. Accessed December 8, 2009.

4. Fields MJ, Lohr K, eds. *Guidelines for Clinical Practice: From Development to Use.* Washington, DC: National Academy Press; 1992.

5. American Medical Association. Physician Consortium for Performance Improvement (PCPI). *PCPI Measures.* Available at: www.ama-assn.org/ama/pub/physician-resources/clinical-practice-improvement/clinical-quality/physician-consortium-performance-improvement/ pcpi-measures.shtml. Accessed December 8, 2009.

6. National Quality Forum. *The NQF Endorsement Process.* Available at: http://qualityforum.org/ WorkArea/linkit.aspx?LinkIdentifier=id&ItemID=1265. Accessed December 8, 2009.

7. Health Quality Alliance. Available at: www.healthqualityalliance.org. Accessed February 20, 2010.

8. Episodes of Care Framework. Available at: www.qualityforum.org/Projects/Episodes_of_ Care_Framework/Project_Brief.aspx. Accessed December 8, 2009.

9. McGinnis JM, Foege WH. Actual causes of death in the US. *JAMA.* 1993;270(18): 2207–2212.

10. CeCity. Available at: www.cecity.com. Accessed February 20, 2010.

11. The Healthcare Imperative: Lowering Costs and Improving Outcomes: Brief Summary of a Workshop. Institute of Medicine. Washington, DC: National Academy Press. 2009. Available at: http://books.nap.edu/openbook.php?record_id=12750. Accessed December 8, 2009.

12. Davidoff F, Batalden P, Stevens D, Ogrinc G, Mooney SE. *Qual Saf Health Care.* 2008;17, (suppl) i3-9.

13. Stevens DP. *Qual Saf Health Care.* 2009;18;(5)332.

CHAPTER 11

The Future—Where to Next?

David Collins, MHA, CPHQ, CPHIMS, FHIMSS; Joan R. Duke, BS, MA, FHIMSS; Alice Loveys, MD, FAAP, FHIMSS; and Patricia B. Wise, MA, MS, RN, FHIMSS

"Change is the law of life. And those who look only to the past or present are certain to miss the future."

—*John F. Kennedy*

INTRODUCTION

By David Collins, MHA, CPHQ, CPHIMS, FHIMSS

Everyone is a patient, everyone is a healthcare consumer. Whether a provider or a "frequent flyer" of healthcare services, all affect and are affected by the healthcare system. As such, "we," the healthcare consumer, will ultimately change expectations in healthcare delivery. Awareness of the value, consistency, convenience, improved safety, and quality of care and outcomes associated with an improved system, one facilitated by health IT, healthcare consumers will expect, and begin to demand, that their healthcare be managed in a digital environment.

Technology has changed expectations for other common consumer services, such as banking and phone service, with access and convenience now part of routine life and the lack thereof met with displeasure and impatience. Prescriptions sent via e-prescribing, medication histories readily available among various providers, including out-of-town visits to the ED, will become the new reality of healthcare delivery, rather than the "wouldn't it be nice" metaphor.

The reality that the healthcare system needs to be fixed is being aligned with the technology, the talent, and the knowledge of lessons learned to enable positive change. Lessons learned from pioneers, such as the Office of the National Coordinator's Health Information Exchange (ONC's HIE) pilots, blaze a trail for spearheading new efforts, with more grounded expectations of how to make things work for today's healthcare sector.

Health reform has taken on a new life with the passage of the Patient Protection and Affordable Care Act and the Health Care and Education Reconciliation Act of 2010. Supported by commitments and backed by extraordinary money earmarked for health IT, the United States is on an expansionary path to the EHR and to health information exchange (HIE). Health IT, not a panacea, but a tool to leverage and revolutionize "business as usual" for healthcare, will help achieve these overdue repairs, improve processes, reduce medical errors and support a realization of cost efficiencies.

Many surgical procedures have become "common" and are streamlined in the outpatient setting, as opposed to requiring lengthy inpatient stays, resulting in a new consumer expectation. The human genome has been mapped out, and the ability to know whether you are genetically predisposed to certain high-risk morbidities is no longer "Star Trek" medicine. Receiving healthcare in the 21st century is on a glide path to realize new expectations and value, value based on solid data and clear trends, driven by technology.

MEANINGFUL USE

By Joan R. Duke, BS, MA, FHIMSS

The American Recovery and Reinvestment Act (ARRA), passed in February 2009, provides for Medicare incentive payments to hospitals and providers that can demonstrate "meaningful use" of "certified EHR technology." The use includes criteria for use of electronic records by providers delivering care in their institutions, as well as the secure transmission of the medical data to external organizations and for submission of clinical quality measures.

The definitions of meaningful use terms have been finalized by the Secretary of Health & Human Services (HHS), and the direction has been set to provide financial incentives to providers and hospitals under Medicare and Medicaid to those who can demonstrate meaningful use of their certified EHR.

A total of $34 billion has been appropriated to expand the use of the EHR, which when combined with projected savings, will provide a net outlay of $19 billion in federal dollars over the next several years. Within this funding, there will be grants for state HIEs and regional extension centers to support adoption, use, and realization of the full potential of EHRs to improve the coordination, efficiency and quality of care. "By focusing on 'meaningful use' we recognize that better healthcare does not come solely from the adoption of technology itself, but through the exchange and use of health information to best inform clinical decisions at the point of care," notes David Blumenthal,[1] National Coordinator for Health Information Technology.

The legislation empowered the Office of the National Coordinator (ONC) to determine the criteria for HHS's certification, which establishes the minimum set of criteria that is necessary to meet the requirement of the statute and to achieve the MU objectives.

The objectives of MU and the criteria for determining such use is about the use of EHRs and is not about the technology. It is not sufficient to install an EHR system to meet the functional certification criteria; the organization must demonstrate MU based on the final definition of meaningful use, which were embodied in draft regulations from the CMS in January 2010, and which were published in final form in July 2010.

MU has identified and organized specific goals to be achieved by 2011, 2013 and 2015. There are also metrics for these goals to evaluate hospitals' and providers' progress in meeting them. The overall priorities are as follows:
- Improve quality, safety, efficiency and reduce health disparities.
- Engage patients and families.
- Improve care coordination.
- Improve population and public health.
- Ensure adequate privacy and security for personal health care information.

Under each of these priorities are care goals, objectives and measures. The goals include such items as access to comprehensive patient health information for the patient's health care team, the use of evidence-based order sets and CPOE, the application of CDS at the point of care, etc. The objectives to achieve those goals are identified on a year to year basis and include the use of CPOE, drug checking, up-to-date problem lists, medications lists, allergies, etc.

The measures are the key to the achievement of MU. Those measures include being able to report CMS and AHRQ quality measures, the ability to include lab results in the EHR in a coded format, the percent of claims to payors being submitted electronically, the ability to do electronic eligibility checking, and many others. The objectives and the measures become more rigorous year by year. The point is that payment is not based on implementation of the technology but on the use of the technology to improve the efficiency and quality of care.

This is similar to the approach taken by the Nicholas E. Davies Committee in creating guidelines for the Davies Award. The criteria ask about the pervasiveness of the technology, but to win the award the organization must report how it has changed to gain financial and clinical value from the implementation of EHR. It is not the technology itself but the value produced from the implementation of technology that demonstrates the difference EHR can make in the delivery of higher quality, lower cost care.

The importance of this legislation, in establishing standards; providing payment; and insisting that EHR make a clinical quality difference, cannot be underestimated in the impact it will have to encourage the use of electronic data within and among provider organizations. The legislation drives the implementation of the EHR and the creation of HIEs. The objectives for meaningful use set criteria, not just for the implementation of EHR within an organization, but also on the need to share data among providers and patients for better coordination of care.

This momentum will build over time as the incentives increase from Medicare and Medicaid payments. There are also disincentives which increase with penalties for the lack of use for electronic data; and as more providers and their patients require these capabilities to support the practice of information-based medicine.

ARRA legislation, particularly the meaningful use provisions, defines what is needed to achieve safe, efficient care and improved outcomes. It sets the goals for the EHR and the results to be archived, the requirement for certification of EHR products with the functions needed, and the support for the right way to implement and use an EHR.

The right way to implement, according to ARRA, aligns with the following topics covered in this book:

- Support for provider communications to coordinate care.
- Guides for usability that ensures that the necessary patient care information is accessible and easy to use.
- Process improvements.
- Physician and staff adoption and training.
- Technical support program.
- Standards for interoperability.
- Data capture methods that make the data available and reusable by clinicians involved in the patient's care.
- Retrospective use of data to assess the quality of healthcare services and outcomes.

All these are embodied in the current definition of meaningful use and are supported by ARRA funding of EHR software, information exchanges and supporting programs.

REGIONAL EXTENSION CENTERS

By Alice Loveys, MD, FAAP, FHIMSS

"Since 1994, the HIMSS Nicholas E. Davies Awards of Excellence Program honors achievement in the implementation and use of health information technology, specifically electronic health records, for healthcare organizations, private practices, public health entities, and community health organizations."[2]

This recognition program supports the HIMSS vision of advancing the best use of information and management systems for the betterment of healthcare. Many of the winning organizations' team members have gone on to lead educational programs and consult in the healthcare industry. Their efforts stress what can be done "right" in an implementation, describe how value is delivered, as well as highlight valuable lessons learned.

Adoption rates for EHRs plateaued in recent years, despite advances in the industry with certification and greater competition. Cost remained the number one cited reason in multiple surveys of EHR use and plans for implementation. Physicians and health system executives have also expressed concern about the overwhelming amount of information and the lack of unbiased information from vendors or consultants regarding EHR implementation.

The federal government is addressing these concerns by funding regional extension centers through a series of grants as part of ARRA of 2009, more specifically two sections of the act that combine to form the Health Information Technology for Economic and Clinical Health Act (HITECH).

Seventy regional extension centers will be funded throughout the country to help providers select and implement certified systems to improve the quality and value of healthcare and to use technology consistent with HIEs. Primary care providers will have priority for receiving such support with a broad scope of services specified. The scope of services outlined in the act encompasses objectives of bolstering local area resources and implementing work force support to help providers toward meaningful use of their EHR.

Local area resources are critical during EHR implementations. An analysis by HIMSS Analytics™ regarding health IT workers needed for EHR adoption in hospital settings alone predicted the need for approximately 150,000 persons. It is likely an almost equal number will be needed to support the approximately 63 percent of U.S. primary care providers who practice in office settings of four or fewer providers.

Thus, the HITECH Act will look for collaboration with the Regional Extension Centers and local area educational institutions to train the needed workforce. Training would likely build upon the certification programs offered by a variety of organizations such as HIMSS's Certified Professional in Healthcare Information and Management Systems (CPHIMS), the American Medical Informatics Association 10 x 10 program, or Health IT Certification granting Certified Professional in Electronic Health Records or Certified Professional in Health Information Technology. Regional Extension Centers (REC) would provide internship opportunities at every stage of EHR implementation and optimization.

Provider and office staff education will also be a key service component of RECs. Through lectures, peer group facilitation, and self-study materials, RECs will bolster the skill set needed throughout a successful implementation. Providers and staff alike will need to understand the dynamics of change management and improve skills in project management and communication. Key leaders of the implementation team will be encouraged to do self-assessment of these skills and use a variety of resources to augment them. Physician practices will need guidance for overall assessment of staff readiness and computer and IT network skills. Through hands-on classroom learning or Web learning, office members can gain the confidence needed to navigate their new environment.

The transition from paper to electronic records is an opportunity for practices to make work flow and process improvement. The REC may facilitate peer groups with like practices in specialty and size to examine current processes and how they might change with technology. Lean Six Sigma manufacturing process principles are being adapted for use in the medical setting. Again, RECs may be a key source for teaching these techniques and bringing them to fruition in the practice setting.

The 70 RECs will participate in a National Learning Consortium. This is to assure rapid dissemination of best practices and development of learning materials; tools; and marketing strategies. It will be a forum for shared experiences with barriers and solutions, use of client management tracking, and reporting applications for data collection regarding contracting as well as program and evaluation purposes. The RECS will be expected to participate in regional and national network meetings supporting this consortium.

Some of the data to share will involve the process for vendor selection and negotiations for group purchasing. Providers lament the large number of vendors on the market and are unsure how to sort through the myriad of options. Yet, given the unique needs of different specialties, practice settings and populations served, no single vendor can be a perfect fit. RECs will need to provide reasonable guidance in apples-to-apples comparisons of vendor company information and pricing.

Again, practice self-assessments will be key in delineating and prioritizing functionality needed. Practices will also need to understand functionality required to achieve meaningful use and assure their eligibility for possible Medicare or Medicaid Incentives. Since cost is a major barrier, RECs can shed light on vendor pricing models, as well as perform group negotiations for purchasing.

EHR vendors are just one partner needed for implementation. A healthcare provider and physician practice must have a strong technical infrastructure that is cost-effective and secure. Support must be able to provide on-site guidance. In as much, RECs can identify and support local area resources. There may be overlap with interns in local area educational programs as well. This infrastructure is also essential in proper disaster preparedness and recovery. An IT partner can assist in hardware purchase, support and maintenance, network set-up, as well as data back up and testing.

The infrastructure is intertwined with the security of data within the practice and in its participation in data exchange. Practices must understand their obligations in complying with state and federal privacy and security regulations. Again, RECs can provide tools for completing the HIPAA Privacy Manual and the often overlooked HIPAA Security Manual. Both of these manuals require documentation of personal training on privacy and security issues. In as much, the RECs can distribute standard assessments and best practices and provide the necessary training sessions.

Health information exchange may require patient consent depending on the type of information to be exchanged, the exchanging entities, and the age and mental status of the patient. Technology may facilitate appropriate consent and information exchange. RECs can educate practices on policies and functionality to assure compliance.

Physician practices will need a trusted source to turn to for the latest requirements of meaningful use, so they can realize the full potential to improve the quality and value of healthcare they provide and receive the full incentives to support the investment in the EHR.

DISRUPTIVE TECHNOLOGIES IN THE EHR AND MEDICAL SOFTWARE APPLICATION MARKET

By Patricia B. Wise, MA, MS, RN, FHIMSS

Clayton Christensen and Joseph Bower introduced the term *disruptive technology* in 1995 in their article *Disruptive Technologies: Catching the Wave*.[4] In this article, Christensen identifies disruptive technology or disruptive innovation as an advance that improves a product or service in an unexpected way. This may be related to price or a design for a newly targeted market. Disruptive technologies are particularly threatening to market leaders because they generate unpredictable competition and may have the potential to gain sufficient market share to dominate a market.

Emerging Trends in EHR and Medical Applications

Healthcare is one of the few segments of the economy that has been largely untouched by the current recession. At the same time, the steady rise in healthcare expenses has made it the target for reform efforts and made the field a target of stimulus spending. A few months ago, the hardware side made its play as Intel and GE announced a new initiative that would see them join forces to develop and market healthcare monitoring devices. Shortly thereafter, software giants made sure their successes were noted, as Google and Microsoft both announced progress in their EHR efforts. The nation's largest retailer, Wal-Mart, announced its intention to enter the EHR marketplace. Unlike most providers in this space, Wal-Mart is focusing on the smallest healthcare practices through collaboration between its Sam's Club division, Dell, and private software firm, eClinicalWorks. Augmenting this effort are Wal-Mart's new initiatives in the personal health record space.

EHR software with support for PDAs and tablet PCs can streamline workflow, improve office efficiency, and assist in personalizing the patient encounter. Designed to give physicians access to patient records wherever and whenever they need it, these mobile devices provide greater flexibility and usability than desktop systems. Some of the basic features to look for in a tablet PC or PDA system include: multiple input options including voice and handwriting recognition, HIPAA compliance to ensure secure transfer and storage of patient data, and; secure and powerful networking capabilities.

New Platforms

The term clinical groupware captures the basic notion that the primary purpose for using IT systems is to improve clinical care through communications and coordination involving a team of people, the patient included, and to do so in a manner that fosters accountability in terms of quality and cost.

Clinical groupware is a departure from the client-server and physician-centric EHR technology of the past 25 years, a fixed database technology that never really became popular. It is a substantially new and disruptive technology that offers lower price of purchase and use, greater convenience, and is capable of being used by less skilled customers across a broader range of settings than the technology it replaces.

Characteristics of this technology answers questions such as:

- Is it Web-based and networkable and is therefore, highly scalable and inexpensive to purchase and use?
- Does it provide a "unified view" of a patient from multiple sources of data and information?
- Is it designed to be used interactively—by providers and patients alike—to coordinate care and create continuity?
- Does it offer evidence-based guidance and coaching, personalized by access to a person's health data as it changes?
- Does it collect, for analysis and reporting, quality and performance measures as the routine byproduct of its normal daily use?
- Does it aims to provide patients and their providers with a collaborative workflow platform for decision support?
- Does it creates a care plan for each individual and then monitors the progress of each patient and provider in meeting the goals of that plan?[5]

As the name indicates, clinical groupware is intended for use by groups of people and not just independent practitioners or individuals. It is not the same thing as an EHR but may share a number of features in common with EHRs, such as e-Prescribing, decision support, and charting of individual visits or encounters, both face-to-face and virtual.

Some clinical groupware may look and feel like a Web-based "EHR lite." But clinical groupware aims to create a unified view of the patient, assembling health data and information that may be stored in many different places and in several different organizations, including HealthVault or Google Health, which most EHRs cannot do.

Clinical groupware is an evolutionary approach to a shifting health economy in which doing more is not always equated with better care and an environment in which the physician or provider role is transforming from autonomous expert to advisor, partner, and guide. It is also an organic response to the reality that most healthcare data in electronic format are dispersed across numerous organizations and companies—e.g., hospitals, labs, pharmacies, and devices—and provide a means of accommodating patient demands for a more participatory practice of medicine.

Modular Platforms

The analogy of the iPhone or Facebook, serves to describe the modular evolution. Utilizing a common platform, the developer could add functionality to an existing EHR in a modular fashion without having to change the core code. This would allow flexibility and rapid innovation and advances a business model that is remarkably different from having hundreds of companies all competing with different EHRs.[6]

A well-established stable platform could have mix-and-match functional modules based upon the need of the institution, organization or practice. Interoperability would be engineered through the common platform. This is the approach that has been noted with open source development with modular architecture. Proprietary EHR vendors are also adopting business models to accommodate modular purchasing.[6]

Mobile Platforms (mHealth)

The impact of mobile healthcare platforms cannot be underestimated. Delivering healthcare services via mobile communications, commonly referred to as mHealth, has emerged as a potentially revolutionary solution for a wide array of pressing healthcare and healthcare system needs. Mobile technology represents a high reach, cost-efficient method for making healthcare more accessible and effective for urban and rural populations and has the capacity to expand access to communications and to transmit voice and data at the precise time they are needed, which will empower healthcare workers to make better informed diagnoses and medical decisions. Mobile technology is easy to use, does not present cost as a barrier and has been quickly adopted by providers and health care consumers.[7]

New 3G cellular technology is now prevalent throughout the world. Currently, there are more than 150 million subscribers worldwide on more than 100 different networks. Applications running on these networks include live video, video mail, video sharing and video conferencing—both stationary and mobile. The potential exists that in the near future millions of patients or caregivers will have the ability to video conference with health providers.

The 4G cellular network is now being launched within the United States. Explosive growth is anticipated within the next 12 to 18 months. Clinical applications of 4G technology include wearable sensors or devices for hypertension, the trauma ambulance with videoconferencing between paramedics at the scene and the receiving trauma physicians and a marked increase for providers in patient efficiency (think doc walking into hospital or doc at stoplight immediately checking on a patient's request or need in response to an alert signaled from her cell phone) with features that could include a download of updated patient list, a download of new consultations and updated versions of patient tracking.

Hybrid EHR

The continued success of the hybrid EHR has prompted extensive debate about what actually constitutes a hybrid EHR. While the Internet is now filled with discussions about EHRs, the number of conversations regarding hybrid EHRs has exploded. In 1997, the first hybrid EHR was created, which concentrated on performance-driven practices, in which high-volume physicians demanded unencumbered productivity. This market segment is growing with hybrid EHRs designed with efficiency and speed in mind. This emphasis on performance criteria contrasts sharply with traditional EHRs, which place functionality at a premium. The SRS hybrid contains functionality currently attributed to a traditional EHR combined with the ease of dictation.[8]

CONCLUSION

This chapter describes a few of the initiatives and technology advances that are on the horizon pushing the implementation of the EHR and providing ever more sophistication and functionality. Other initiatives that might be called "pull" measures include the pay for performance and incentive payment structures that are meant to drive a willingness to make the significant investments needed. Still further incentive to implement the EHR is found in the dis-incentive payment policies that have been enacted, such as the ending of payment for never events and for certain re-hospitalizations.

At the underpinning of all these push and pull initiatives and the promises and possibilities of new technology is the demand for more efficient and effective healthcare delivery, improved quality, reduction in medical errors, and reduction in the rate of cost increase that the US has been experiencing. Healthcare IT can serve as the infrastructure to achieve these goals and, in fact, they cannot be achieved without this infrastructure. The Nicholas E. Davies Award-winning EHR implementations have been used by their organizations to advance improved quality and improved business results. They are achieving measurable improved results and serve as a beacon for others to do likewise.

References

1. A Message from Dr. David Blumenthal, National Coordinator for Health Information Technology. Available at: http://healthit.hhs.gov/portal/server.pt?open=512&objID=1350&parentname=CommunityPage&parentid=5&mode=2&in_hi_userid=11113&cached. Accessed January 3, 2010.

2. HIMSS Davies Award. [Web site] Available at: www.himss.org/davies/index.asp. Accessed December 12, 2009.

3. Centers for Medicare and Medicaid Services. Available at: www.cms.hhs.gov/apps/media/press/factsheet.asp?Counter=3564. Accessed February 20, 2010.

4. Bower JL, Christensen CM. (January/February, 1995). Disruptive Technologies: Catching the Wave. *Harvard Business Review.* 73(1).43–55.

5. Kibbe DC. *Why Clinical Groupware May Be the Next Big Thing in Health IT.* Available at: www.thehealthcareblog.com/the_health_care_blog/2009/02/why-clinical-groupware-may-be-the-next-big-thing-in-health-it.html. Accessed November 12, 2009.

6. Kibbe, DC. *Toward a Modular EHR.* Available at: www.aafp.org/fpm/20090700/8towa.html. Accessed November 15, 2009.

7. United Nations Foundation, Vital Wave Consulting. *mHealth for Development: The Opportunity of Mobile Technology for Healthcare in the Developing World.* Available at: www. unfoundation.org/global-issues/technology/mhealth-report.html. Accessed November 15, 2009.

8. Steel E, CEO, SRSsoft. *Straight Talk, What is a Hybrid EMR?* Available at: http://blog.srssoft. com/?p=186. Accessed November 16, 2009.

Index